TOMBS.
TREASURES.
MUMMIES.
Seven Great Discoveries
of Egyptian Archaeology
in
Five Volumes

BOOK FIVE

CATALOGUES
of the
ROYAL MUMMIES
from
TT320 & KV35

plus
SEARCH FOR THE MUMMIES OF HATSHEPSUT & RAMESES I

plus
THE EGYPTIAN MUMMIES PROJECT
and
THE FAMILY OF TUTANKHAMEN

ISBN-13: 978-1539534310
ISBN-10: 1539534316

Book design by the Author in QuarkXpress & Adobe Photoshop

Cover images: Front, Egyptian Supreme Council for Antiquities; Back, Salima Ikram

Other Egypt-themed Books by the Author

Imperial Lives: Illustrated Biographies of Significant New Kingdom Egyptians
        Volume One: The 18th Dynasty through Thutmose IV

Intimate Egypt: Black & White Photography of the Ancient Monuments in Seven Volumes

Tombs.Treasures.Mummies. Seven Great Discoveries of Egyptian Archaeology

        Book One: The Royal Mummies Caches (TT320 & KV35)

        Book Two: The Tombs of Maiherpri (KV36) & Kha & Merit (TT8)

        Book Three: The Tomb of Yuya & Thuyu (KV46) & The Amarna Cache (KV55)

Ancient Egypt, Modern Hues: Relief Images Digitally Colorized in Two Volumes

TOMBS.
TREASURES.
MUMMIES.
Seven Great Discoveries
of Egyptian Archaeology
in
Five Volumes

BOOK FIVE

CATALOGUES
of the
ROYAL MUMMIES
from
TT320 & KV35

plus
SEARCH FOR THE MUMMIES OF
HATSHEPSUT & RAMESES I

plus
THE EGYPTIAN MUMMIES PROJECT
&
THE FAMILY OF TUTANKHAMEN

DENNIS C. FORBES

This study is dedicated to

G. Elliot Smith
&
Zahi Hawass

Contents

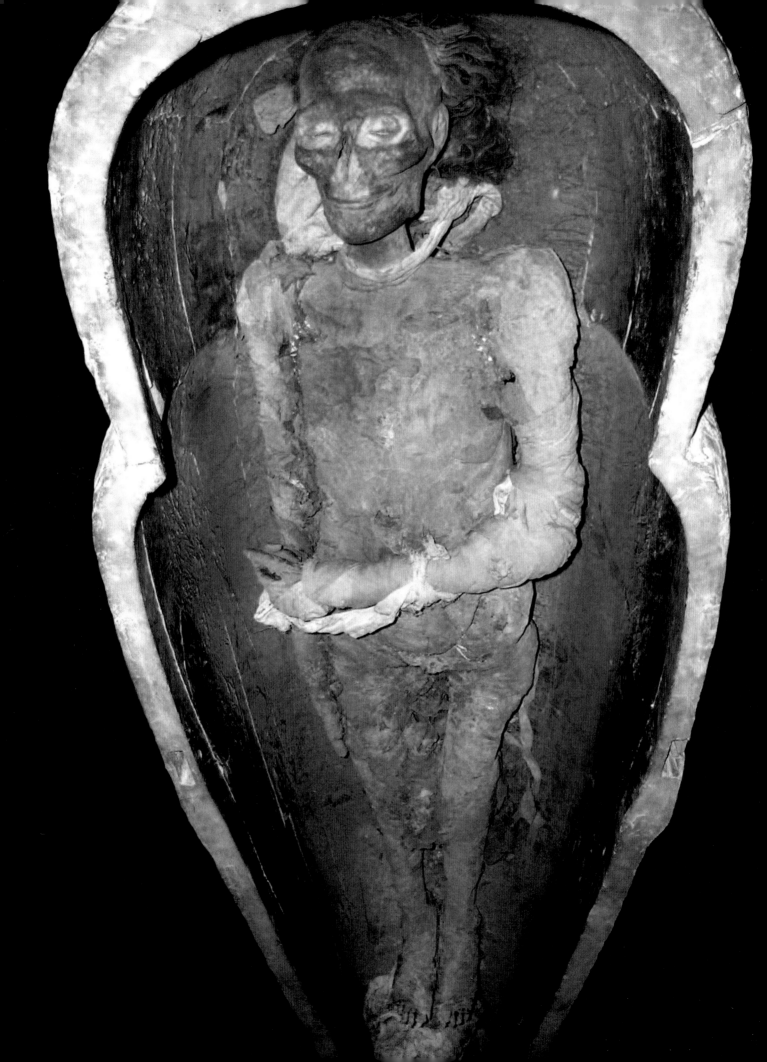

Introduction

Ancient Egypt is unique in countless ways, but especially so because it is the only high civilization of antiquity from which the actual physical bodies of a great many of its rulers have survived the vicissitudes of time and fortune, due to the artificial preservation afforded by mummification, so that today those once-powerful individuals' petrified-in-time-if-withered faces can be gazed upon, with the effect of awing or else repulsing the viewer. Would that we could today behold the actual visages of Julius Caesar and Napoleon Bonaparte in the same way we may look upon the haughty one of mighty Usermaatre Rameses II, resting — quietly if not exactly serenely — in his display case in the Royal Mummies Gallery at the Cairo Egyptian Museum.

The Egyptians of pharaonic times believed human bodies (and those of select sacred — and pet — animals) were revivified in the Afterlife, so needed preservation for this eventuality following the Final Judgment of Osiris. When most of the Valley of the Kings tombs of the rulers and their relations of the Eighteenth, Nineteenth and Twentieth dynasties were located, broken into and plundered during the twilight years of the New Kingdom (ca. 1100 BC), the mummified royalty occupying those sepulchers were treated ruthlessly by the plunderers: turned out of their sarcophagi and coffins, their wrappings torn apart in the frantic search for jewelry adornments, limbs often torn from bodies, chest cavities hacked open, heads even decapitated, these human ruins were then left behind among the wreckage and debris of burial goods deemed of no intrinsic value by the thieves.

As the economy of the Third Intermediate Period teetered on total collapse, the priest-kings ruling at Waset (Thebes/Luxor) ordered the total dismantlement of the Valley of the Kings royal necropolis, in order to recover any precious metals that had been overlooked by the thieves, so that these could be turned into bullion for the government treasury. In the process of officially relooting the royal tombs, the necropolis priests given this task took it upon themselves to rescue the desecrated royal remains, identify and rewrap them (if somewhat haphazardly in most cases), supply them with replacement coffins (only rarely the deceased's) and then gather

Opposite, The female mummy identified as KV60-B, seen resting in the coffin basin where she was found in 1902 in Valley of the Kings Tomb 60, which belonged to Sitre-In, a nurse of the early-18th Dynasty female pharaoh Hatshepsut. A second uncoffined & mostly denuded female mummy rested on the floor of the same roughly hewn small two-chambered tomb (& was identified as KV60-A). The latter was left in the reburied tomb & in ca. 1906 KV60-B was removed to the Cairo Egyptian Museum, where she & the coffin basin (made for Sitre-In) were placed in storage in the attic & subsequently forgotten. She was rediscovered by the Egyptian Mummy Project in 2005 & along with KV60-A became a candidate for the previously unknown mummy of Hatshepsut, the identification finally going to KV60-A, with -B being tagged as Sitre-In. S. Ikram photo

them ultimately into two groups for re-internment in the family tomb of the high-priestly Pinudjem family and in KV35, the well-plundered Tomb of Amenhotep II, whose rescued, rewrapped and re-coffined mummy was still residing there.

As sheer luck would have it, these royal individuals and a few retainers lay undisturbed for two and one-half millennia, until the largest of the two caches, TT320 (the Pinudjem group-sepulcher), was found quite by accident in 1871; the some three-dozen occupants were "rescued" a second time, in 1881, by the Egyptian Antiquities Service, to be taken to Cairo, where, during the 1880s, they were informally and unceremoniously unwrapped by French Egyptologists — specifically Gaston Maspero, Georges Daressy and Emilé Brugsch — and a physician, Daniel Fouquet, who wrote descriptions of each speciman, many of his observations and inferences mistaken, however.

Then in 1898 the second, smaller royal cache in KV35 was discovered by Director of the Antiquities Service Victor Loret. After some confusion/indecision over whether these royal mummies should be left where they had been found or taken to Cairo, they finally were removed and shipped north, to become objects of scholarly and scientific inquiry. Amenhotep II himself and three unwrapped anonymous mummies thought to have been original occupants of the king's tomb were left behind (eventually, except for one, later to be removed to Cairo, as well).

Antiquities Director Maspero enlisted the services of a professor of Anatomy at the Cairo School of Medicine, Australian G. Elliot Smith, to formally and officially examine and describe all of the Royal Mummies, which he did over the first decade of the Twentieth Century. Smith's examinations did not amount to autopsies, inasmuch as the remains were neither cut open nor dissected, rather only observed visually. Smith's written descriptions were published in 1912 as a folio volume of the Cairo Egyptian Museum's Catalogue Général (*The Royal Mummies*), heavily illustrated by gravure photographs of the mummies (presumably taken by Brugsch); this stood as the definitive work on the subject of mummified ancient Egyptian royalty, until the publication in 2015 of *Scanning the Pharaohs: CT Imaging of the New Kingdom Royal Mummies* by Zahi Hawass and Sahar N. Saleem, that being the official findings of the Egyptian Mummy and the Family of King Tutankhamun joint projects of the early first decade of the Twenty-first Century.

This present volume presents what is known about the Royal Mummies in 2016.

Dennis C. Forbes

Engraved illustration (made from a photograph) for the French weekly magazine La Science Illustrée, *which shows, at left, Frenchmen Georges Daressy (1864-1938) & Dr. Daniel Fouquet (1850-1921) posed as if examining a wrapped Egyptian mummy, with unidentified onlookers.* Internet image

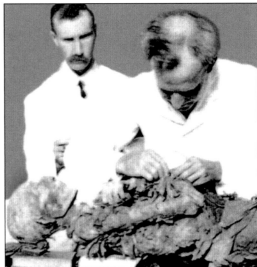

Top, Studio portrait of Australian anatomist Grafton Elliot Smith, who examined & described the Royal Mummies from caches TT320 & KV35, his observations published in 1912 as a volume of the Cairo Museum's Catalogue Général (The Royal Mummies). Above, Smith & unidentified assistant examining the 19th Dynasty mummy of King Baenre-Meriamen Merneptah. Adapted archival photos

CHAPTER ONE

Catalogue
of the Mummies from
the First Royal Cache, TT320

Forty mummies, whole or partial, poorly and well-preserved, were recovered in 1881 by Émile Brugsch from the royal cache at Deir el Bahari South, TT320 (alternately DB320), first discovered by the Brothers Abd er Rassul in 1871 (see Book One, this series). Sixteen of these are of identified royal and non-royal individiuals, male and female, dating to the late Sevententh and early Eighteenth dynasties of ancient Egypt's New Kingdom. Two are kings of the Nineteenth Dynasty, two kings of the Twentieth Dynasty. Eleven are mummies of the male and female members and an associate of the so-called "priest-king" family of Pinudjem I of the Twenty-first Dynasty. And the balance (nine individuals, male and female) are anonymous, probably mostly to be dated to the Eighteenth Dynasty.

A first detailed discussion of these remains was done by Gaston Maspero in his *Les Momies Royales de Déir el-Baharî* of 1889, although he had earlier made an initial presentation of this material in the slender text-volume which accompanies Brugsch's album of photographs of several of the mummies and their coffins, *La Trouvaille de Deir-El-Bahari* (1881). In 1912 Australian anatomist G. Elliot Smith authored a full scientific description of these mummies and those from the second royal cache found in 1898 in the Tomb of Amenhotep II, KV35 (see Book One, this series), as a volume in the Catalogue Général series of the Cairo Egyptian Museum. It is titled *The Royal Mummies* and is accompanied by 110 photographic plates of the mummies, their coffins, in some cases, and relevant wrappings, these also taken by Brugsch, but uncredited. Another Catalogue Général volume, authored in 1909 by Georges Daressy, *Cercueils des Cachettes Royales,* describes and illustrates the coffins from both TT320 and KV35. Likely these photographs are also by Brugsch.

What follows is a chronological presentation of the named mummies from TT320, plus significant anonymous ones, and their coffins. The various photographic and engraved illustrations are chiefly from the Brugsch images and other archival and popular sources of the period, with additional available new color photos.

Opposite, The gilded & polychrome wooden outer coffin of 21st Dynasty Amen priestess Maatkare, from the royal Mummies Cache.

Adapted from *Cercueils*, 1909

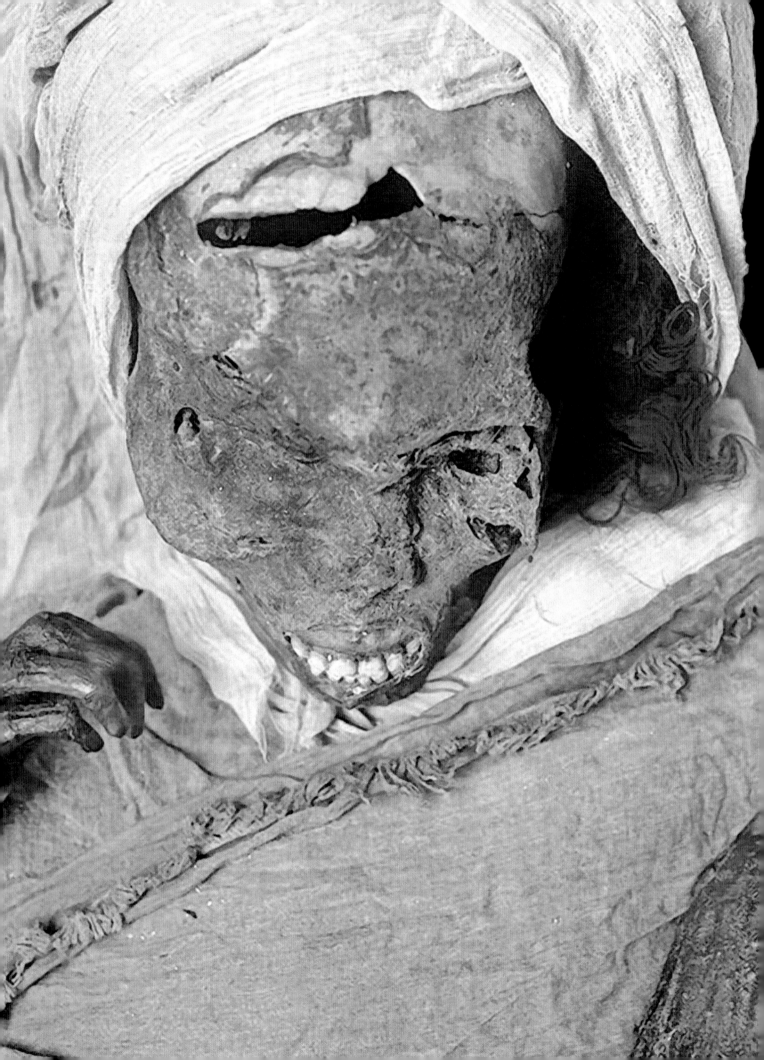

No. 61051
Seqenenre Tao II
End of the 17th Dynasty
Died c. 1555 BC

The likely oldest mummy from the TT320 cache is that of the next-to-last ruler of the Wasetan (Theban) Seventeenth Dynasty. Seqenenre Tao II, who is best known for having initiated the War of Liberation against the Hyksos foreign rulers of Egypt at the end of the Second Intermediate Period. In fact, it would appear from the condition of his mummy that Tao II died on the battlfield: his remains consist of *"a badly damaged, disarticulated skeleton enclosed in an imperfect sheet of soft, moist, flexible, dark brown skin, which has a strongly aromatic, spicy odour"* (Smith, 1). Additionally, his head and face exhibit numerous wounds that were almost certainly the cause of his death, which would have been quite violent, as might be expected in battle.

From the contortions of the mummy (head turned to one side, legs not fully extended, arms and hands twisted as if in a death spasm) and the grimace of the face (lips pulled back from the teeth so that the mouth is a distorted oval), it is apparent that the body of Tao II was not formally mummified, but rather was recovered already in a state of putrefaction on the field of battle. Although the slain king's brain was not removed through the nasal passages, an incision was made in the lower-left side of the abdomen and the viscera and thoracic organs extracted by those who embalmed and wrapped the body. The abdomen (but not the thorax) was then tightly packed with linen, which now forms a solid mass. The "mummification" of the body *per se* was probably limited to its being liberally sprinkled with powdered aromatic wood (sawdust), which accounts for its spicy odor today.

Opposite, Detail of the head of the mummy of Seqenenre Tao II, as displayed today in the Cairo Egyptian Museum. Above, Painting by Winifred Brunton of the discovery of the slain king on the battlefield. Archival image

The five wounds to the head of Tao II suggest that he was attacked by at least two persons wielding an axe and spear, and a blunt instrument — possibly an axe or spear handle, or a club. The horizontal nature of four of the five wounds suggest that the Theban king was attacked while lying down — which has caused speculation that he may have been assassinated while sleeping; this would necessarily preclude the battlefield scenario for the condition of his mummy. Rather, he was probably felled by the non-horizontal blow, the other wounds being *coups des grâces*.

Above, Massive anthropoid coffin of Tao II, of wood gessoed & painted yellow, but originally gilded with a rishi-*pattern. It is 2.12. meters long (6 ft., 11.46 in).*

Cercueils, 1909

Seqenenre Tao II in life stood approximately 1.702 m. (5 ft. 7 in.) tall, had a thick head of curly black hair, and a remarkably (for the time) good set of teeth. He was apparently slightly built, but muscular. The warrior-king was at least thirty but less than forty when he died.

Tao II originally would have been interred in a rock-cut tomb surmounted by a small mud-brick pyramid at the Seventeenth Dynasty's necropolis, Dra Abu el Naga, in Western Thebes. He was reburied in TT320, housed in his original large anthropoid wooden coffin, this having been stripped of its original *rishi*-patterned gilding, either by tomb robbers or in the Twenty-first Dynasty.

Above, The rewrapped mummy of Tao II, as it is displayed today in the Cairo Egyptian Museum. Cairo Egyptian Museum

Opposite, Bottom right, Detail of the contorted hands of the king's only summarily mummified remains. Adapted from *Royal Mummies*, 1912

Below, 19th Century engraving of the poorly preserved mummy of Tao II, as it appeared following its unwrapping. Anonymous

No. 61053
Ahmes-Inhapi
Queen
17th Dynasty

The mummy of the daughter of King Senakhtenre Tao I and wife of her half(?)-brother Seqenenre Tao II was found in the coffin inscribed for the wet-nurse of Queen Ahmes-Nefertari, Lady Rai (see following). Ahmes-Inhapi was identified by a cursive hieratic inscription on the shroud of her rebandaged body. There has been some disagreement among scholars as to whether her tomb — recorded in antiquity as in a *"high place"* — might, in fact, be TT320, which was later appropriated and enlarged for the Priest-King Pinudjem family, and subsequently became the Royal Mummies Cache.

Ahmes-Inhapi was a somewhat tall (1.685 m., 5 ft. 6.34 in.), stout, but small-breasted youngish woman. The mummification technique employed on her remains is very similar to that used for her slain husband; i.e., the dark-brown skin has the quality of oiled leather, being soft and moist, although tough. The body, however, is in no better state of preservation than that of Tao II, even though there seems to have been no haste involved on the part of the embalmers, the body being arranged in the conventional position of the time, with the arms extended, hands resting on the thighs. That Ahmes-Inhapi was stout in life is evidenced by the fact that shrinkage of the subcutaneous tissues has left the skin in numerous folds. The pelvic viscera are still in place, *"a very exceptional state of affairs in a New Empire mummy"* (Smith, 10). The face is coated with a resinous paste, which bears the impression of a complicated pattern, perhaps a pectoral ornament which was pressed against the right temple when the mummy was being wrapped. So much pressure was applied to the bandages of the head that the queen's nose was completely flattened. Ahmes-Inhapi's own dark hair (a section of which on the left crown is missing) is braided into plaits resembling wheat ears.

Tomb robbers treated this mummy roughly, the head being separated from the torso above the neck and the right hand is missing.

The head of Ahmes-Inhapi seen in profile, opposite, shows how the nose was completely flattened by the pressure of the bandaging. Also note the complicated marks on the right temple, where an ornament of some sort was pressed into the resin coating the queen's face. Part of her own hair is missing on the left crown (at left). The full-length image above was made after the royal lady had been devested of her bandaging.

All images adapted from *Royal Mummies*, 1912

No. 61052
"Unknown Woman A" (Meritamen?)
17th Dynasty
Possibly Earlier

One of the more problematic mummies from the TT320 cache is that of a poorly preserved, badly damaged elderly female, whom Gaston Maspero — based on hieratic writing on the shroud — thought might possibly be a Princess Meritamen of the late Seventeenth/early Eighteenth dynasties. Or else these remains were a substitute for the lost mummy of that same royal lady, inasmuch as the style of mummification in this case might be as early as Middle Kingdom in date.

Elliot Smith described No. 61052 as *"a small, old woman, roughly embalmed, shrunken, distorted and desiccated"* (Smith, 7). The mummy is not in a *"customary mummy-position,"* inasmuch as the head is tilted to one side and the legs are partially flexed, the left foot crossed over the right, with the lower legs bandaged together; the arms were torn off by tomb robbers in antiquity, and are missing, so it is not possible to say how they were situated. Additionally, the lady's mouth is wide open, so that she appears to be in great agony. The skull is completely bald; whether shaved or its hair lost in the rudimentary embalming process, it cannot be determined. The lower thorax frontal wall has been smashed in, revealing that the pelvic area is packed with resin and aromatic sawdust.

The mouth of No. 61052 is wide open in a "grimace," right, & the legs are crossed, left over right, at the ankles; since the arms are missing, it is not possible to know how they were positioned. Images adapted from *Royal Mummies*, 1912

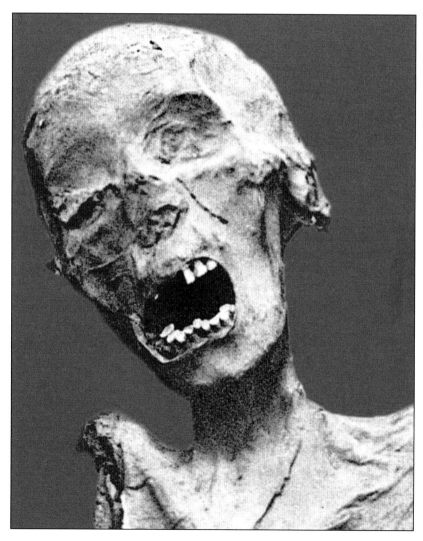

No. 61056"

"Unknown Woman B (Tetisheri?)"

17th Dynasty/18th Dynasty, Died after 1550 BC

Although it may be only wishful thinking, it has been suggested that the mummy of a little old woman found resting in TT320 in a coffin of Twenty-first Dynasty date (but inscribed with the name of Rameses I) is that of the famous Queen Tetisheri, the non-royal wife of Senakhtenre Tao I, mother of Seqenenre Tao II, and grandmother of kings Kamose and Ahmose I. Along with her daughter/daughter-in-law, Queen Aahotep I, Tetisheri was a driving force behind the expulsion of the Hyksos and the reunification of Egypt under King Ahmose, into whose reign she in all probability lived.

Identifiable officially only as "Unknown Woman B," the mummy in question is that of a white-haired, partially bald, petite (1.57 m., 5 ft. 1.8 in. tall) female of very advanced years, who is embalmed in the manner of the early part of the Eighteenth Dynasty. She has a short ovoid face, a pointed but receding chin, and the exaggerated overbite characteristic of the members of the royal family of that dynasty.

The skin of the body is blackened, the face coated with a shiney black resin, to which bandage fragments adhere. Artificial braids are woven into the scant hair.

"Unknown Woman B" seen in three views. The head became detached from the body in antiquity, as was the right hand, both probably through rough handling by tomb robbers. Images adapted from Royal Mummies, 1912

Princess Ahmes-Hentempet

Princess Sitkamose

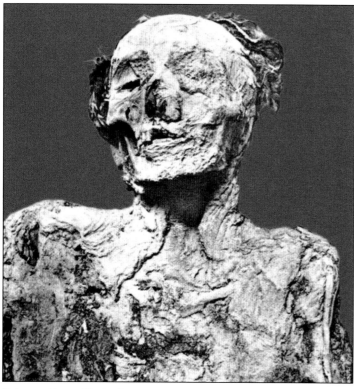

Princess Ahmes-Hettimehu

Images adapted from *Royal Mummies*, 1912

No. 61062
Ahmes-Hentempet
Princess
17th Dynasty/18th Dynasty

A large hole bored into the chest of this mummy was undoubtedly the work of one of the Rassul brothers, looking for a heart scarab. When the mummy was unwrapped, it proved to be the superficially intact body of an old woman (opposite, top left), who, from the inscription on her wrappings was Ahmes-Hentempet, a daughter of Seqenenre Tao II and his sister, Queen Aahotep. Judging from her advanced age and the mummification technique employed, she would very likely have lived somewhat beyond the reign of her brother, Ahmose I.

The mummy, 1.613 m. (5 ft. 3.5 in.) in height, was severely damaged in antiquity, both forearms being torn off (to remove jewelry?); only fragments of the right remain, and the left was placed in a transverse postion across the midsection. Intense pressure applied by the embalmers to the bandaging around Ahmes-Hentemet's head totally flattened her nose, causing plugs of linen, which had been insert into the nostrils to be squeezed out, so that they now hang over the upper lip and create a particularly grotesque appearance.

The skin of the face is paper thin and, as though it had been painted with ochre, a pale-yellow color. Because no resinous paste was applied to the body, it would seem that the princess was mummified following the reign of Ahmose. The embalmer's incision is on the lower-left side of the abdomen and vertical. The vagina was plugged with linen.

When unwrapped the princess was wearing a wig askew on the left side of her head. Additionally there was a large and elaborate wig resting on the chest of the mummy. Both of these wigs are made of wavy brown human hair, although Ahmes-Hentempet's own hair is well-streaked with gray.

No. 61061
Ahmes-Hettimehu
Princess
17th Dynasty/18th Dynasty

This mummy (opposite, bottom left) was greatly damaged in antiquity, and again while it was being transported from Luxor to Cairo, following discovery of the TT320 cache. Originally wrapped in an enormous quantity of bandaging saturated with a resin solution, ancient tomb robbers chopped a great deal of this away; but no attempt was made to remove what remained when the necropolis priests of the Twenty-first Dynasty rewrapped the mummy.

Ahmes-Hettimehu was a daughter of Seqenenre Tao II and Queen Ahmes-Inhapi; and, since her mummy is that of an old woman, she would seem to have lived into the reign of her half-brother (or not; see below), Ahmose I, and perhaps beyond. Standing a little over 1.52 m. (4 ft. 11.8 in.) tall in life, when she died Ahmes-Hettimehu was nearly bald, having only scanty locks at the sides and back of her head, which are dyed reddish, probably with henna. Into these a few plaits of black hair have been interbraided.

The face of the mummy is very damaged, most of the nose and parts of the cheeks having disappeared, although the linen plugs which were inserted into the nostrils during mummification are still visible. The cavity of the body is packed with resin-saturated pads of linen. The elderly princess's arms are extended, with the hands placed in front of the thighs.

No. 61063
Sitkamose
Princess, King's Wife
17th Dynasty/18th Dynasty

Like the other mummies of early New Kingdom royal ladies found in the TT320 cache, that of Sitkamose (*opposite, right*) was badly damaged by ancient tomb robbers, who chopped through her bandaging, hacked away most of the anterior wall of the torso (exposing the tight linen packing inside), tore off the left arm at the shoulder and smashed the entire back of the skull (revealing the well-preserved brain, which had not been removed during mummification).

Her name suggests that she was the daughter (*sit*) of the last king of the Seventeenth Dynasty, Kamose. If so, then her titles, *"King's Daughter, King's Sister, King's Wife,"* might suggest that Kamose's successor, Ahmose, was his son rather than brother, as is most often thought (for, if she was Kamose's daughter, what other king would she be the sister of?). Elliot Smith estimated that Sitkamose was probably not much more than thirty when she died (based on the only moderate wear of her teeth and that her hair, while sparse, is not streaked with white). The princess/queen was probably taller than most of her female contemporaries in the royal family, her mummy being 1.62 m. (5 ft. 7.8 in.) long. Sitkamose was also a *"powerfully built, almost masculine woman"* (Smith, 21).

Somewhat peculiarly for this time period, the dead princess/queen was mummified with her arms extended so that the hands cover the pubic area instead of resting on the thighs. A thick coat of resin completely covers the perineum, a technique which is also seen in the near-contemporary mummy of Ahmose I. A black resinous paste was smeared over the entire body, including the face, and impressions of fine linen bandages and of a pectoral ornament are embedded in it. Still visible on the toes are impressions of the string used to secure the nails.

Regrettably, Sitkamose's right gluteus maximus and the rear left thigh have been nibbled on by mice.

No. 61054
Lady Rai
Royal Nurse
17th Dynasty/18th Dynasty

An ink inscription on the bandages enveloping this mummy indicated that her name was Rai; and from the fact that the embalming style here is of early Eighteenth Dynasty date, it is almost certain that she is the same Rai who is known to have been the nurse of Queen Ahmes-Nefertari, sister-wife of Ahmose I and mother of Amenhotep I. She was found in a Twentieth Dynasty coffin inscribed for one Paheripedjet, her own coffin being occupied by the mummy of Queen Ahmes-Inhapi. The site of her original tomb is unknown but was possibly at Dra Abu el Naga, which at the beginning of the Eighteenth Dynasty may have been used for royal-related interments.

Lady Rai in life was a petite (1.510 m., 4 ft. 11.45 in. tall), very full-breasted young woman with well-proportioned limbs. Because her teeth are only slightly worn, it is probable that she was still fairly young at death. Elliot Smith said of her mummy that it *"is the most perfect example of embalming that has yet come down to us from the time of the early Eighteenth Dynasty, or perhaps even of any period,"* and is *"the least unlovely of all the mummies of women that have been spared"* (Smith, 11, 12).

Mummification was done with the arms fully extended, the child-like hands resting on the thighs. Pubic hair is present. The embalming incision on the left side of the abdomen is fusiform and vertical. Rai has an abundance of her own hair, elaborately plaited and arranged in two club-like masses on either side of her head and hanging well past her shoulders. Each of these was separately wrapped in a downward-spiraled linen bandage.

The mummy's skin is reddish-brown, the body and face having been dusted with a thin layer of mixed sand and powdered resin. On the right wrist, tomb robbers and necropolis workers missed a large barrel-shaped carnelian bead worn as a bracelet.

The hair of Lady Rai, her own, is elaborately plaited & arranged into two club-like masses falling on either side of her face to past her shoulders. Images adapted from *Royal Mummies*, 1912

22

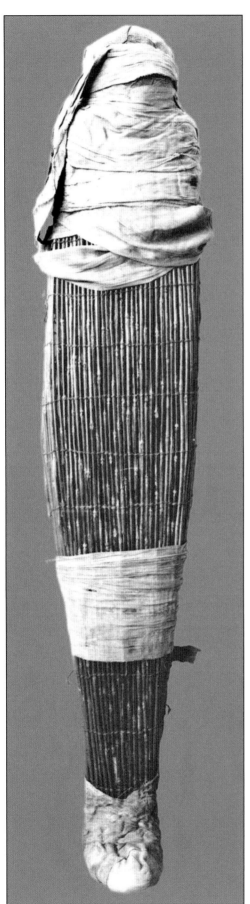

No. 61059
Prince Siamen
18th Dynasty

Probably a son of Ahmose I, the remains of a Prince Siamen found in TT320 consist of the bones of a young child *"simply thrown pell-mell into an oblong bundle"* (Smith, 18) by the necropolis priests of the Twenty-first Dynasty. These remains are not illustrated in *The Royal Mummies* Catalogue Général volume, nor are they here.

No. 61060
Princess Sitamen
18th Dynasty

Maspero decided against unwrapping the "false" mummy of a child identified by the inscription on the shroud as Royal Daughter Sita-men, probably an offspring of Ahmose I and Ahmes-Nefertari. This decision was prompted by the fact that it is *"so curious and its general appearance so singular"* (Smith, 19). The princess's remains consist of a *"bundle of reeds surmounted by a skull"* (ibid.). It is also not illustrated in *The Royal Mummies*, and the unidentified photo at left — from the archives of the Cairo Egyptian Museum — may or may not represent the Sitamen remains.

No. 61076
Unknown Woman (Likely Bakt)
Probably 18th Dynasty

Contained within an Eighteenth Dynasty coffin bearing the name "Bakt" were the garlanded rewrapped skeletal remains of a young woman of about twenty-one years, who it has been supposed was the owner of the coffin. A piece of a Twentieth Dynasty varnished-yellow coffin lid and the handle of a mirror were found wrapped with the bones. Smith could not determine whether the young woman had been mummified, but based on the bandages found closest to the bones, he dated "Bakt" to the Eighteenth Dynasty.

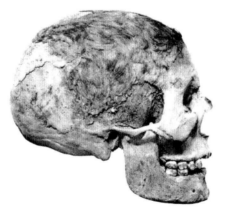 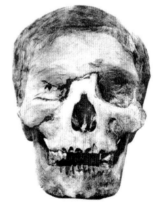

Above, Two views of the skull presumed to be Bakt's. Adapted from *Royal Mummies*, 1912

Left, An unidentified photograph from the archives of the Cairo Egyptian Museum may or may not be of the "mummy" of an 18th Dynasty princess named Sitamen (No. 610-60); but it illustrates the concept of a "false" mummy consisting of bones wrapped in reeds & topped by a skull. Cairo Egyptian Museum

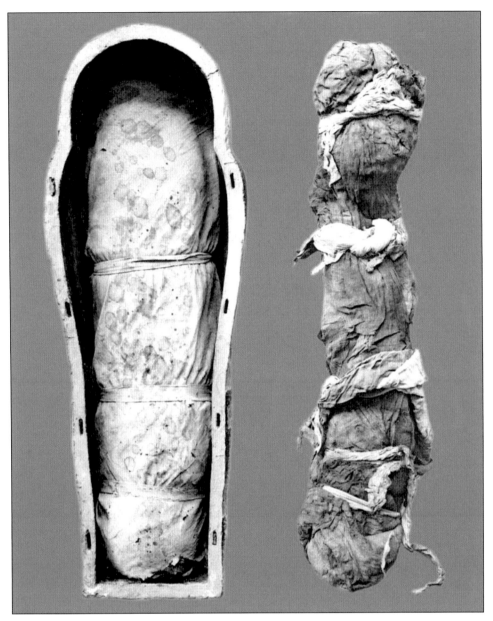

No. 61064
Prince Ahmose-Sipair

Early 18th Dynasty

One of the most peculiar mummies found in the TT320 cache is that of Prince Ahmose-Sipair, who was a son of Ahmose I and his sister-wife, Queen Ahmes-Nefertari. Interred in a small coffin of the black-and-gold style (similar to those housing the fetal mummies in the Tomb of Tutankhamen, but larger), the mummy bundle first seemed to be of expected shape (above, left). But in the unwrapping, it was discovered that most of this was padding, to disguise a rather oddly shaped inner bundle (above center). When this was opened it was found to contain what at first appeared to be the flayed skin of a young boy (above, right). Many of the skeletal bones are missing, leaving a mostly hollow shell of soft, pliable skin *"which has become grossly distorted by pressure* [of the bandaging]...*the face so flattened that the mouth is almost vertical"* (Smith, 25).

Elliot Smith offered no explanation in The Royal Mummies *as to why one identified as an early-18th Dynasty prince, Ahmose-Sipair, should have been mummified & wrapped as essentially a bag of skin containing a skull & a few bones.*

Adapted from *Royal Mummies*, 1912

25

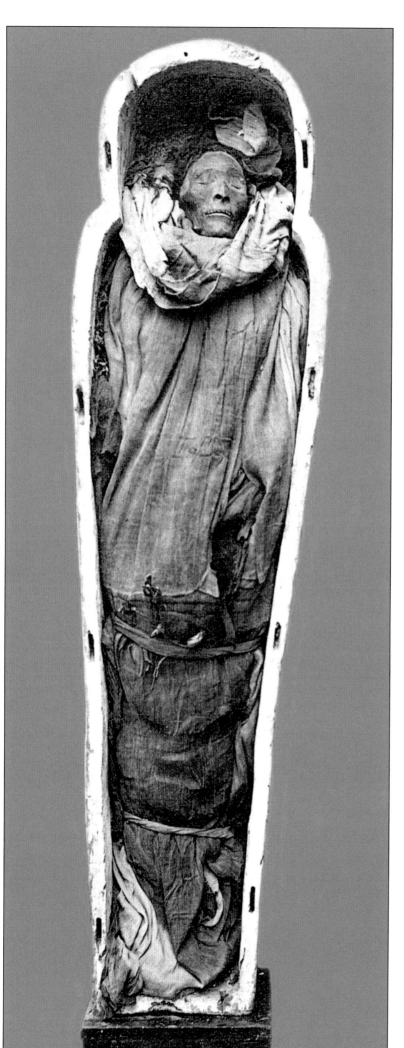

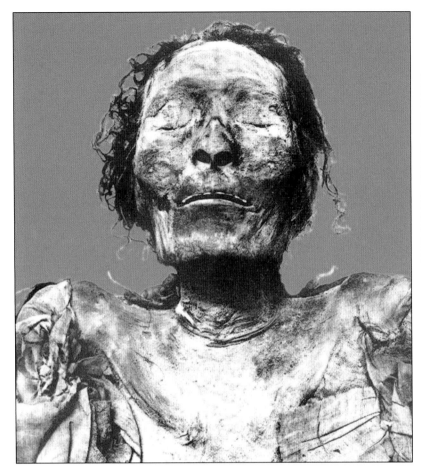

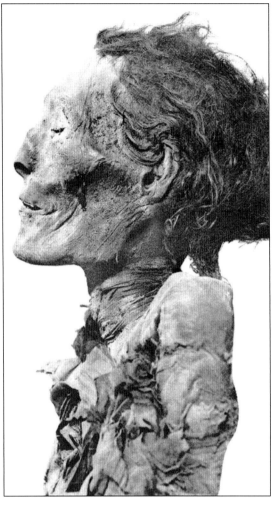

Opposite, left: The mummy of Unknown Man C as first seen, resting in the basin of the coffin of a 21st Dynasty scribe named Nebseni. The face was probably exposed by the Rassul brothers between 1871 & 1881. Adapted from *La Trouvaille*, 1881 *The unwrapped mummy of Unknown Man C (above & opposite, right) was judged by Elliot Smith to be too robust & tall to have been a member of the Thutmosid royal family. He concluded, therefore, that "C" was a high official of the early/mid-18th Dynasty.*

Adapted from *Royal Mummies*, 1912

No. 61067
"Unknown Man C"

Early/Mid-18th Dynasty

When found in TT320 in 1881, the face of Unknown Man C already had been revealed by the shroud being pulled back — almost certainly the work of the Brothers Rassul during one of their foraging visits to the Royal Mummies Cache.

This especially well-preserved mummy of a man in late middle age (judging from the wear of his teeth) was resting in the coffin of a Twenty-first Dynasty scribe named Nebseni; but Elliot Smith was positive that its mummification technique places the individual between the reigns of Ahmose I and Thutmose II. He briefly hinted that the mummy might be that of Amenhotep I, if the unwrapped individual found in that king's coffin was, in fact, someone else, placed there by mistake in the Twenty-first Dynasty. Smith's entertaining this possibility perhaps was prompted by the fact that the mummy of Ahmose I and that supposed to be Thutmose I both were embalmed with the arms fully extended — as is the case with Unknown Man C — instead of crossed on the torso, as is seen in the mummy identified as Thutmose II. However, Smith also states that *"the features of this man present no likeness to any of his possible contemporaries among the royal family"* (32). At 1.739 m. (5 ft. 8.46 in.) in height, Smith thought he would *"have seemed a very giant amongst them, and is hardly likely to have sprung from such a puny stock"* (ibid). He concludes, therefore that Unknown Man C was a high official during the early part of the Eighteenth Dynasty.

The mummy has abundant black hair streaked with gray and about 15 c. (5.9 in.) long. The face is strong with pronounced features: heavy, broad jaw and broad cheeks; prominent brow ridges; sloping forehead; and fairly prominent nose. The ear lobes are pierced for earrings. Smith thought that, *"On the whole his features conform, not to the indigenous Egyptian type, but to that of the alien, so-called Armenoid group"* (ibid.).

In his examination of Unknown Man C, Smith was unable to detect the presence of any genitalia. He would not have, he wrote, *"hesitated to call this man a eunuch, if it had not been for the fact that the mode of treatment of the genitalia is almost equally puzzling in the mummies of the three others members of this group (Thoutmosis I, II and III), who were certainly not eunuchs, if we accept the history of their reigns"* (ibid.).

No. 61057
Nebpehtire Ahmose I
Reigned c. 1550-1525 BC

Very few contemporary depictions of Nebpehtire Ahmose are known; one of those is the painted-limestone head (above) of a colossal Osiride statue of The Liberator in the collection of the Brooklyn Museum. Author's photo

The identity of this mummy as that of the first ruler of the Eighteenth Dynasty seems almost certain, inasmuch as the name of his son and successor (Amenhotep I), occurs on a fragment of original wrapping which was in contact with the skin. Hieroglyphs on the coffin — this of early-Eighteenth Dynasty date, but of a non-royal type — also name the occupant as Nebpehtire Ahmose I.

Best remembered as the vanquisher of the Hyksos rulers of Lower Egypt, and so known as The Liberator, Ahmose took over the struggle against the foreign occupiers from the king of Waset (Thebes), Kamose, who was either his brother or father. Thus he was also the son or grandson of Seqenenre Tao II, who had initiated the campaign against the Hyksos. Ahmose had at least two principal wives, Ahmes-Inhapi and Ahmes-Nefertari, both of whom were also his sisters, the latter being the mother of his heir, Prince Amenhotep. The location of his tomb is unknown, but in all likelihood was most probably in the Seventeenth Dynasty royal necropolis at Dra Abu el Naga on the Luxor west bank.

Ahmose was 1.635 m. (5 ft. 4.37 in.) tall and very slightly built. He seems to have been especially well-endowed, however; but the penis is uncircumcised, suggesting that he may have been a hemophiliac or else was in too frail health generally to have undergone the operation, which was usually performed at puberty. X-rays taken of the mummy in 1970 indicate that King Ahmose had to endure severe arthritis in his knees and back.

The mummy was prepared with the arms fully extended, fingers unflexed, the left hand positioned with the palm against the side of the thigh, the right resting in front of the thigh. Ahmose suffered at the hands of the robbers of his tomb, his head being torn from the torso and the nose smashed. The body likely would have been even more damaged except for the fact that it was coated by the embalmers with a thick layer of resin which dried to a stony hardness. The head was likewise coated in this resin, but even so it is apparent that the king had abundant dark-brown hair in long ringlets. An area under the chin covered by the resin reveals that at death Ahmose had a growth of whiskers about 4.0 mm. long.

Because of the resin coating the body, it is not possible to observe the embalmer's incision; but the cranium is tightly packed with linen. Smith thought that the extreme narrowness of the mummy's thorax was due to excessive compression by the original bandaging. He estimated Ahmose to have been about forty when he died.

The Liberator's remains were moved from the Cairo Egyptian Museum to the Luxor Museum during the first decade of the present century, where his mummy now rests in a special small gallery alongside the remains which have been tentatively identified as those of Rameses I of the Nineteenth Dynasty.

Opposite, Ahmose I's facial features were refined, his nose (albeit missing from the mummy) was fairly narrow & not prominent. Like other members of his family, he had a pronounced overbite. Adapted from *Royal Mummies*, 1912 *Right, The cedarwood coffin of Ahmose I is of early-18th Dynasty date, but not of the royal type. Gilding & inlays were removed in antiquity.* Adapted from *Cercueils*, 1909

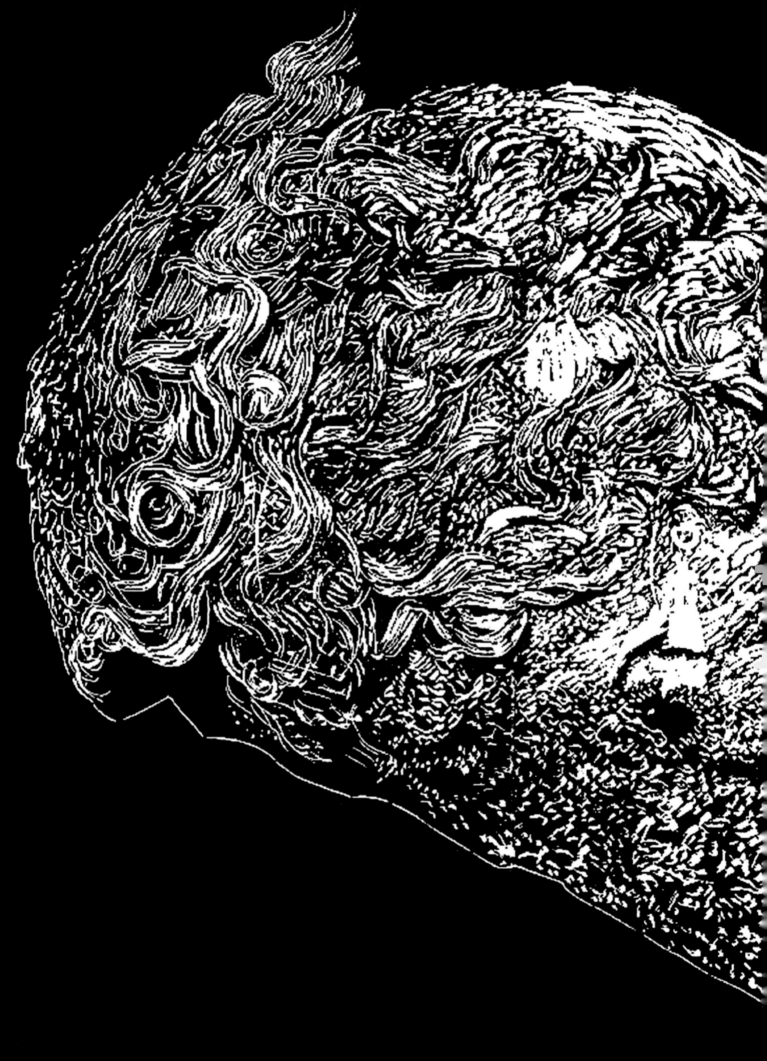

Left, Wood engraving of the head of Ahmose I in profile. Note abundant hair in curly ringlets. Egyptian Mummies, 1924

His mummy, right, indicates that Ahmose I was short & of slender build. His endowment was generous, but the well-preserved penis is uncircumcised, suggesting that he was perhaps a hemophiliac, so that operation — performed at puberty — was not possible. The pendant position of the arms would indicate that the folding of these across the upper torso in the case of New Kingdom rulers had not yet been introduced.

Royal Mummies, 1912

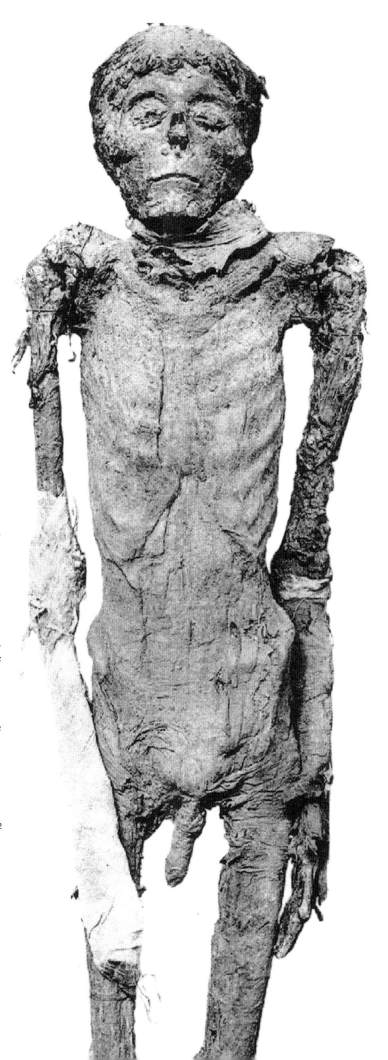

No. 61055
Ahmes-Nefertari
Early 18th Dynasty

Ahmes-Nefertari apparently was the daughter of Seventeenth Dynasty ruler Seqenenre Tao II and his principal wife, Queen Aahotep, and so she was also the full sister of Ahmose I (or else his aunt), whom she married and by whom she was the mother of the next king, Amenhotep I, living well into the latter's reign (and possibly even that of his successor, Thutmose I). She apparently was quite advanced in years at the time of her death, her teeth being heavily worn and her head almost bald.

The mummy identified as Ahmes-Nefertari was found in a gigantic coffin of the type employed for queens of her era. She shared this with the intrusive mummy of Rameses III. The queen was unwrapped in 1885 by Émile Brugsch in Gaston Maspero's absence. Due to putrefaction, the body was found to be quite odoriferous.

Ahmes-Nefertari was short in life, at 1.61 m. (5 ft. 3.39 in.) height. Her mummy is extremely emaciated and lacks any sign of breasts, which may be due to a combination of senile atrophy and desiccation. Her baldness is disguised by tightly braided long plaits of human hair attached to twenty strings placed across the top of the head. Additionally, other plaits were tied to her own sparse white locks.

The queen's mummy was roughly handled by tomb robbers in antiquity, the left hand being broken off and lost, and the right forearm and hand as well. Nonetheless it is evident that embalming took place with the arms fully extended, the hands either resting on the fronts of the thighs or possibly partially covering the pubic area. The embalming incision is plugged with linen and smeared with resinous paste, which bears the impression of a leaf-shaped plate (gold?) which once covered it.

As typical of mummies of the period, that of Ahmes-Nefertari was coated all over, including the face, with resin. A few of the original resin-impregnated bandages still adhere The queen's mouth is partially open. In profile it is quite apparent that she has the same dental overbite first observed in her grandmother, Tetisheri (No. 61056?), and which would be characteristic of her descendants, male and female, in the Thutmosid line of the Eighteenth Dynasty.

One of the few depictions of Queen Ahmes-Nefertari from her lifetime is seen in a sandstone sunk relief, above, now on view in the Open Air Museum at Karnak, & originating from a dismantled monument of her son, Amenhotep I. The numerous extant statuettes of her in various materials date from the later-18th & the 19th dynasties & her features on these are certainly idealized. Author's photo *Opposite, The royal lady's mummy is coated with resin, which was a mummification technique found in several of the early New Kingdom royal remains.* Adapted from *Royal Mummies,* 1912 *Below, Human-headed calcite canopic vessel inscribed for Q. Ahmes-Nefertari & found in the Royal Mummies Cache, TT320.* Archival photo

Opposite, The overbite seen in Ahmes-Ne-fertari's mummy is typical of both female & male members of the royal family of the 18th Dynasty. Adapted from *Royal Mummies*, 1912 *Above & detail right, Ahmes-Nefertari's colossal (3.78 m. long, including the feathers) wood-en coffin, which housed both her rescued remains & those of Rameses III in TT320.*

Adapted from *Cercueils*, 1909

No. 61058
Djoserkare Amenhotep I

Reigned c. 1529-1508 BC

The first Amenhotep succeeded his father, Ahmose I, when he was still a minor, and his mother, Ahmes-Nefertari served as his regent at the beginning of his twenty-one-year reign. In fact, he remained intimately associated with her throughout the New Kingdom, as both came to be regarded as patrons of the Theban tomb-builders' community (at modern-day Deir el Medina), and were worshiped as deities there. Djoserkare Amenhotep campaigned in both Nubia and Western Asia, further consolidating the fledgling empire begun by his father.

When his mummy was discovered in the Deir el Bahari royal cache, it was found to be so well-wrapped (and adorned with a replacement cartonnage-mask and garlands) that Gaston Maspero refused to unwrap it, a decision respected to this day. X-rays taken of the king's remains show him to have been not much over thirty at death, with arms folded across his lower thorax, the earliest instance of this so-called royal pose seen in the mummies of New Kingdom rulers; however, both forearms had been broken off by tomb robbers, so the Twenty-first Dynasty priests who rescued and rewrapped the king's remains may have positioned them thusly according to tradition rather than reality.

Opposite, Pigmented raised-relief image of Djoserkare Amenhotep I on a dismantled limestone block of a monument of the king, now displayed in the Open Air Museum at Karnak. Author's photo *Below, The king's painted-cedarwood replacement coffin, with his garlanded mummy* in situ, *photographed not long after its 1881 discovery in TT320, the Royal Mummies Cache.* La Trouvaille, 1881

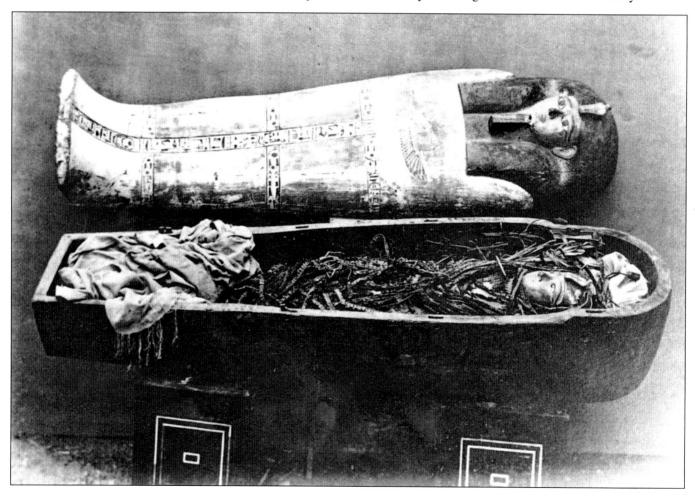

Carefully rewrapped & garlanded in the 21st Dynasty, the mummy of Amenhotep I (opposite & above) has never been viewed or examined directly; but x-rays taken of it in the late 1960s reveal that the king's arms are crossed on the lower thorax, although both forearms had been broken off by tomb robbers & their subsequent repositioning by the necropolis priests may not represent their original arrangement. Adapted archival photo (opposite) & Cairo Egyptian Museum (above)

The coffin (right) in which the 21st Dynasty necropolis priests placed the rewrapped remains of Amenhotep I had originally belonged to an unknown non-royal 18th Dynasty individual named Djehutnefer. It was adapted for its new royal occupant by the addition of a urae-us. *Note the hieratic inscription added by the priests to the coffin at the time of its reinterment (written in the blank space above the figure of the Nekhbet vulture).*
Cercueils, 1909

Below, 1960s x-ray of the Amenhotep I mummy, skull visible through the cartonnage mask. Adapted archival photo

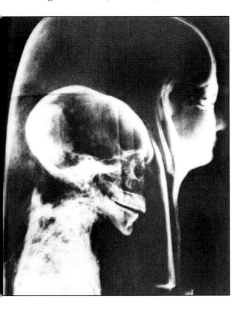

No. 61065
Anonymous Young Man originally thought to be Akheperkare Thutmose I

Early 18th Dynasty

Identities of the individual who called himself Thutmose I, his original burial place and the TT320 mummy originally thought to be his are problematic. It is certain that Amenhotep I died relatively young and without surviving male issue. The origins of his successor — with whom he may have associated himself briefly in a coregency — are unclear. Early commentators on the history of the Eighteenth Dynasty saw Akheperkare Thutmose as a likely comrade-in-arms of Amenhotep I, a general with sons whom the childless king named to succeed him. It is more probable, however, that, rather than being a commoner, the new (co-) king was an adult member of a collateral branch of the royal family, thus probably Amenhotep's cousin, once or twice removed, likely a member of the Taosid line. The name of the first Thutmose's mother is known (Senseneb), although his father is anonymous, suggesting it was more likely through the former that he counted his connection to the Taosids. Probably somewhat before his accession, he married Ahmes, who was herself almost certainly a member of the same royal family, arguably a sister or half-sister of Amenhotep I.

Whoever he was, Thutmose I came to the throne as a mature adult, probably somewhat senior in age to his predecessor (who died in his mid-to-late twenties). It is with him that the subsequent Thutmosid line of the Eighteenth Dynasty originated. He continued the expansionist policies of Ahmose I and Amenhotep I, vigorously campaigning in both Nubia and Western Asia, and expanding even further the boundaries of the empire. After a reign of only some dozen years, Akheperkare died (having been predeceased by two sons mothered by King's Great Wife Ahmes) and was succeeded by his namesake, Thutmose II, his still-youthful offspring by a secondary wife (or concubine), Mutnofret, who seems not to have been royal.

Where exactly Thutmose I was buried originally is not certain. His tomb architect, Ineni, apparently cut for him — *"No one seeing, no one hearing"* — a sepulcher in a hidden place, thought to have been the west-bank wadi at Waset (Thebes), which subsequently came to be known (in modern times) as the Valley of the Kings, and that Akheperkare Thutmose was the first occupant thereof. It has been argued that the location of Thutmose's secret burial place is to be seen as Kings' Valley Tomb 20 (KV20), which was subsequently enlarged to accommodate the interment, as well, of his daughter, Hatshepsut — when the latter, as female pharaoh, needed a sepulcher suitable to her unique status. Others believe the tomb Ineni made for Thutmose I to be Kings' Valley Tomb 38, in which a quartzite sarcophagus and canopic chest inscribed for the king were found; although another view is that KV38 is a "replacement" tomb prepared for Akheperkare when his mummy eventually was removed from KV20 by his grandson, Thutmose III. Architecturally, however, KV38 would seem to predate the burial place which the third Thutmose prepared for himself in the Valley of the Kings (KV34).

Opposite, Head of No. 61065, photographed by Émile Brugsch following its discovery. La Trouvaille, 1881 *Right, full-length view of the mummy originally identified as "supposed to be" that of Thutmose I, although this has been challenged because of several anomalies: the apparent youth of the individual at death; the lack of cranial-morphology correspondences with the mummies identified as Thutmoses II & III; & the non-royal extension of the mummy's arms (as opposed to the crossing of same on the torso, seen with certainty only as early as the mummy of Thutmose II).* Royal Mummies, 1912

Mummy No. 61065 was discovered in TT320 in 1881, housed in a nest of two wooden coffins — one of Eighteenth Dynasty date, the other of Twenty-first Dynasty type — which, although greatly damaged by the adzing of their gilded surfaces, were found to be inscribed for Priest-King Pinudjem I of the Twenty-first Dynasty, even though evidence remained to indicate that the outermost of the pair seems to have been made, originally, for Thutmose I. The mummy therein, consequently, was identified by Gaston Maspero as Pinudjem; it was not until 1896 that the Frenchman changed his mind and re-identified No. 61065 as Thutmose I, who previously had been missing (another mummy from the Royal Cache by this time being recognized as the first Pinudjem).

In his 1912 Catalogue Général description of the royal (and related) mummies, G. Elliot Smith identified No. 61065 as *"supposed to be"* (Smith, 25) the remains of Thutmose I, based on Maspero's expressed opinion that the mummy's head presented *"a striking resemblance to those of Thoutmosis II and III"* (ibid.). Smith was convinced that, based on mummification technique, the remains in question were later than Ahmose I and earlier than Thutmose II, placing the individual neatly within the range of Maspero's arbitrary dating.

Unlike royal mummies of the earlier Eighteenth Dynasty, that of "Thutmose I" was not coated in resin. Although its hands had been broken off in antiquity (by tomb robbers removing bracelets, almost certainly), and were lost, it was apparent to Smith that the extended position of the arms (missing hands originally placed over the pubic region) was very similar to those of Ahmose I's mummy (at the time the remains of Amenhotep I had yet to be x-rayed, so the anatomist was unaware of the [original?] position of that king's arms). Smith thought the 61065 mummy's stature (1.545 m., 5 ft. .83 in. tall) placed him among the *"group of short men"* (ibid., 27) who were the Eighteenth Dynasty kings. And he concluded that the wear of the mummy's teeth fully accorded with Maspero's view that Thutmose I was *"over fifty years old"* (ibid., 28) at the time of his demise.

Subsequent examinations — most recently by the Supreme Council for Antiquities' Egyptian Mummy Project in 2004-2005 — have concluded, however, that the No. 61065 individual is considerably younger — only eighteen or twenty at death — and that there is little similarity in his cranial morphology to those of the almost-certain mummies of Thutmose II and III, therefore arguing against a father-grandfather relationship to the latter.

Additionally, the EMP study determined by CT-scan that there is a small metallic object embedded within 61065's upper-right chest cavity, which was assessed to probably be an arrowhead, thus almost certainly the cause of the individual's death. Although historically he was a warrior-king, there is no textual record of Thutmose I having been slain in battle.

Thus, the current viewpoint holds that No. 61065 — who, through a mixup in antiquity, was cached in Thutmose I's appropriated coffin(s) — must be regarded as anonymous. It has been suggested that he may possibly be an attested Ahmose-Sipairi and even the unnamed father of the actual Thutmose I.

The EMP has suggested that an unwrapped male-mummy found several years ago in scree outside the entrance to KV15 (Tomb of Seti II) — and for several years displayed under glass in a cheap wooden coffin positioned on a stairwell ledge of the tomb — may possibly be the phantom first Thutmose. A published image of the new Thutmose I candidate would suggest that this heavy-jawed individual may be none other than Seti II himself, which would accord with G. Elliott Smith's suggestion that KV35 mummy No. 61081 — labeled as Seti II by the Twenty-first Dynasty necropolis priests as the second Seti — is, in fact, the otherwise-missing Thutmose I (see below, pp. 124-125). If DNA and other testing of the KV15 interloper was done by the EMP, the results have not been published at this writing. The pendant arms are a problem, however.

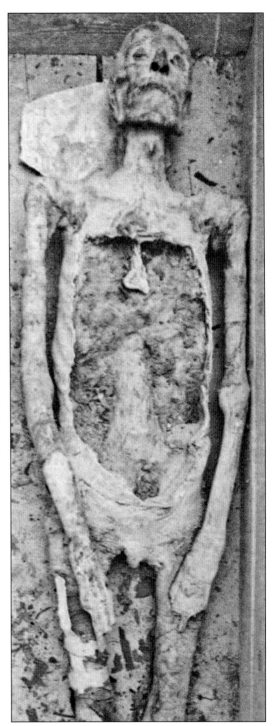

Above, Photo of the male mummy found in the loose-rock debris outside the entrance of KV15 (Tomb of Seti II) which has been proposed as a candidate for the otherwise-missing Thutmose I, despite pendant position of the arms. Archival photo

Opposite, The TT320 pair of coffins which housed No. 61065 when found. The one at left is of 18th Dynasty date, & seems to originally have been made for Thutmose I. The one at right dates to the 21st Dynasty. Both coffins subsequently were altered for the employment of Priest-King Pinudjem I. Cercueils, 1909

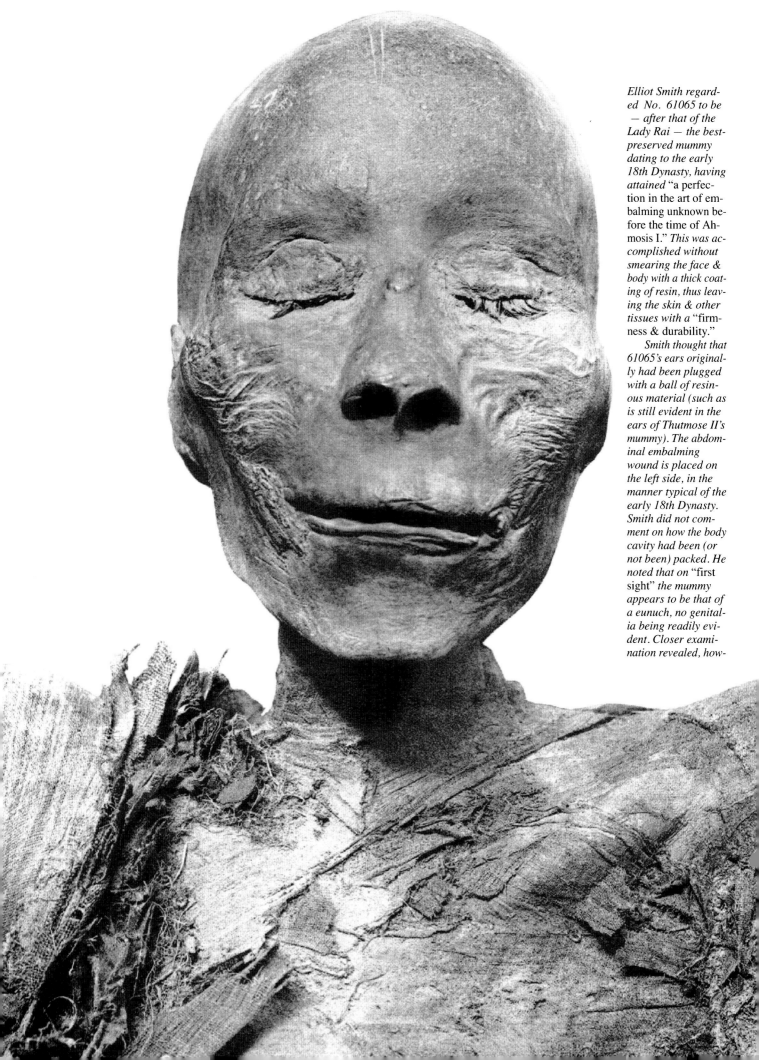

Elliot Smith regarded No. 61065 to be — after that of the Lady Rai — the best-preserved mummy dating to the early 18th Dynasty, having attained "a perfection in the art of embalming unknown before the time of Ahmosis I." *This was accomplished without smearing the face & body with a thick coating of resin, thus leaving the skin & other tissues with a* "firmness & durability."

Smith thought that 61065's ears originally had been plugged with a ball of resinous material (such as is still evident in the ears of Thutmose II's mummy). The abdominal embalming wound is placed on the left side, in the manner typical of the early 18th Dynasty. Smith did not comment on how the body cavity had been (or not been) packed. He noted that on "first sight" *the mummy appears to be that of a eunuch, no genitalia being readily evident. Closer examination revealed, how-*

Above, 1880s engraving of TT320 mummy No. 61-065 seen in profile. It was identified at the time of discovery as the remains of both Pinudjems I & II, neither of whom it is.

ever, that the scrotum & penis had been flattened against the perineum & left thigh respectively. For Smith this seemed to be a transitional treatment between the separately wrapped genitalia of Ahmose I & the total absence of any visible penis & scrotum in the subsequent TT320 mummies of Thutmoses II & III & Unknown Man C.

Smith noted that, apart from the eyelashes, the head of 61065 is completely hairless — the scalp being quite smooth — with no sign of a moustache or beard. He thought that the evident wrinkles on the face were as they had been in life (further proof of his estimate of an advanced age for the mummy), without considering that this might have resulted from the desiccation of rather full, fleshy cheeks (as almost certainly would have been the case if No. 61065 was as young at death (18-20) as recent estimates have made him.

Maspero described the mummy's features as "refined," with the mouth still giving the impression of "shrewdness & cunning." Smith, on the other hand, saw in the face "an aspect of weakness" (Smith, 27-28). *Royal Mummies, 1912*

No. 61066
Akheperenre Thutmose II

Reigned c. 1492-1479 BC

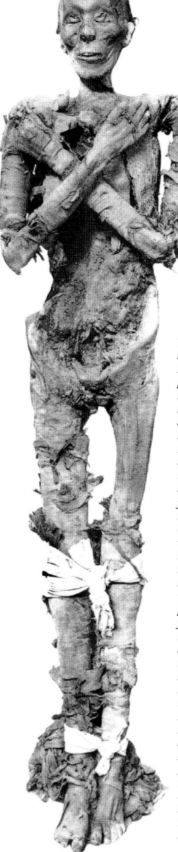

The successor of Thutmose I remains one of the lesser known rulers of the Eighteenth Dynasty, in part because Thutmose II's relatively short reign was uneventful: he seems not to have been a warrior-king in the mode of his immediate predecessors (because of lack of temperament or absence of necessity is not known); and because he was overshadowed during his lifetime, it would seem, by his strong-willed half-sister/spouse, Hatshepsut.

Akheperenre came to the throne only because Thutmose I's two elder sons by King's Great Wife Ahmes predeceased him, leaving as successor his namesake by an auxiliary commoner-wife named Mutnofret. The semi-royal second Thutmose was married on his accession (or perhaps before?) to his fully royal half-sister, Hatshepsut, the eldest daughter of Thutmose I and Ahmes. By Hatshepsut he fathered a daughter, Neferure, but no surviving sons. It was by a concubine, Iset, that he produced his own heir and namesake, who succeeded him as a minor child with the prenomen Menkheperre.

Where the deceased Thutmose II was buried is a puzzle. Lacking any other option, some scholars would like to see as his tomb KV42 in the Royal Valley, inasmuch as this seems to be architecturally transitional between KV38 (Thutmose I) and KV34 (Thutmose III). However, foundation deposits of the uninscribed (but still only partially cleared) monument belong to Meritre-Hatshepsut, principal queen of Thutmose III. Thus, if Thutmose II possibly was the original owner of the tomb, he ultimately would have been displaced from it by his son for the interment therein of the latter's wife; where Osiris Akheperenre subsequently would have resided until his remains were recovered, rewrapped, recoffined and reinterred by the necropolis priests in the Twenty-first Dynasty is, for now, unknown.

There never has been any question about the identity of the mummy found in TT320 housed in an early-Eighteenth Dynasty private coffin to which a *uraeus* had been added and painted text bands inscribed with the name and titles of Thutmose II. Gaston Maspero unwrapped these remains on the first of July in 1886, and found that the body had been badly damaged by tomb robbers: the arms torn and chopped off (one at the shoulder, the other at the elbow), the right leg completely severed from the body, and a great portion of the abdominal and thoracic walls hacked away. Additionally, Thutmose II's mortal remains had suffered numerous knife cuts about the neck and face — probably as a result of the original bandaging being sliced away by his ancient violators. It was in this broken-up condition that anatomist G. Elliot Smith found No. 61066 in September 1906. In the course of his examination of Thutmose II, he was able to restore the mummy's limbs to their proper positions, although it was necessary to tie the legs together at the knees and ankles with new bandages in order to hold them in place.

Smith observed that the king's skin was covered on the thorax,

Opposite, Sunk-relief pigmented depiction of Akheperenre Thutmose II on a block from a dismantled monument of his & Hatshepsut's reconstructed in the Open Air Museum at Karnak. Author's photo

The badly damaged mummy of Thutmose II, at left, as it appeared following restoration of the severed limbs by anatomist G. Elliot Smith in 1906. Tomb robbers had torn off the left arm at the shoulder & chopped off the right forearm just above the elbow. When Gaston Maspero unwrapped the mummy in 1886, it was found that the right leg had been completely severed from the body, probably by a blow from an axe. Additionally, the frontal abdominal & thoracic walls were missing, having been hacked away by an instrument that was sharp enough to slice through several ribs in the process. Numerous cuts or gashes on the neck & face were also observed. The bandages seen here at the knees & ankles are modern.

Royal Mummies, 1912

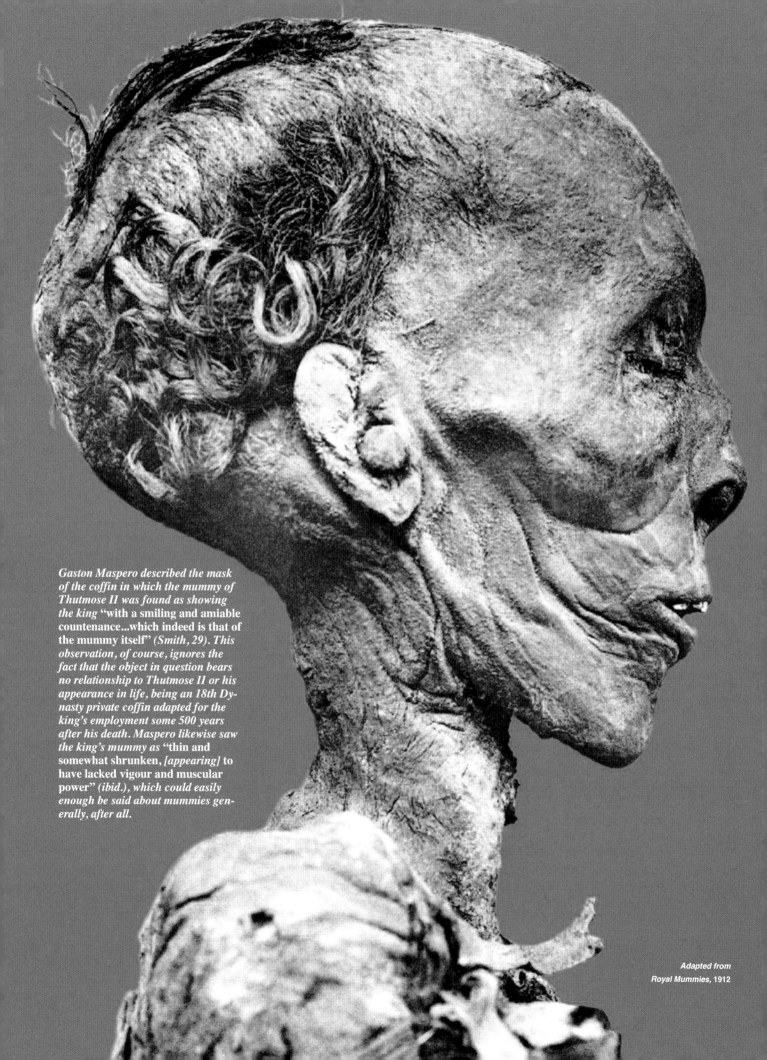

Gaston Maspero described the mask of the coffin in which the mummy of Thutmose II was found as showing the king "with a smiling and amiable countenance...which indeed is that of the mummy itself" (Smith, 29). This observation, of course, ignores the fact that the object in question bears no relationship to Thutmose II or his appearance in life, being an 18th Dynasty private coffin adapted for the king's employment some 500 years after his death. Maspero likewise saw the king's mummy as "thin and somewhat shrunken, [appearing] to have lacked vigour and muscular power" (ibid.), which could easily enough be said about mummies generally, after all.

Adapted from
Royal Mummies, 1912

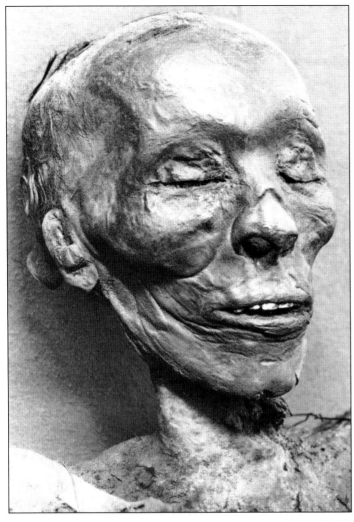

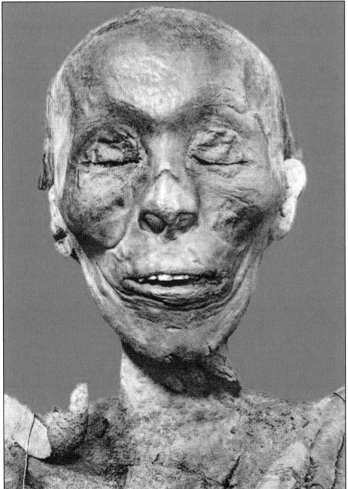

body, and a great portion of the abdominal and thoracic walls hacked away. Additionally, Thutmose II's mortal remains had suffered numerous knife cuts about the neck and face — probably as a result of the original bandaging being sliced away by his ancient violators. It was in this broken-up condition that anatomist G. Elliot Smith found No. 61066 in September 1906. In the course of his examination of Thutmose II, he was able to restore the mummy's limbs to their proper positions, although it was necessary to tie the legs together at the knees and ankles with new bandages, in order to hold them in place.

Smith observed that the king's skin was covered on the thorax, shoulders, arms (but not the hands), back, buttocks and legs (excluding the feet) with hundreds of raised or scabrous eruptions ranging in size *"from minute points to patches a centimetre in diameter"* (Smith, 29). Like the hands and feet, the skin of the head and face was free of these maculae. Maspero had surmised that this condition was the result of a disease which had felled Thutmose II. Smith, however, was inclined to attribute the eruptions to a reaction caused by irritants in the preservative salts used in the mummification process — inasmuch as the same (or *"precisely similar"* [ibid.]) skin condition was to be observed in the mummies of Thutmose II's two immediate successors, Thutmose III (to a lesser degree) and Amenhotep II. Smith did allow that *"this irregularity of the skin"* (ibid.) in father, son and grandson could be the result of some congenital condition.

Smith's measurements of Thutmose II found him to have stood 1.684 m. (5 ft. 6.3 in.) tall. Maspero estimated the king's age at death to have been barely thirty years, based upon the condition of the upper incisor teeth visible through the partially open mouth; Smith, however, thought Thutmose II was somewhat older, considering his partial baldness and *"the wrinkled skin of his face"* (ibid., 30). The latter condition — as seen in No. 61065 — could just as well have resulted from desiccation of fleshy facial features, however. Certainly thirty years of age would accord with the historical Thutmose II.

Despite a severely receding hairline, the mummy displays dark-brown wavy locks (about 12 cm. long) on the temples and sides of the head. Missing patches in the occipital region Smith attributed to the hair having *"fallen off during or after mummification"* (ibid.). The only evidence of a beard are a few scattered hairs just forward of the ears.

The king's ear openings are sealed with plugs of resin, as are the nostrils. The ears apparently were not perforated for earrings (not yet in vogue for royal males at this time). Although the nostrils are rather extended by the resin-impregnated linen plugs, the nose, in any case, seems to have been somewhat broad with a low bridge. Thutmose II's finger- and toenails are clean and neatly trimmed.

Smith was unable to find any evidence of external genitalia, but thought the penis and scrotum may have been flattened against the perineum, as in No. 61065.

The mummy of Thutmose II was included in the SCA's Egyptian Mummy Project in 2005. CT-scanning showed that the king had an enlarged heart, and it was speculated by the examining team that coronary disease may have contributed to his early demise. It was also determined that brain extraction had not been performed. Thutmose's penis was identified. Interestingly no DNA testing was undertaken to determine No. 61066's familial relationships to the Thutmose III mummy (No. 61068) or that of the declared Hatshepsut remains (KV60-A; see below).

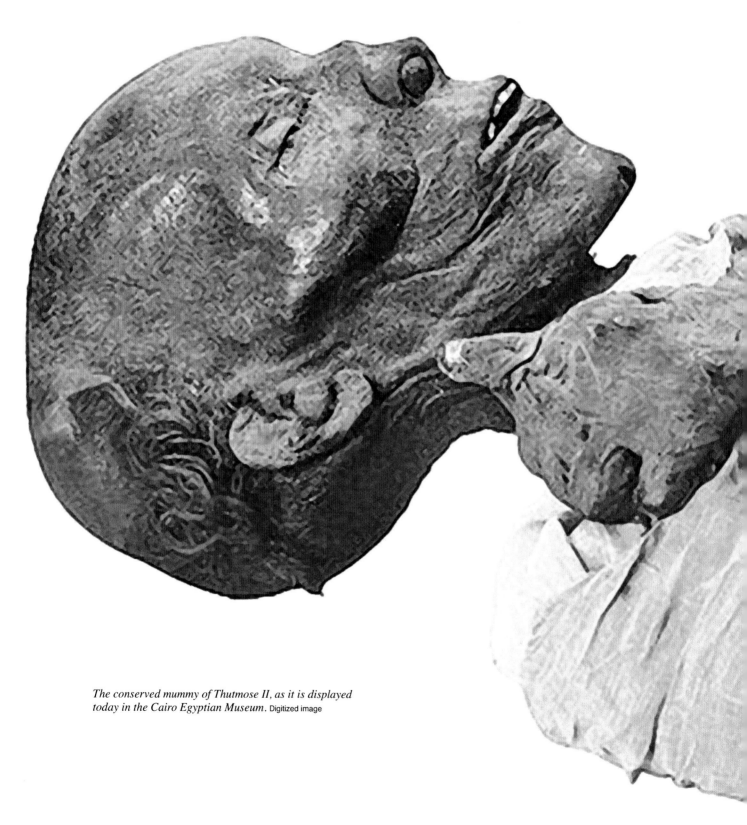

The conserved mummy of Thutmose II, as it is displayed today in the Cairo Egyptian Museum. Digitized image

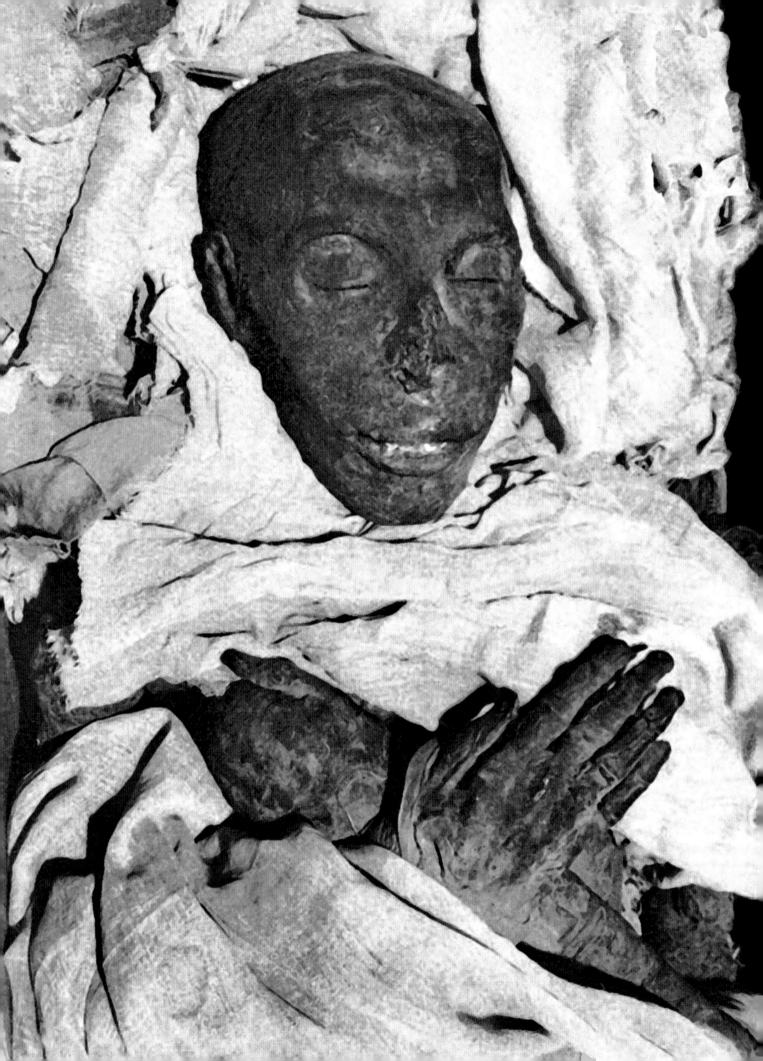

No. 61068
Menkheperre Thutmose III
Reigned c. 1479-1425 BC

F ew Egyptologists would quarrel with the statement that the third Thutmose was, everything considered, the most capable of all the kings who ruled Egypt during the thirty-two dynasties of the pharaonic period. As the "Napoleon" of the Bronze Age, his military genius was responsible for expanding the Egyptian empire to its greatest extent. As a builder he was exceeded only in scope and scale by the efforts of Amenhotep III and, of course, the egomaniacal Rameses II. But neither of those great kings demonstrated the personal aptitudes for which Menkheperre Thutmose was noted in his day: amateur botanist and biologist, artisan and author. He was in many ways the "Renaissance Man" of antiquity.

Ironically, the outstanding Thutmose did not fare so well in death. When found resting in his original wooden coffin (albeit thoroughly adzed of almost all gilding), the bundle containing the king's mummy was held together by three wooden oars, one bound to the exterior and the others contained within the wrappings. This was the first mummy to be exposed — in 1881 by Émile Brugsch, in Gaston Maspero's absence — and when the shattered condition of Thutmose III was revealed (all four limbs torn from the torso, both arms separated at the elbows, the feet broken off, the head detached, the nose mostly obliterated), it was so discouraging that further unwrappings of the Royal Cache mummies were not undertaken until 1886.

Elliot Smith gave the height of Thutmose III's remains as 1.615 m. (5 ft. 3.58 in.), but this, of course, was not inclusive of the absent feet; thus, the king's modern-day reputation as being especially short is not deserved.

Similar to the mummies of his father and son, the blackened skin of Thutmose III is studded on the abdomen, perineum and shoulders with small eruptions. Except for scant eyebrows, the head is completely devoid of hair. Smith could find no visible trace of genitalia.

Above, Imaginary portrait of Thutmose III by Edwardian artist Winifred Brunton. Opposite, The restored mummy of Thutmose III (No. 61068) today in the Cairo Egyptian Museum. Digitized image *Below, Two views of the detached head of the king display (especially in profile) the overbite chracteristic of the Thutmosid dynasty. The king's nose was greatly damaged by tomb robbers, but enough remains to confirm its size & shape in his contemporary 3-dimensional images.*

Royal Mummies, 1912

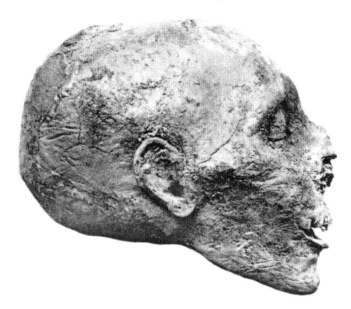

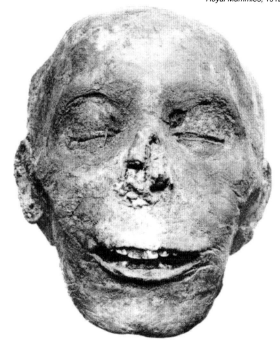

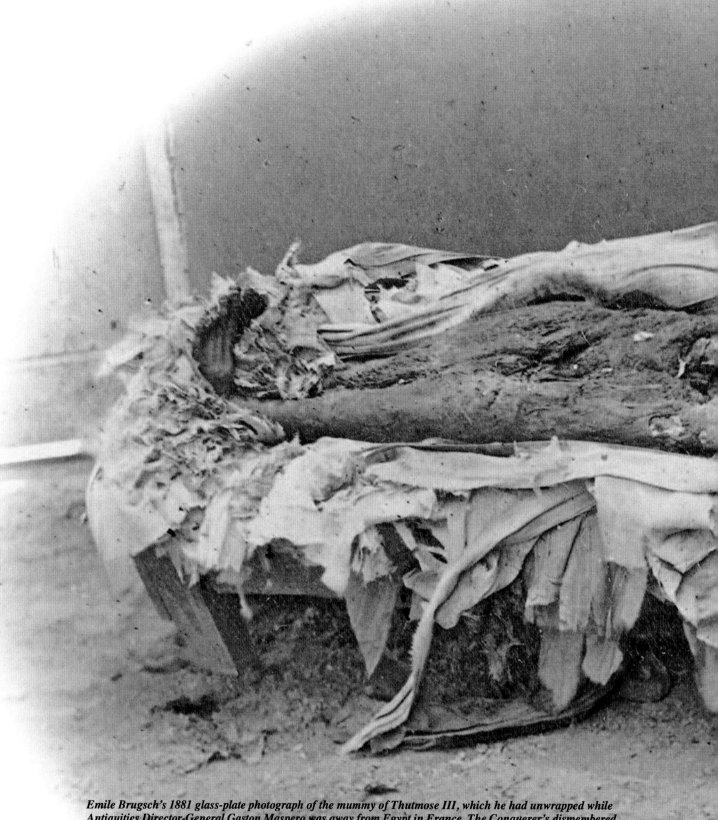

Emile Brugsch's 1881 glass-plate photograph of the mummy of Thutmose III, which he had unwrapped while Antiquities Director-General Gaston Maspero was away from Egypt in France. The Conquerer's dismembered remains had been badly ravished by ancient tomb robbers. Upon his return to Cairo, a greatly displeased Maspero ordered No. 61068 to be rewrapped, exposing it again himself at a public unwrapping five years later, in 1886. Trouvaille, 1881

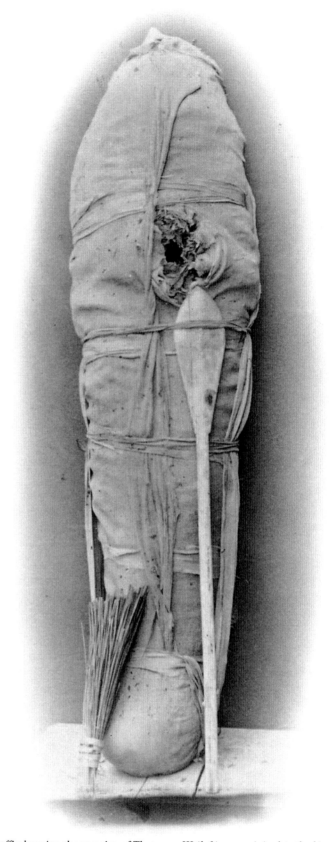

The coffin housing the remains of Thutmose III (left) was original to the king, although it had been hacked all over to remove its gilding. Cercueils, 1909 The bundle containing his mummy (seen in Brugsch's photo above) was torn into by the Brothers Rassul in their search for a heart scarab. Trouvaille. 1881

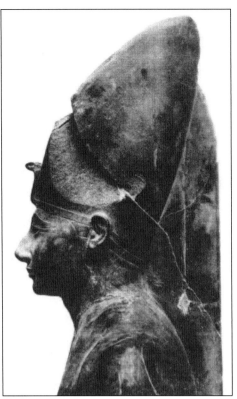

Green basalt just-over-life-size standing statue of Thutmose III found in the Karnak Cache in 1905 is surprisingly naturalistic in depicting the king's strong profile, the large nose being close to the fact of his mummy's (albeit this was largely broken away in antiquity). Archival photo

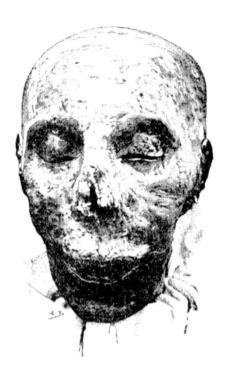

Above, 19th Century engraving of the head of Thutmose III. Archival image Below, The conserved mummy of the king, as displayed today in the Cairo Egyptian Museum. Digitized image

No. 61077
Menmaatre Seti I

Reigned c. 1306-1290 BC

Very likely one important reason the childless King Horemheb selected his aged comrade in arms and confidante, the non-royal Vizier Rameses, to succeed him was that the latter was the father of a fully mature and highly capable son, Seti, who himself had a minor son named for his grandfather. Thus, with the Thutmosid line having run its course (the last true scion of that house being Tutankhamen), the prospect of firmly establishing a vigorous new dynasty, the Ramessides, must have seemed very appealing to Horemheb.

Certainly Menpehtyre Rameses I was not long for this world after donning the Double Crown. He ruled fewer than two years and was succeeded by Seti, who took the throne name of Menmaatre (*"Eternal Justice of Re"*). Whereas Horemheb had focused his energies domestically — in order to restabilize the country politically and economically in the wake of the disastrous Aten-cult experiment — King Seti took as his mission the reestablishment of Egyptian authority in the long neglected "empire" abroad. As early as the first year of his reign, he led the Egyptian forces into Syria, initiating a series of successful campaigns there over the next several years. He also waged war against Libya to the west, although there is no record that he ever marched south into Nubia. All in all, Menmaatre Seti succeeded in his goal of recapturing the foreign territories brought under Egyptian control 250 years earlier by Thutmose III.

But Seti demonstrated the renewed vitality of the state at home by ordering several major building-projects, including: the addition of a great Hypostyle Hall to the mansion of Amen-Re at Ipet-Isut (Karnak); the erection at Abdjw (Abydos) of a chapel for his father, as well as a great temple dedicated to himself and several deities; the raising of his own mortuary temple at the edge of the flood plain west of Waset (Thebes/Luxor); and the cutting in the Valley of the Kings of a large and thoroughly decorated tomb, the grandest royal sepulcher hewn there up to that time. The quantity and quality of reliefs which adorned these several monuments represent a high point of Egyptian art.

In the waning days of the New Kingdom, King Seti's great tomb (KV17) was violated like most others in the Royal Valley and his mummy desecrated, the head being torn from the body and the anterior wall of the abdomen caved in. That the king's body did not suffer greater damage may be due to the fact that its entire surface — except the face — is encased in rock-hard resin-impregnated bandages, which presented a certain amount of protection from tomb robbers' knives and axes.

Gaston Maspero unwrapped Seti I's mummy on June 9, 1886. Even though today — and at the time of Elliot Smith's examination — the head and a few exposed areas of skin are quite black in color, Maspero told Smith that, at the time of the unwrapping, these were of a distinctly brown hue.

Although some bandaging remains on the soles of the mum-

Imaginary 1917 portrait of Menmaatre Seti I by Winifred Bunton. Kings and Queens of Ancient Egypt *Opposite, Of all the surviving royal mummies, the head of that of Seti I, seen opposite in Émile Brugsch's photograph, is certainly one of the best preserved & the most life-like. G. Elliot Smith wrote of it that* "it reveals to us one of the most perfect examples of manly dignity displayed in a mummy that has come down from ancient Egypt" *(Smith, 57).* Adapted from Royal Mummies, 1912 *Below, Relief portrait of the king in the Hypostyle Hall, Karnak.* Author's photo

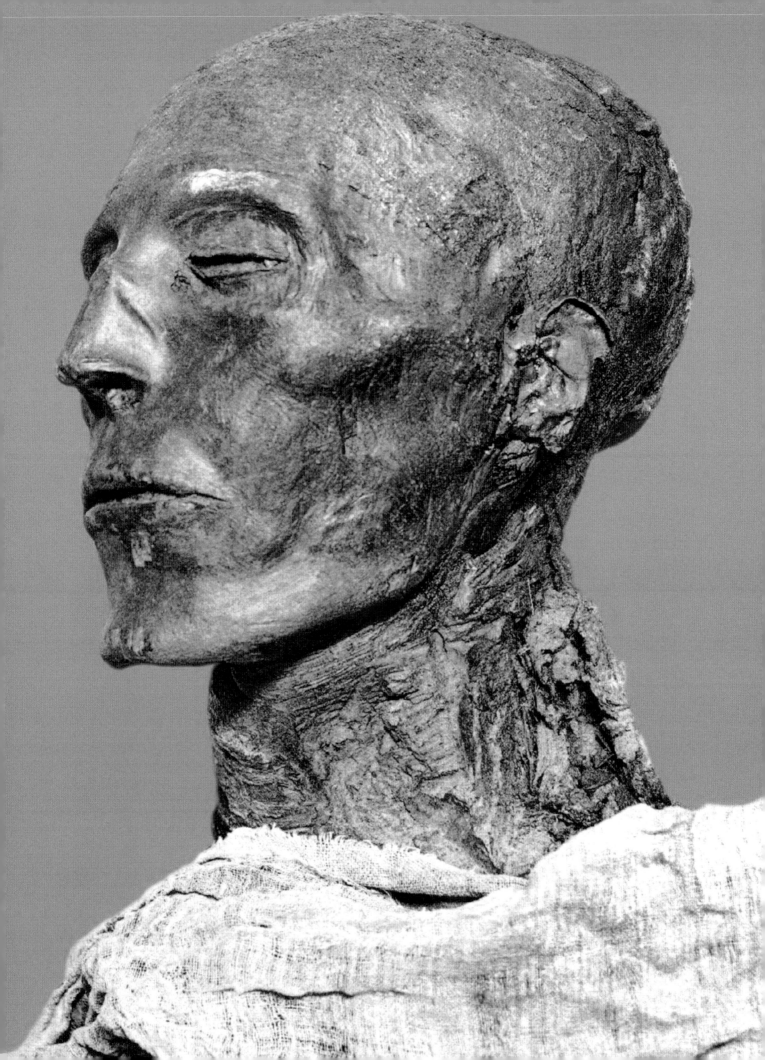

my's feet, Smith estimated the height of Seti I at 1.665 m (5 ft. 5.55 in.). The king was embalmed with his forearms crossed over his chest, the palms flat, fingers extended. *"The left side of the chest is stuffed with black masses of resin-impregnated linen, now of stony hardness"* (Smith, 57). In the upper right side of the thorax *"is a solid black mass about the size of a closed fist. It is not linen, but some brittle jet-black material, with a shining surface when fractured"* (ibid, 57-58). Below this Smith noted another mass of stony consistency which he thought was probably the king's heart — typically left in the body by embalmers. Its position was due, Smith suggested, to its having been displaced during removal of other viscera.

In his Catalogue Général commentary on No. 61077, Smith remarked on Seti I's facial features, which he found distinctly different from the kings of the preceding dynasty (as would be expected), and possibly reflecting "alien (Asiatic)" traits. He wrote, *"there can be no doubt that he* [Seti] *and his successors are less characteristically Egyptian than his predecessors were"* (ibid., 59). The king's head is shaven and there is no trace of a beard.

Although Smith recorded no observation regarding the royal

The large cedarwood coffin that housed the mummy of Seti I in DB320 (lid at left) is probably the husk of one of the king's original coffins, thoroughly scraped of all of its original gilding, the damaged face recarved in the 21st Dynasty. Note hieratic inscriptions of the necropolis priests who retrieved & reburied Seti. Cercueils, 1909 *Although the identity of the mummy of Seti I is confirmed by the hieratic inscriptions on the king's coffin, any question about who No. 61077 was in life could be resolved by a comparison of the mummy's facial features with the many known representations (mostly relief) of Menmaatre Seti.* Adapted from Royal Mummies, 1912 & an archival photo (above)

genitalia in Seti's case, it would seem from the full-length photograph of the mummy that these are present, albeit covered by the bandage-resin carapace. This fact was not commented on in the very thorough discussion of No. 61077 in the *Scanning the Pharaohs* 2015 official report of the Egyptian Mummy Project.

The EMP CT-scanning of the Seti I remains revealed that the king's corpse had been broken by ancient tomb robbers into three parts: the head severed (between the third and fourth dorsal vertebrae) and the torso separated at the lower back (above the iliac crest). The brain had been removed and the thoraxic cavity filled with resin-soaked packs of linen. The body overall had been subjected to ample amounts of liquid (molton) resin during the mummification process, this material having penetrated the soft tissues and infiltrated the bones, spinal canal and body cavities. Additionally, the skin of the face and body had been painted with resin, which over time darkened, giving the mummy its present glossy-black appearance. Atypical of mummification of Seti's time — in fact not seen generally until the Third Intermediate Period — the king benefited from ample amounts of subcutaneous packing of the face, neck, torso and limbs, even palms of the hands and soles of the feet, which enhanced the body's contours and give his mummy an exceptionally lifelike appearance. The scan also revealed several amulets within the mummy and its wrappings.

Interestingly, because it is not commented on in *Scanning the Pharaohs*, there apparently were no DNA comparisons made between the mummy of Seti I and the mummies believed to be those of his father, Rameses I, and his son, Rameses II.

Above, Revealed full-length Seti I mummy, showing its intact but badly damaged condition. The arms are crossed over the chest, fingers extended, palms flat.
Royal Mummies, 1912

Opposite, Archival photo of the king's mummy lying in its coffin basin, as formerly displayed in the Cairo Egyptian Museum.

Right, Profile view of Seti I's head, showing the damaged left ear, the lobe missing.
Adapted from Royal Mummies, 1912

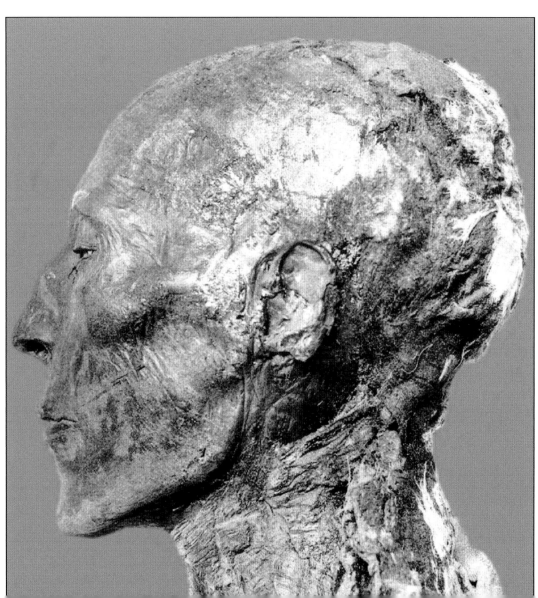

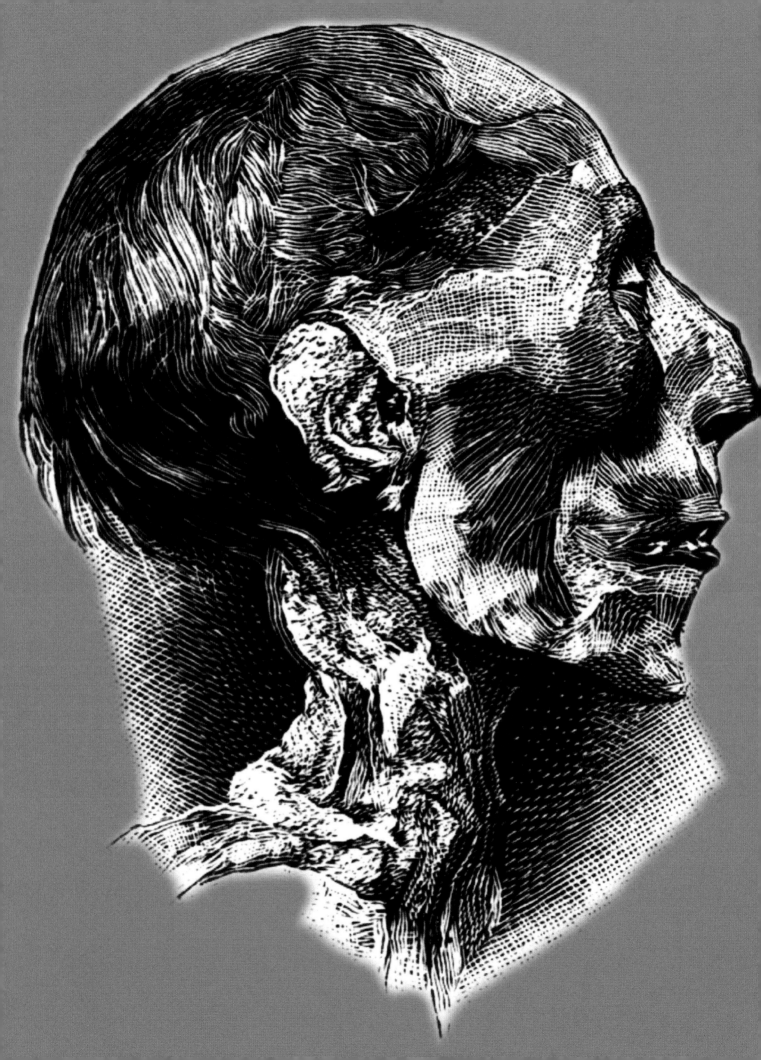

No. 61078
Usermaatre Rameses II

Reigned c. 1290-1224 BC

Except perhaps for the historically somewhat inconsequential Tutankhamen, no ruler of ancient Egypt is more universally known today than the third king of the Nineteenth Dynasty, Usermaatre-Setepenre Rameses-Meriamen (*"The Justice of Re is Powerful, Chosen of Re, Re Has Fashioned Him, Beloved of Amen"*), Rameses II, "Rameses the Great."

In many ways he deserves the last accolade. Other than Pepi II of the Old Kingdom, at sixty-seven years Rameses reigned longer than any other ancient Egyptian monarch. He sired over 100 children, a record for a pharaoh. He built, rebuilt or added on to more monuments than all who preceded or followed him on the throne of the Two Lands. He built a new capital for Egypt in the eastern Delta, which bore his name (Per-Rameses). He raised up score upon score of statues of himself, or else reinscribed the stone images of others with his own names. And he had those names cut so deeply that no later ruler would ever be able to erase or overwrite them.

The second Rameses fancied himself a warrior-king in the mold of Thutmose III, even though his own military campaigns were more public-relations spins than real victories: the text relating Rameses II's fanciful coup against the Hittites at the Battle of Kadesh became the most-often-repeated public record ever cut in stone.

When he died at over ninety years of age, Rameses went to rest in the grand sepulcher (KV7) he had caused to be hewn in the royal necropolis at Waset (Thebes). But ancient tomb robbers harbored no respect for dead kings, however mighty the latter may have been in their own lifetimes; and — just like his great and not so illustrious New Kingdom predecessors, and his mostly lack-luster later-Nineteenth and Twentieth Dynasty successors — Rameses II was turned out of his coffin and his mummy denuded of the funerary finery that had adorned it. And whatever wealth of Egypt he had stocked his tomb with was carried off as well.

When the time came to rescue the royal remains and to officially dismantle their already-plundered burials in the Valley of the Kings, the still remarkably intact body of Rameses II was collected from KV7 by the necropolis priests, rewrapped and installed in a denuded cedarwood coffin which had originally been part of the funerary equipage of one of his predecessors at the close of the Eighteenth Dynasty (Aye or Horemheb). It was then moved on more than one occasion, until it came to rest with others of the royal ancestors in the Pinudjem family sepulcher at Deir el Bahari, TT320, to be found there by modern-day tomb robbers in 1871 and rescued from them a decade later.

The garlanded mummy of Rameses II was publically unwrapped by Gaston Maspero in the presence of Khedive Tewfik on June

Opposite page, An engraving from the late-1880s of the Rameses II mummy in profile. It was obviously this or a profile photograph of the king's head which inspired Egyptologist/artist Winifred Brunton to paint her gouache-on-ivory imaginary portrait of Rameses the Great in 1917 (above). Kings and Queens of Ancient Egypt *Below, The famous Turin black-granite seated statue of Rameses II wearing the* Khepresh *helmet-crown; it is thought to depict the king in the prime of life.* Author's photo

1, 1886. Unlike the unfortunate, shattered remains of Thutmose III, the second Rameses's mummy was found to be in fairly good condition, with only the king's genitals having suffered at the hands of his desecraters, these being broken away and lost (in G. Elliot Smith's opinion).

The great king was mummified with his arms crossed over his chest, the left slightly elevated, both hands flexed, one only partially so.

Opposite, Adaptation of one of the earliest photographs of Rameses II's mummy, published in G. Maspero's Les Momies Royales *(1889).*

Right & detail below, The handsome cedarwood coffin which Rameses II was found occupying in TT320, although reinscribed for him in the 21st Dynasty, was almost certainly not his own. On stylistic grounds it can be dated to the end of the 18th Dynasty, & was likely part of the funerary furnishings of one of the last two kings of that lineage, Aye or Horemheb (neither of whose mummies survived or, if so, are unknown). At one time gessoed, gilded & possibly inlaid, all of that original surface was neatly scraped from both lid & basin in antiquity. Traces of yellow paint are visible, & details of bracelets, etc., are picked out in black pigment. Because of their inferior workmanship, it is probable that the uraeus & crook & flail elements are 21st Dynasty replacements of lost gilded-metal originals.

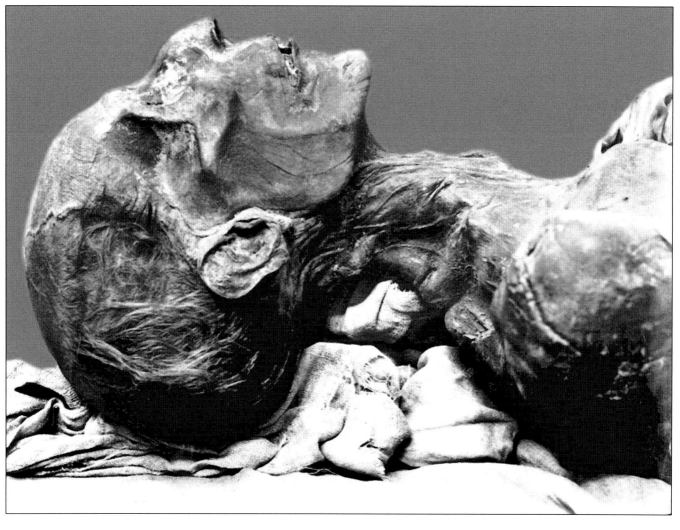

Smith does not indicate in his lengthy (seven-page) Catalogue Général discussion of the Rameses II mummy exactly when he made his examination. Clearly the remains of this particular king held a special fascination for the Australian anatomist, as his description is much more detailed in this case than in any of the other royal and associated mummies recovered from the two caches, TT320 and KV35. Perhaps this was due to Smith having personally regarded Rameses II as the greatest of the pharaohs (whose remains also happened to be in relatively good condition, unlike those of other greats — Thutmose III and Amenhotep III, for instance).

In his discussion of the Rameses II mummy (*Momies Royales*, 253-255), Maspero remarked upon the reddish color of its finger- and toenails, and concluded that this was due to the application of henna to the king's hands and feet during his lifetime. Smith, on the other hand, wrote : *"It is open to question whether the discolouration of the finger and toe-nails may not be due to the staining by resinous embalming-materials and not to henna..."* (Smith, 61).

Whereas Maspero was of the opinion that the king's genitals intentionally had been removed during the embalming process, Smith took the view that — due to apparent broken edges of the flesh area around the missing genitalia, and the bandaging there, as well — it was more likely post-mummification desecration which resulted in their loss.

Rameses II was bald on top at death, with longish white hair (stained yellow by the embalming) on the temples, sides and in back. Smith noted peculiar cross and crescent markings (one each) on the top of the head, but was unable to determine if these were *"intentional or only accidental."* Both ears are pierced, as was the fashion for men in the later New Kingdom. The face had been painted with red ochre by the embalmers, who also accentuated the brows in black pigment.

Certainly the mortal remains of Rameses II are the most thoroughly examined & described of all of the TT320 & KV35 mummies. This is in part due to the king having been sent in 1976 to the Musée de l'Homme in Paris, because of concern over the state of his preservation. As a consequence the mummy was examined using a variety of scientific techniques unavailable in Elliot Smith's day. Some hair strands surreptitiously were taken at the time, but the Egyptian government allowed no tissue samples to be removed from the

Above, The full length view of the Rameses II mummy, as revealed by G. Elliot Smith & photograped by Emile Brugsch for The Royal Mummies, *1912. The absence of genitalia is probably to be attributed to a postmortem event at the hands of tomb robbers. The mummy is 1.733 m. tall (6 ft. 7.75 in.). X-rays made in the late '60s & mid '70s showed that the octogenarian king suffered from degenerative arthritis in both hip joints, & arteriosclerosis in the lower legs — conditions which would have made the act of walking very painful. Fused vertebrae would have given him a stooped stance, as well.*

Opposite, The right profile of Rameses II's face. Both images adapted from *Royal Mummies, 1912*

Below, The mummy of Rameses II as displayed today in the Royal Mummies Room of the Cairo Egyptian Museum. Mummification has turned his longish white hair blond. Cairo Egyptian Museum

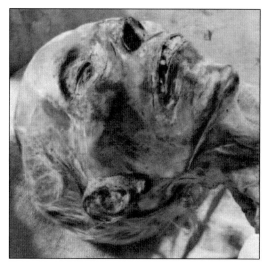

mummy. When it was learned in 2006 that some of Rameses II's hair had, in fact, remained in France when the mummy was returned to Egypt, a formal request was made for the return of the strands. This happened on April 11, 2007, along with pieces of linen and resin samples from the mummy.

No. 61078 was included in the Egyptian Mummy Project CT-scanning of select Royal Mummies in the Cairo Museum during 2005. In the published results (*Scanning the Pharaohs*, 2016), it was reported that Rameses II suffered from massive arthritis consistent with his greatly advanced age (approximately eighty-seven years), with fusions of the spine which would have caused him to

Below, View of the left side of the Rameses II mummy's upper torso & head. Note the elevated position of the left forearm & hand crossed over the right hand resting on the upper chest. The fingers of the left hand are clenched, as if holding a scepter.

Adapted from *Royal Mummies*, 1912

have walked limping with a hunched back during during his final years. Also in keeping with the age factor, the EMP CT-scan revealed that the king had very poor dentition, with marked tooth wear and a root-abcess of the mandible left second molar, which would have caused the second Rameses considerable constant pain, and making eating difficult.

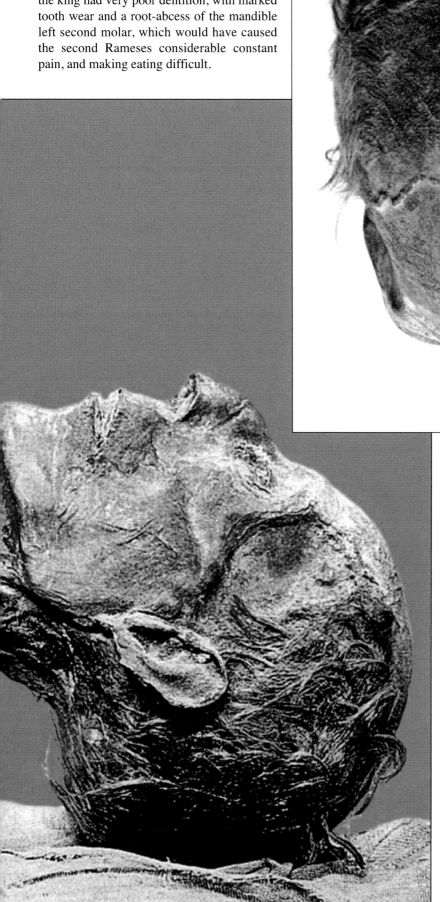

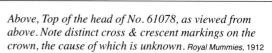

Above, Top of the head of No. 61078, as viewed from above. Note distinct cross & crescent markings on the crown, the cause of which is unknown. Royal Mummies, 1912

No. 61083
Usermaatre-Meriamen
Rameses-heqaiunu III
Reigned c. 1194-1163 BC

Although he aspired to the achievements and reputation of his namesake, the third Rameses only managed to be regarded by historians as the last great king to govern Egypt. The second pharaoh of the Twentieth Dynasty (third and last of the New Kingdom), succeeded his father, Setnakhte — who founded the new line, but wore the Double Crown only briefly — and took as his throne name Usermaatre-Meriamen (*"Powerful Justice of Re, Beloved of Amen"*), appending to his birth name (*"Re Fashioned Him"*) the epithet *"heqaiunu," "Ruler of Iunu* (Heliopolis)." It is probable that King Setnakhte (and Rameses III through him) was, in fact, a descendent of Rameses II, a grandson or even one of the unnamed younger sons to be counted among the over fifty sired by the first Usermaatre. The "Set" element of his nomen may reflect the earlier Ramessides' special affinity for that particular deity.

Whatever his roots, Rameses III was a mature man when he followed his father on the throne, no doubt with several sons of his own (whom he had named in imitation of the first several sons of Rameses II). Soon after after his ascension, the second Usermaatre became a warrior-king in spite of himself. He had spent the first four years of his reign continuing his father's program of restabilizing the country in the wake of the political confusion (even civil wars) that characterized the last years of the Nineteenth Dynasty. In his Year 5, however, Egypt came under assault from a coalition of Libyan tribes bent on immigrating into the fertile Delta from their western-desert homelands. Rameses III met this invasion with the full force of the Egyptian military; and the Libyan tribes were fully routed, with many prisoners taken. But Egypt's and Rameses's domestic tranquility was short-lived, as in Year 8 the country was under siege once again, this time by a somewhat enigmatic collective-group known to history as the Sea Peoples. To counter this attack on the Delta

Above, Winifred Brunton's imaginary portrait of Rameses III, based in large part on his mummy. Kings and Queens of Ancient Egypt *Opposite, Head of Rameses III's mummy, inspiration for the Hollywood "Mummy" movies of the 1940s.* Adapted from an archival photo *Below, Rameses III's mummy in the cartonnage case found within the colossal coffin of Ahmes-Nefertari — which contained the queen's mummy as well.* Trouvaille, 1881

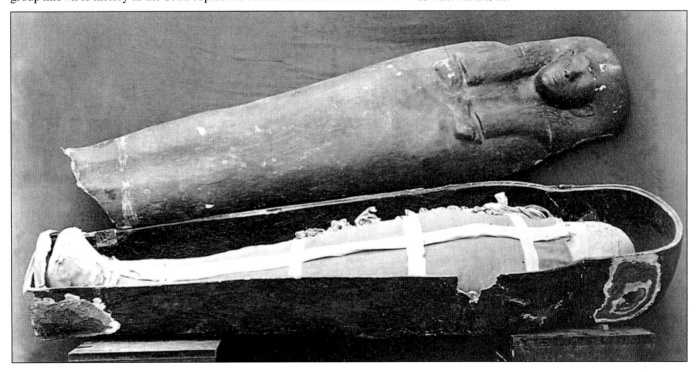

by land from the Levant and via the branches of the Nile, Rameses was compelled to utilize the Egyptian navy, as well as his land forces. Once again the invaders were repelled. But in only three years Rameses was leading his troops yet one more time against a new wave of Libyan invaders from the western desert. And still again Egypt was victorious in defending the Delta from foreigners bent on settling there.

Rameses III recorded all of these military campaigns in reliefs and texts on the walls of his greatest surviving architectural accomplishment, his mortuary temple, still remarkably well preserved today at Medinet Habu on the Luxor west bank. Another principal monument of the king, today still nearly intact, is a small temple built to one side of the Second pylon at Ipet-Isut, the mansion of Amen-Re at Karnak. Usermaatre Rameses III's third architectural achievement is his large and well-decorated tomb (KV11) in the Valley of the Kings.

Rameses was sent to occupy the latter after a reign of thirty-one years, almost certainly as the result of a plot to assassinate him, in order to place one of his sons by a secondary wife on the throne, an event known as the Harem Conspiracy (see below).

The king's mummy was found in TT320 enclosed in a cartonnage replacement coffin of crude workmanship, this latter contained within the gigantic coffin of Queen Ahmes-Nefertari, which was spacious enough to house her mummy as well. Dockets on the wrappings confirmed the king's identity. Neatly rewrapped in an orange-colored linen shroud tightly bound by a longitudinal and four transverse bandages, Rameses III's remains were revealed by Gaston Maspero in the presence of the Khedive Tewfik on June 1, 1886, the same day as the unwrapping of Rameses II (a coincidence which undoubtedly would have pleased Rameses III).

When the outer bandages were removed, it was discovered that the king's mummy was literally encased in a carapace of rock-hard resin-impregnated linen. Maspero subsequently caused this to be cut away from the area of the head, but left it intact over the rest of the body. As a consequence, when Elliot Smith examined the Rameses III mummy (on a date not given by him in his Catalogue Général account), he was unable to make any direct observation of the mummification technique or the condition of the remains.

Above, Relief depiction of Rameses III in his memorial temple at Medinet Habu. Author's photo *Opposite, Right profile view of the head & shoulders of the Rameses mummy.* Adapted from *Royal Mummies*, 1912

The king had been embalmed with his arms crossed on his chest, the hands unflexed and resting on the shoulders. This latter condition seems to have been *"a distinctive feature of XXth Dynasty mummification"* (Smith, 87). Also new was the insertion of artificial eyes of resin, the earliest example of this technique known to Smith.

Rameses III stood 1.683 m. (5 ft. 6.26 in.) tall.

More specific data concerning the mummy was obtained when No. 61083 was CT-scanned in 2005 by the Egyptian Mummy Project. The remains were in generally good condidtion, having escaped tomb-robbers' mutilations due to its resin-linen carapace. The united epiphyses of all bones and full closure of cranial sutures indicated the Rameses III mummy was of a mature individual; and an age estimate of sixty years was given, which would conform with the historical record: a mature man reigning just over three decades. His teeth were in fair periddontal health and exhibited moderate wear and attrition in keeping with his age at death.

The most interesting revelation of the EMP examinations was that the soft tissues king's neck had been slit diagonally from the fifth to the seventh vertebrae, to a depth reaching the bones, causing a gap measuring 35.0 mm, and slicing through the trachea, esophagus and large blood vessels, so definitely fatal. The wound was probably caused by a pointed blade such as a dagger. Thus, one of the questions surrounding the Harem Conspiracy was solved: Rameses III had been slain instantly, rather than only wounded by the conspirators and dying later, as had been speculated on textual evidence by some historians.

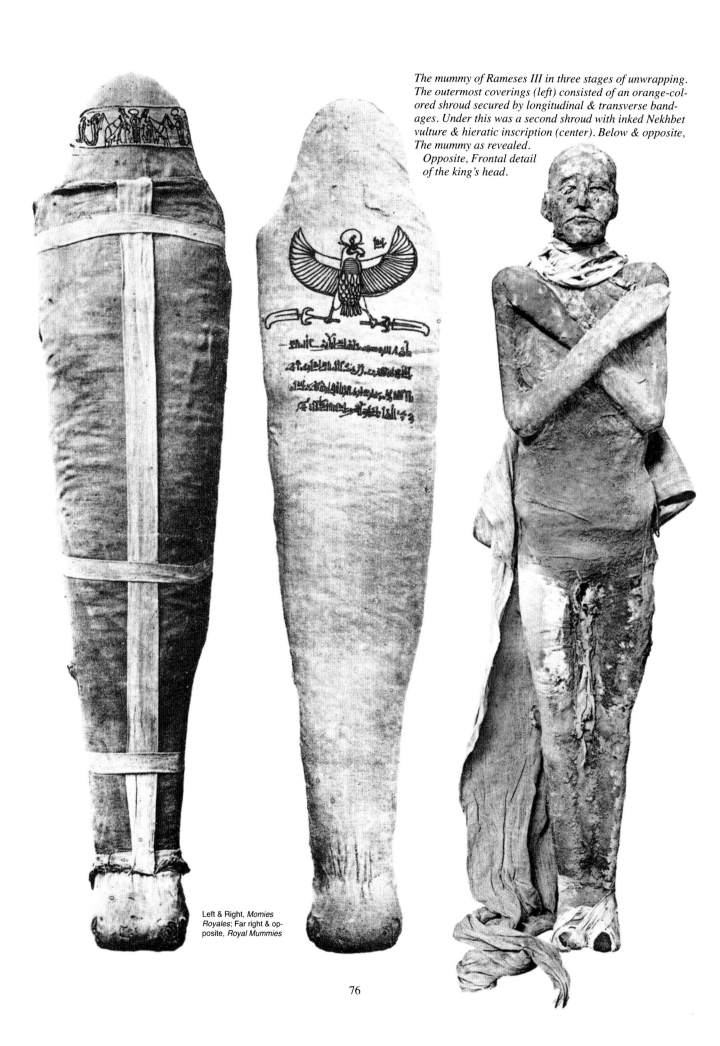

The mummy of Rameses III in three stages of unwrapping. The outermost coverings (left) consisted of an orange-colored shroud secured by longitudinal & transverse bandages. Under this was a second shroud with inked Nekhbet vulture & hieratic inscription (center). Below & opposite, The mummy as revealed.

Opposite, Frontal detail of the king's head.

Left & Right, *Momies Royales*; Far right & opposite, *Royal Mummies*

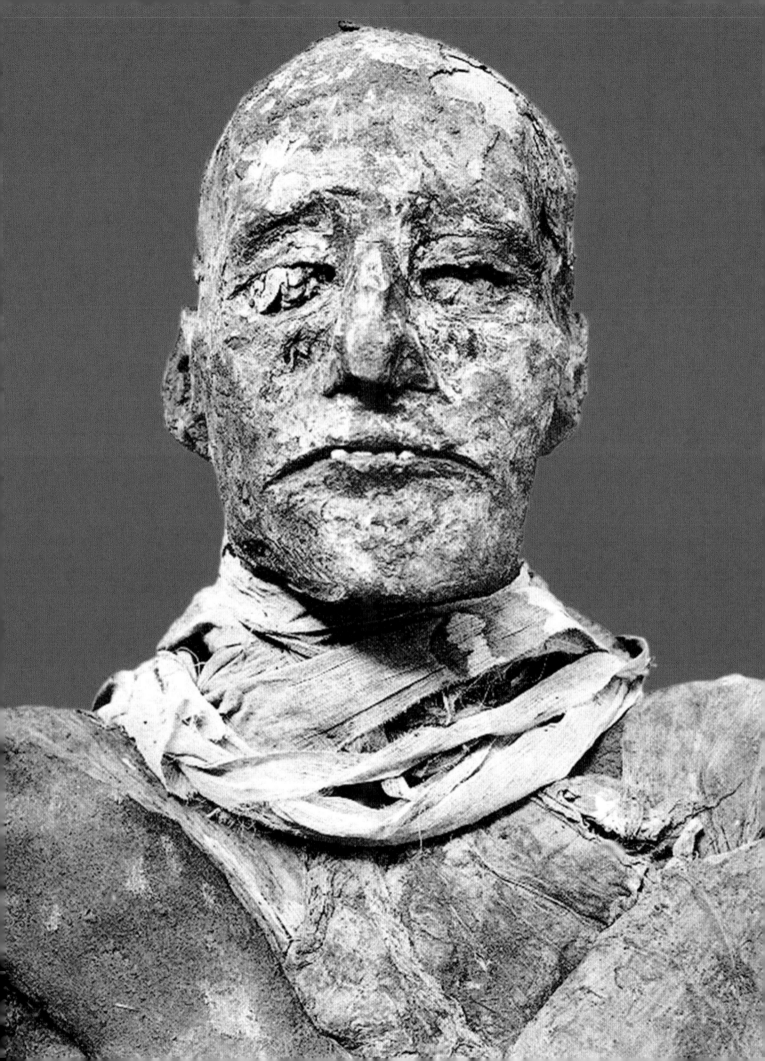

No. 61098
"Unknown Man E"
Probaby Prince Pentawere

20th Dynasty, Reign of Rameses III

Certainly the most disturbing of the mummies from the TT320 cache is the one given the identification of Unknown Man E. Because of the peculiar situation of these remains, there has been considerable speculation as to who he might have been and how he died. Of medium height (1.709 m., 5 ft. 7.28 in.), he was apparently a young man, inasmuch as his teeth are only slightly worn. His hair is long and plaited and encrusted with cheese-like matter. Both ears are pierced and there is no sign of facial hair. Like Unknown Man C and Thutmoses I, II and III, Unknown Man E's genitalia have been removed — whether ante- or postmortem cannot be said.

What is strange about this mummy is that the individual apparently was not embalmed but desiccated naturally. There is no incision for evisceration, so presumably the internal organs are intact. The arms are extended, with the hands side by side over the pubic area, but not touching. The head is thrown back at an oblique angle on the neck, and the mouth is wide open — as was the case with Unknown Woman A — giving the face a horrific grimace. Because of the lack of artificial mummification, it was not possible for Elliot Smith to advance an opinion as to when Unknown Man E may have died.

This mummy was found contained in a well-carved anthropoid coffin painted white without inscriptions of any sort (left); on a stylistic basis it probably is to be dated to the Twenty-first Dynasty, and therefore may be a replacement coffin. When it was opened at the Cairo Egyptian Museum, it was discovered that the enclosed mummy was sewn inside of a sheepskin, and that some natron had been packed around the bundle. Two sticks were also found in the coffin, but the relationship of those to the mummy is unknown.

The sheepskin was removed in 1886 and the fetid-smelling body was found to have its hands and feet bound together with leather thongs. It was examined by Gaston Maspero's anatomist at that time, Dr. Daniel Fouquet, who put forth the theory that Unknown Man E had either died of poisoning or was buried alive. This prompted Maspero to speculate on the identity of the mummy and to suggest in his *Momies Royales* that he might have been the son of Rameses III who was to have been the benefactor of the so-called Harem Conspiracy, Prince Pentawere.

Smith, however, rejected the idea of Unknown Man E having been poisoned, stating that, *"A corpse that was dead of any complaint might fall into just such an attitude as this body has assumed"* (116). And he concluded, *"Without any clue whatsoever to indicate the period in which this individual lived or to suggest his identity it is idle to speculate on the history of his death"* (Ibid.).

The Egyptian Mummy Project (EMP) examined and tested the mummy in 2006, determining that the individual was eighteen to twenty years of age, based on the incomplete fusion of the long bones. It was thought that, because of an inflated larnyx that he had died from strangulation or by hanging. To test the theory (Maspero's) that No. 61098 was the son of Rameses III, Prince Pentawere, a genetic analyis was done by comparing DNA samplings from the king and Unknown Man E. Various Y-chromosome markers were shown to exist, so that the EMP postulated a father-son relationship was highy probable. Thus it safely can be concluded that "E" is Pentawere and that he was executed for his guilt-by-association role in the infamous Harem Conspiracy initiated by his mother, King's Great Wife Teye

Above & opposite, TT320 mummy No. 61098, dubbed "unknown Man E" but now pretty certainly Prince Pentawere of the 20st Dynasty, son of Rameses III. Momies Royales; Royal Mummies, 1912 *Below, The mummy's well-carved, undecorated wooden anthropoid coffin, probably of 21st Dynasty date & so a replacement.* Cercueils, 1909

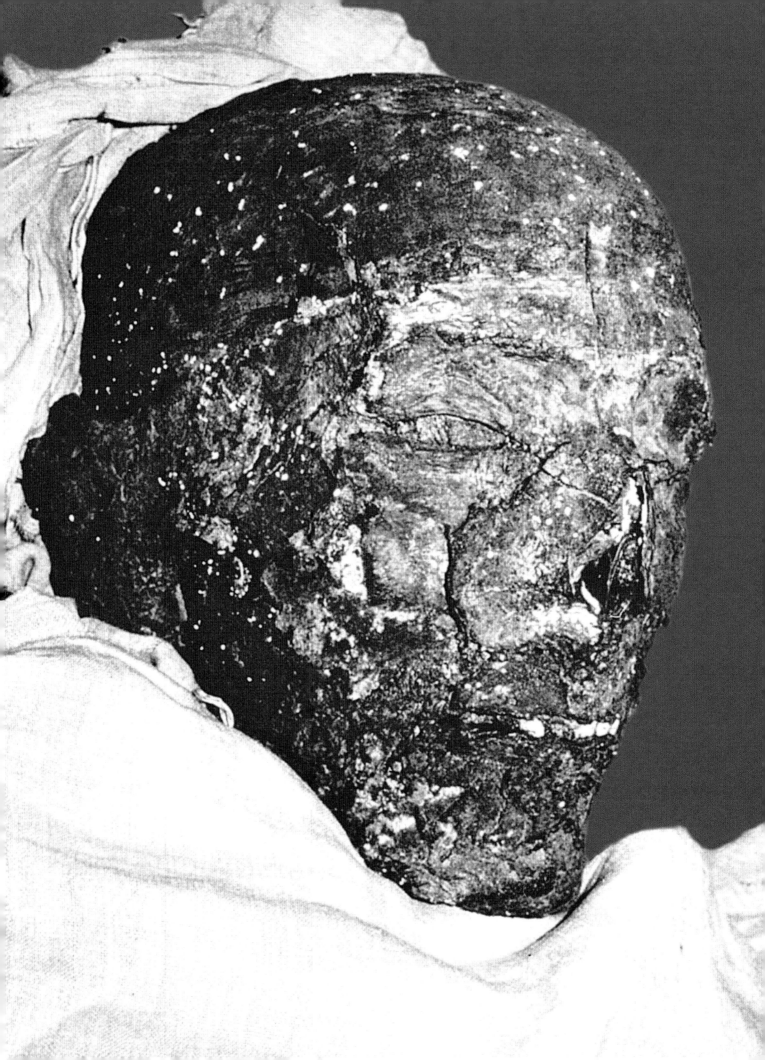

No Number Assigned

Neferkare-Setepenre
Rameses IX

Reigned c. 1131-1112

The ninth Rameses was one of the shadowy rulers of the later Twentieth Dynasty about whom relatively little is certain — regarding both his personal origins and his reign of some nineteen years. It is thought that he was possibly a Prince Khaemwaset (D), son of one of Rameses III's non-ruling sons, Prince Montuhirkhopshef (B) and his wife Takhat (B). He was likely also the father of his successor, Rameses X; and his queen, mother of the latter, was apparently the Baketwernel who was buried in the reused Tomb of Amenmesse (KV10). Rameses IX took as his throne name Neferkare-Setepenre, *"Beautiful Soul of Re, Chosen of Re."*

Despite his relatively long time on the throne (as reigns went in the days of the last Ramessides), there is not much extant evidence of Rameses IX's rule. He apparently built at Iunu (Heliopolis), but his principal monument is his tomb in the Valley of the Kings, KV6, which is of the "syringe" type characteristic of the Twentieth Dynasty, and fairly well decorated. It was standing open and was superficially examined in the early years of the Nineteenth Century, then more thoroughly cleared by Georges Daressy in 1888. There is evidence that it had received the interment of Rameses.

His mummy was among those discovered in TT320 in 1881, housed in a coffin which belonged originally to Princess Nesikhons, wife of High-Priest Pinudjem II; although which of her three TT320 coffins this was is not recorded. Also found in the Royal Mummies Cache was an ivory-veneered casket bearing Rameses IX's name. Strangely enough, the king's remains apparently were never assigned a Catalogue Général number and were not examined, it would seem, by Elliot Smith — at least Rameses IX is not included in his *Royal Mummies* of 1912.

Rameses IX nonetheless was x-rayed and his head photographed by Dr. James E. Harris and the University of Michigan Expedition in the late 1960s. The apparently unwrapped body is superficially intact, although the forearms are missing. The mummy's head — all that has been exposed — is without a nose, and the skin is heavily encrusted with salt deposits resulting from the mummification. Harris and his team, for reasons unexplained, were uncertain in their identification of the king's mummy, referring to it in *An X-Ray Atlas of the Royal Mummies* (Chicago, 1980) as either Rameses IX or Rameses XI.

Along with Pinudjem I, Rameses IX (head at right & opposite, adapted from James E. Harris photos*) is one of the "neglected" royal mummies, never having been assigned a Catalogue Général number, photographed by Émile Brugsch or examined by Elliot Smith (& thus not included in the 1912* Royal Mummies *by the latter). Rameses IX's mummy has lost its nose & the skin of the head is encrusted with salt deposits — resulting no doubt from the mummification process. The king's forearms are also missing.*

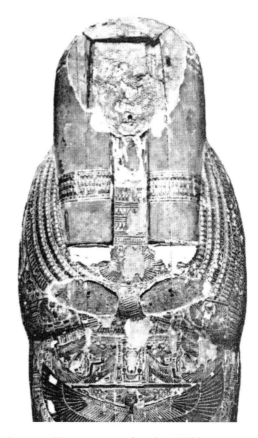

Rameses IX's mummy was found in TT320 resting in one of the three coffins of Nesikhons, wife of Pinudjem II, although which of these is unrecorded. The middle one of the Nesikhons set (from which the gilded facepiece & hands have been torn away by [modern-day?] tomb robbers) is seen above. Cercueils, 1909

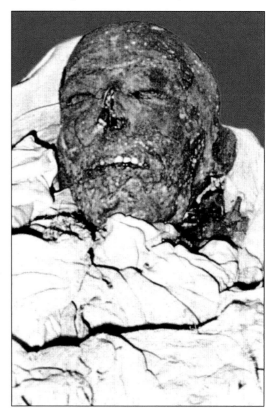

No. 61087
Nodjmet
Queen
20-21st Dynasty. c. 1075 BC

Nodjmet was the wife of Herihor, the high-priest of Amen who established a line of priest-kings ruling from Waset (Thebes) contemporaneously with the Twenty-first Dynasty royal line at Tanis. Herihor's own antecedents are uncertain, but he seems to have had Libyan ancestry. He attained the positions of viceroy of Kush and vizier prior to assuming royal prerogatives.

Nodjmet is thought to have possibly been a sister of Rameses XI, alongside whom Herihor ruled for a period of six years, predeceasing that last ruler of the Twentieth Dynasty. A docket found on the mummy of Nodjmet indicates that she was buried in Year 1 of Smendes, successor of Rameses XI and founder of the Tanite Twenty-first Dynasty. Thus she outlived her husband by several years.

Of the Third Intermediate Period mummies found in TT320, that of Nodjmet is chronologically the earliest, and already reflects the changes in mummification techniques introduced in the Twenty-first Dynasty. It was during the floruit of Herihor that the collecting and rewrapping of the plundered mummies of the New Kingdom began; and it may have been the first-hand observation of these (for the most part) pitifully shrunken remains that inspired the embalmers of Herihor's time to strive to improve upon their art by devising a *"means of restoring to the embalmed body the fulness of limb and features that it had possessed during life but had lost during the process of mummification"* (Smith, *Royal Mummies*, 95).

In the case of Nodjmet, this was accomplished by the application of sawdust padding to the surface of the body, which was held in place by bandages impregnated with resinous material, forming a complete carapace such as was first seen in the mummy of Rameses III. The body was then painted all over with ochre and gum. The neck and cheeks were tightly packed internally with sawdust, artificial stone eyes were inserted and eyebrows of hair stuck in position. An artificial brown wig composed of elaborate plaits was applied to the head, covering Nodjmet's own scanty locks. The body cavity was packed with sawdust, the embalming wound plugged with a lump of wax.

The mummy of Nodjmet was damaged by tomb robbers both in antiquity and following the initial discovery of TT320 in 1871. The limbs are broken in several places and there are numerous wounds about the face and chest made by knives cutting through the bandaging.

Nodjmet stood about 1.548 m. (5 ft. .94 in.) tall in life. Smith estimated she was about thirty-five at her death.

Above, Q. Nodjmet's outer coffin (of two), which has been adzed of most ot its original gilding, possibly by the Rassul brothers following their discovery of the TT320 cache in 1871. Cercueils, 1909

The full face of Q. Nodjmet's mummy, left & opposite, is the result of packing with sawdust to give a resemblance of its appearance in life. Her mummy is the earliest example of the use of stone artificial eyes.

Photos adapted from Royal Mummies, 1912

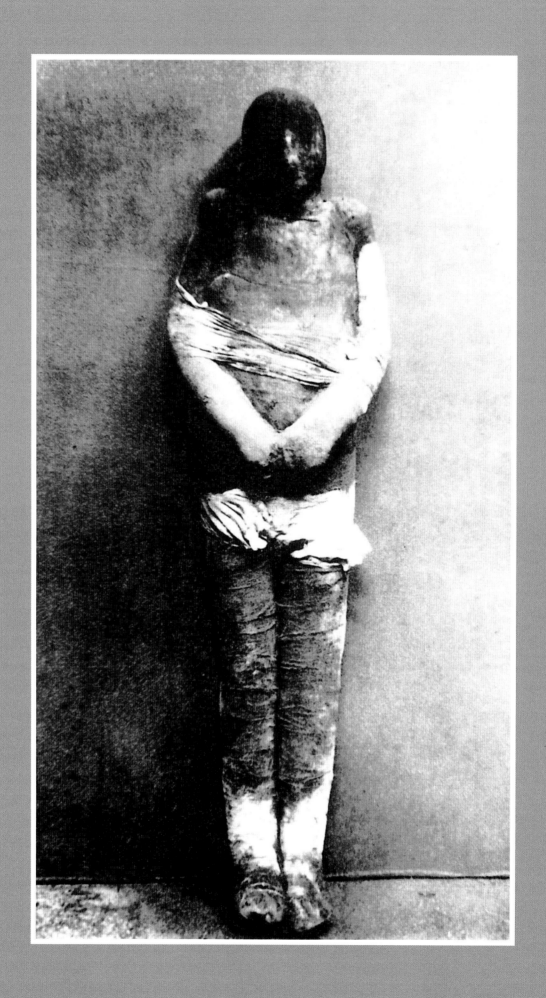

No Number Assigned

Khakheperre-Setepenamen Pinudjem I

Priest-King
Reigned c. 1070-1032 BC

The second high-priest of Amen-Re at Waset (Thebes/ Luxor) to assume royal prerogatives was one Pinudjem, who took as his kingly prenomen Khakheperre-Setep-enamen (*"The Soul of Re Appears, Chosen of Amen"*). His birth name and epithet (Pinudjem-Meriamen) means *"He Who Belongs to the Pleasant One (Ptah), Beloved of Amen."* His pontificate began during the reign of Rameses XI and continued for sixteen years under Herihor and Piankh (his grandfather and father). It was upon the death of the latter that he began reigning fully as king in the south, with Nesbanebdjed I (Smendes) heading up the Tanite Twenty-first Dynasty in the Delta. Pinudjem outlasted that king and his successors, Amenemnisu and Pasebakhaenniut I (Psusennes), for a total rule of eighteen to twenty years. It would seem that Priest-King Pinudjem I had two wives (queens), Hent-tawy and Maatkare.

The mummy of Pinudjem was found in the Royal Mum-mies Cache, not within his own pair of nested coffins (one of which he had usurped from Thutmose I), but rather in an appro-priated colossal queen's coffin which had belonged originally to Aahotep of the late-Seventeenth/early-Eighteenth Dynasty. For reasons that are not understood, Pinudjem I was never assigned a Catalogue Général number, nor were his remains examined (or at least reported on) by G. Elliot Smith. The whereabouts of the mummy today also seems to be unknown (to the EMP).

That the priest-king did not exist in Émile Brugsch's and Gaston Maspero's imaginations only is evident from at least four existing contemporary pictorial records of his mummy. Two pho-tographs were apparently taken by Brugsch. One (opposite) shows the partially wrapped remains (any outer shrouding having been removed) standing upright against a canvas backdrop. It would appear that the mummy was carefully bandaged with per-haps a carapace of resin-impregnated linen covering the head. The arms are extended but partially flexed, with the hands resting side by side over the genital area. Two engravings of the mummy were subsequently published in the 1880s (at right), one showing the priest-king with his head revealed, the other this head in a profile detail. The latter indicates that Pinudjem I was rather well-preserved, his cheeks filled out with padding (sawdust?).

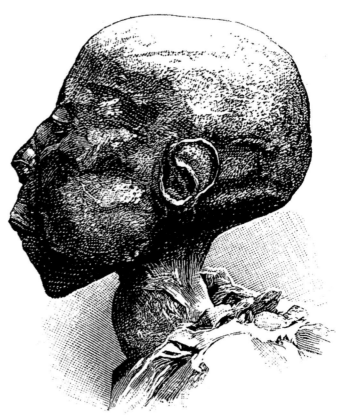

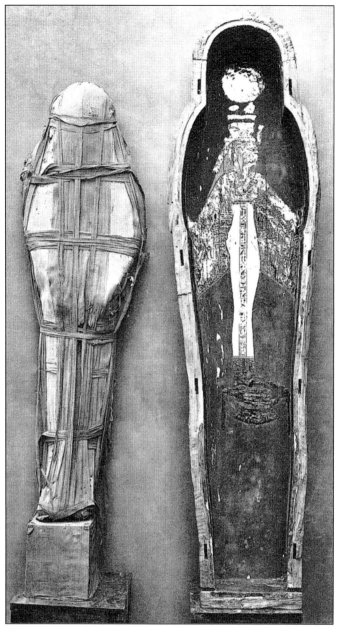

No. 61090
Henttawy

Queen
21st Dynasty. c. 1040 BC

It would seem that Henttawy was the daughter of Rameses XI, and the Great Royal Wife of Priest-King Pinudjem I. She also held the title *"Chief of the Harem of Amen-Re, King of the Gods"* and was a prophetess (priestess) of both Mut and Khonsu at Ipet-Isut (Karnak) and of Inheret-Shu at Thinis. She bore several children to Pinudjem, including Priest-King Menkheperre; King Pasebakhaenniut I (Psusennes); the latter's wife, Mutnodjmet; as well as possibly God's Wife of Amen Maatkare.

Like her husband and other members of her family who were found cached in TT320 at Deir el Bahari South, Henttawy was apparently buried elsewhere originally, although the location of the early Pinudjem family tomb(s) is unknown.

The queen's mummy was discovered in a set of two wooden coffins, both of which had been thoroughly adzed of their gilding and the inlaid eyes removed. This is likely to have been the doing of the Rassul brothers who found the Royal Mummies Cache. The mummy itself was exposed by Gaston Maspero in 1886. It had been damaged by ancient tomb robbers, who, in a search for a heart scarab, had penetrated through the wrappings and the resin-impregnated carapace surrounding the body, into the thorax itself. When G. Elliot Smith examined the mummy in June 1909, he found in the wrappings a large embossed sheet-gold plate covering the abdominal embalming incision, secured there by red-linen-wrapped string passed around body.

Henttawy's mummy was prepared in the manner characteristic of Twenty-first Dynasty embalming techniques. The body is wrapped in particularly fine linen, one of the innermost sheets being dyed red. Resin-impregnated linen encases the body in a hard carapace, which has been broken away in the areas of the head, thorax-abdomen and the right foot (where the toes are missing). The body (1.518 m., 4 ft. 11.76 in. tall) is that of a very heavy-set individual with large pendant breasts, the body cavity being packed with aromatic sawdust. The face has been filled out with a *"cheese-like"* mixture in order to simulate its plumpness in life. Although intact when discovered in 1881 (as evident at left in a photograph taken that year), the face subsequently *"burst"* open on the left side prior to Smith's examination. Artificial stone eyes fill the sockets, although these have disintegrated somewhat. The queen's face is painted with ochre and the lips and cheeks are stained red.

Above left, The wrapped mummy of Q. Henttawy & the trough of her inner coffin. Trouvaille, 1909 Left, The mummy's head, as photographed in the 1880s, when there was minimal damage to the fully packed face. Les Momies Royales, 1889 By the time the queen's remains were photographed for Smith's Royal Mummies *(1912), opposite, the face had burst open on the left side. This is restored today. Royal Mummies, 1912*

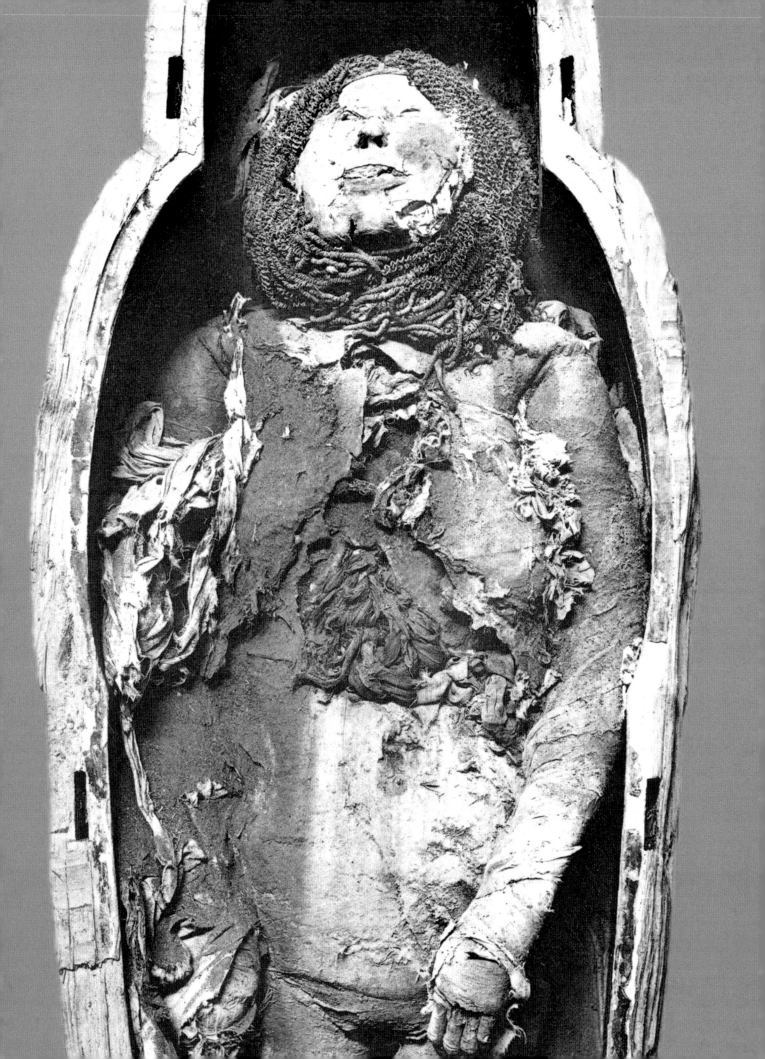

No. 61092
Masaharta

High-Priest, General-in-Chief
Pontificate, c. 1054-1046 BC

Very little is known about Masaharta, except that he was the only son of Pinudjem I and the latter's second wife, Isetemkheb (A). When his father assumed the role of king in the south (at Waset), Masaharta succeeded him in the pontificate of Amen-Re at Ipet-Isut (Karnak). He also held the title of General-in-Chief, and it would appear that he died (after serving as Amen high-priest for only eight years) at the fortress at Teudjoi (modern El Hiba), which apparently served as a some-time home for the Theban priest-kings. Where Masaharta's original tomb was located is unknown, but his mummy was moved along with those of other members of his family to the cache-tomb TT320 at Deir el Bahari South.

When found, the Masaharta mummy occupied a set of two gilded-and-painted cedarwood coffins and was accompanied by a so-called "mummy board." While the outer coffin is largely intact (only one gilded hand of the cover is missing), the inner one and the board are both lacking the presumably gilded face pieces and hands. Whether these were wrenched off and stolen by necropols workers in antiquity or more recently is uncertain.

Gaston Maspero caused the mummy's wrappings to be removed on June 30, 1886, to confirm that Masaharta had been disturbed by the Rassul brothers during the decade between 1871 and 1881. There remains on the soft and flexible skin of the mummy's torso the impressions of a pectoral ornament and of "braces" or suspenders — the latter very likely being the same such items shown by one of the Rassuls to American Charles Edwin Wilbour in Luxor in 1881 (see Book One, p. 23).

The body of Masaharta is that of a very obese man who would have stood 1.696 m. (5 ft. 6.77 in.) tall in life. Peculiarly there is present a short curly white beard around the jaw line, and scattered hairs of a mustache. The mummy's short hair is also white, although now thickly smeared with resinous material.

As typical of the period, the body cavity was filled at the time of embalming with sawdust for packing. Because of the subject's obesity, it was necessary to change the position of the embalming incision, making it parallel: *"In a subject of his bulk the attempt to eviscerate the body through the loins in the way customary at his time would have presented very great difficulties"* (Smith, *Royal Mummies*, 106).

The face and the entire body are painted with a thick layer of red ochre. The face is packed in accordance with the mummification practices of the Twenty-first Dynasty, but in this case excessively so, giving the cheeks *"an unnaturally puffed-out appearance"* (Smith, ibid).

The ears lobes have small perforations and the fingers and toes all bear impressions of strings used to hold on the nails during the desiccation process.

Opposite, The mummy of Masaharta resting in the trough of his inner coffin. Note the impressions of a pectoral & "braces" on the soft, flexible skin of the torso. Adapted from *Royal Mummies*, 1912
Right, The outermost or first coffin of Masaharta, from which only one gilded hand is missing. Cercueils, 1909

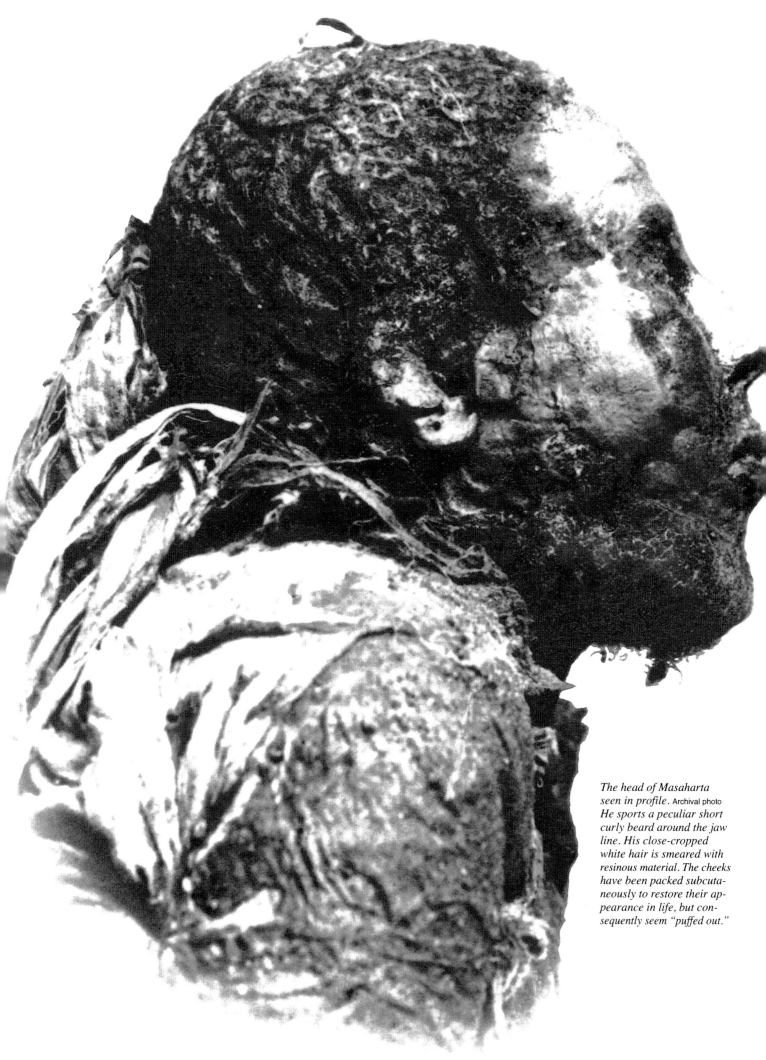

The head of Masaharta seen in profile. Archival photo *He sports a peculiar short curly beard around the jaw line. His close-cropped white hair is smeared with resinous material. The cheeks have been packed subcutaneously to restore their appearance in life, but consequently seem "puffed out."*

Left, The full-length view of Masaharta's mummy, No. 61092. The rock-hard carapace formed by resin-impregnated linen molded around external packing of sawdust has been left on the upper portion of the left arm & on the entire left leg, thus giving a clear idea of the embalmers' intention to give the body a life-like appearance. Masaharta's hands are intended to cross at the genitals, but his gross corpulence interferred with this being fully accomplished. _{Momies Royales} *Below, The upper portion of Masaharta's second or inner coffin, from which the face piece & hands have been wrenched away, either for their gilding in antiquity or disposal on the antiquities market in the 1870s.* _{Adapted from Cercueils, 1909}

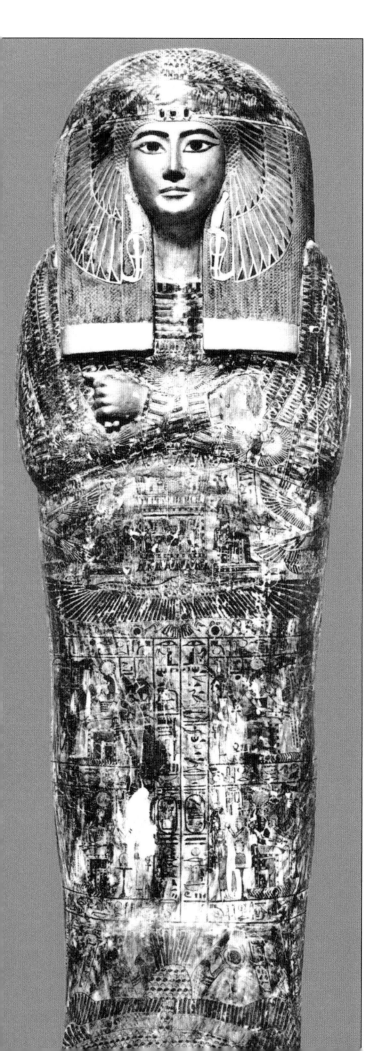

No. 61088
Maatkare

God's Wife of Amen
21st Dynasty, c. 1030 BC

Not a great deal is known about Maatkare, who was apparently the daughter of Pinudjem I and Queen Henttawy. She held the title of *"God's Wife of Amen,"* which meant that she was effectively the virgin female head of the Amen cult at Ipet-Isut (Karnak). It is surmised that she was named for Maatkare Hatshepsut, as her brother, Menkheperre, apparently had been named for Menkheperre Thutmose III, thus reflecting a special interest of Pinudjem I in those particular early-Eighteenth Dynasty rulers.

When Maatkare's inner coffin (of two) was opened following its discovery in the Royal Mummies Cache in 1881, it was found that her neatly wrapped mummy shared the space with a much smaller bundle, which was automatically presumed to be the body of an infant, perhaps stillborn. It appeared to Gaston Maspero and his colleagues, upon their superficial examination, that Maatkare had been embalmed and wrapped so as to seem pregnant. This presented a problem, owing to the presumed virginity of the individual holding the God's Wife of Amen sacerdotal position, and thus led to all sorts of speculation. Which was all put to rest, however, when the "infant" was later x-rayed and found to be an adolescent baboon, probably Maatkare's beloved pet.

Elliot Smith examined Maatkare in June 1909, to observe

Left, The well-preserved coffin of Maatkare only one gilded hand having been wrenched away by thieves) is easily the most attractive of all the 21st Dynasty coffins recovered from TT320. Cercueils, 1909 Above, The mummy of Maatkare resting in her second coffin, accompanied by the wrapped remains of her pet baboon (also opposite). Trouvaille, 1881

that, like her mother, she had been a very short woman in life (1.482 m, 4 ft. 10.35 in. tall) and rather heavyset. To produce her actual proportions, the embalmers had stuffed the body cavity with sawdust and additionally *"Various foreign substances had been introduced under the skin of every part of the body and moulded into some semblance of the queen* [sic]*"* (Smith, *Royal Mummies*, 98). This is the earliest known Twenty-first Dynasty example of inserting filler material under the skin in an attempt to recreate a life-like appearance.

Maatkare's cheeks also were (over) stuffed with a great quantity of mud, the nostrils plugged and artificial stone eyes installed under the lids. The face was painted with yellow ochre and sprinkled with powdered resin, then covered by a sheet of very fine muslin, which subsequently adhered to the skin surface, forming a kind of mask. The mass of wavy and plaited hair on the mummy's head is, to all appearances, Maatkare's own — dark brown with hints of grey. The lobes of the priestess's ears are pierced and greatly stretched.

Maatkare's *"breasts were enormously enlarged, probably because she was lactating,"* Smith mistakenly concluded (Smith, 100), having accepted Maspero's view that the priestess had died following childbirth. Yellow ochre was applied to the entire body, which was carefully wrapped in sheets of very fine linen, several additional layers being added and the whole thickly covered with resinous material to create a strong carapace covering both head and body.

Red-leather *"braces"* were found on the mummy's torso, with parchment *"tablets"* attached; the latter could not be read, however, because of the resin covering them.

The tattered appearance of Maatkare's mummy (right) is due to ancient thieves having torn through the bandages in search of jewelry. Note the carapace of resin-impregnated linen still covering the lower legs. Royal Mummies, 1912

No. 61094
Khakheperre-Setepenamen Pinudjem II

High-Priest
21st Dynasty, c. 990-969 BC

The second Pinudjem was the son of Priest-King Menkheperre and half-brother of High-Priest Nesbanebdjed II (Smendes). Like the latter he did not employ a cartouche when writing his name (as his father and grandfather, the first Pinudjem, had done), and therefore, apparently, he did not otherwise assume royal prerogatives (although he took a prenomen, or throne name — the same as his namesake's). His mother was Isetemkheb, daughter of Pasebakhaennuit (Psusennes) I, who had ruled at Tanis in the Delta.

Pinudjem II had two wives, one of whom, Nesikhons, was buried with him in TT320, as was their daughter, Nestanebtishru — which has led to the speculation that the Deir el Bahari tomb was original to them rather than the site of their reburial.

The undisturbed mummy of Pinudjem II was found in a set of two painted-and-gilded coffins with a mummy board. That both the remains of the high-priest and his coffins were intact suggests that they had been placed in TT320 without having had an earlier interment.

The mummy itself was first exposed by Gaston Maspero on June 28, 1886. Like the remains of Henttawy and Maatkare, it was found to be wrapped in multiple layers of very fine linen, with interspersing layers of resinous paste. Some of Pinudjem's wrappings had colored borders and fringes. The high-priest was found to be wearing crossing strips of red-leather *"braces,"* such as had been stolen from the mummy of Masaharta.

The mummy's face had been liberally sprinkled with powdered resin, which now cakes much of the surface (as can be seen in the detail photo below). Pinudjem sported a short white chin-beard in life, although his upper lip was shaven. The mummy's arms are packed with mud. Packets of viscera are contained within the body cavity.

In life Pinudjem II stood 1.706 m. (5 ft. 7 in.).

What appears to be hair on the head of Pinudjem II's mummy (above & right, Royal Mummies, 1912) is actually the tatters of the linen & resin carapace which covered the remains.

Pinudjem II's set
of two coffins
(the outer one at
left) are intact, &
excellent exam-
ples of the coffin
style of the 21st
Dynasty. Face &
hand pieces are
gilded & the en-
tire surfaces cov-
ered with painted
& gilded funer-
ary vignettes.

Cercueils, 1909

No. 61091
Tayuheret
21st Dynasty

T he identity of the lady Tayuheret is uncertain, but it has been offered that she may have been the wife of High-Priest Masaharta. She apparently was a chantress of Amen during her lifetime. Her body was found among those of the Pinudjem family, housed in a pair of badly damaged coffins with a mummy board in similar condition.

Like the mummies of Henttawy and Maatkare, that of Tayuheret was encased in a carapace composed of fine linen and layers of resinous paste. One of the innermost of her burial sheets is dyed red. The face is packed like those of the other mummies in the Pinudjem group, except that in Tayuheret's case her widely separated lips are filled with a mass of wax and there is a large wax plate over the right eye. The hair visible on her head is probably a wig.

The skin of the lady's face, especially on the forehead, has been badly damaged by insects.

The mummy of Tayuheret (opposite & above, adapted from Royal Mummies, 1912) *has never been completely unwrapped, being encased in a carapace of linen & resin paste. Elliot Smith removed enough of this in 1909 to expose the head. Tayuheret's cheeks had been typically packed so as to extend them, but in her case the nose is buttressed with large pieces of wax. There is a wax plate in front of the right eye, & a large mass of wax protrudes from her widely opened mouth.*

Left & below, The lid & basin of the second, inner, coffin of Tayuheret. The former has been damaged by robbers (possibly modern), who tore away the gilded face piece, wig lapets & hands.
Cercueils, 1909

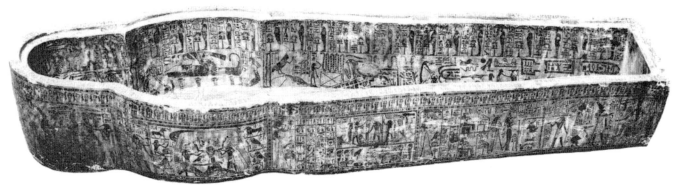

Left, The damaged lid of Iset-emkheb's inner coffin, face piece & hands torn away in antiquity. Right, The intact lid of her outer coffin.

Cercueils, 1909

No. 61093
Isetemkheb (D)

21st Dynasty. c. 980 BC

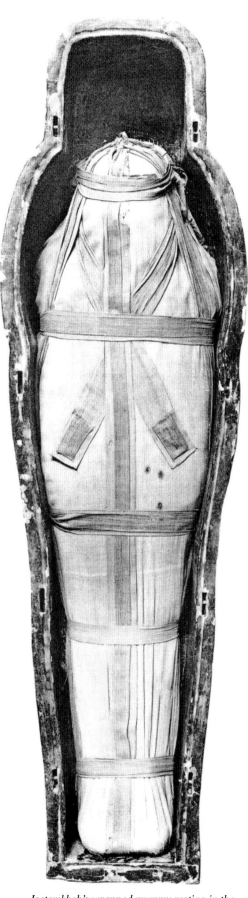

Both sister and wife of High-Priest Pinudjem II, Isetemkheb (D) apparently predeceased him by some years and was interred in TT320, which would become the family tomb, and then the royal cache.

She was buried in a set of two coffins, with a board covering the mummy. The latter were damaged, in likelihood by necropolis workers responsible for actual interments, who would typically tear away the gilded face pieces and hands from inner coffin(s) and mummy boards, their handiwork subsequently undetected, hidden by the closed lid of the outer coffin.

The mummy of Isetemkheb (below, adapted from *Royal Mummies, 1912*) was found to be so beautifully wrapped that Gaston Maspero decided not to disturb it, as he had also decided in the case of Amenhotep I (see pp. 36-39). Later x-rays revealed amulets within the bandages, but no jewelry.

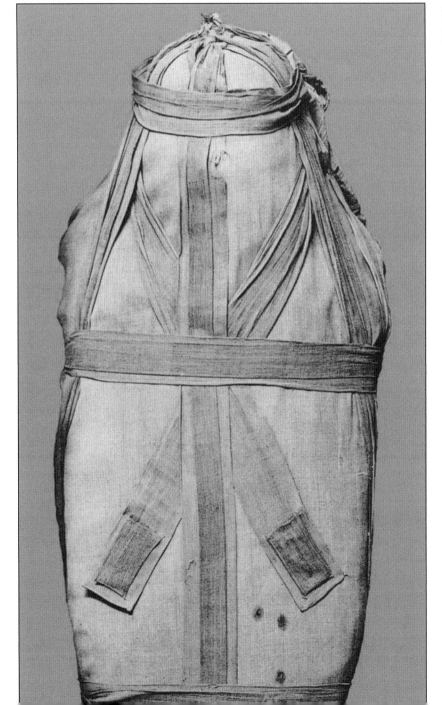

Isetemkheb's wrapped mummy resting in the basin of her inner coffin. Royal Mummies, 1912

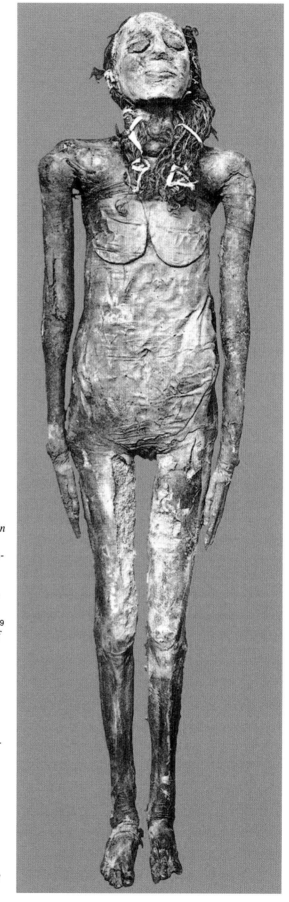

The outer coffin of Nesikhonsu (left) is fully intact, a handsome example of the 21st Dynasty type.

Cercueils, 1909

The mummy of Smendes II's daughter appears not to have been encased in a linen-resin carapace, or else this came completely away when she was unwrapped in 1906. Note packing material filling out the right leg. Left-foot toes are missing.

Adapted from *Royal Mummies, 1912*

No. 61095
Nesikhonsu

21st Dynasty. c. 980 BC

Daughter of High-Priest Nesbanebdjed II (Smendes), Nesikhonsu was a wife of her uncle, Pinudjem II, who succeeded his brother in the Amen pontificate. She died when she was fairly young, predeceasing her husband, and was buried in the family tomb, TT320, in a set of two coffins, the outermost of which was found intact. Gilded face-pieces and hands of the inner coffin and accompanying coffin board had been torn away by robbers, as is typical of most of the Twenty-first Dynasty coffin sets found in the first Royal Cache.

The mummy of Nesikhonsu was partially unwrapped by Gaston Maspero in 1886, and Elliot Smith finished the process twenty years later. Although Smith does not comment on it in his Catalogue Général discussion of No. 61095, the fact that the photographs therein of the mummy show that it is completely denuded of bandages would suggest that Nesikhonsu was not enclosed within a linen-resin carapace, as was the case with many of the other Pinudjem family mummies. Or else this came away easily.

Smith regarded the Nesikhonsu mummy to be the finest example of Twenty-first Dynasty mummification technique. Save for her hands and rather large, pendulous breasts, the entire body of the lady was carefully packed with a mixture of mud, sawdust

and a cheese-like material — but without the distortions seen in other mummies of the period, inparticular of the Pinudjem group. The large breasts and loose, pendulous skin on the abdomen indicate that, like most members of her family, Nesikhonsu was somewhat overweight in life. At 1.615 m. (5 ft. 3.58 in.) tall, she was of average height for her time. There was nothing about the mummy to indicate her age, but Smith noted that there was no gray in her long, dark-brown hair. This hair consists largely of loose strands, most of which have been collected in two large clumps that hang on each side of the head, reaching past the shoulders. These are held together by means of a single bandage spiraled around the hair mass. Nesikhonsu's hair is thickly covered with powdered red-resin.

Powdered resin also encrusts the face, with large cakes of resinous material covering the eyes, nostrils and mouth. Artificial stone eyes were inserted by the embalmers, but these have mostly disintegrated. The lady's ears are pierced and the lobes greatly distended.

The body cavity is packed with sawdust and the characteristic vertical embalming incision is covered by a wax plate of usual Twenty-first Dynasty form, but without a *Wadjet*-eye design. Smith did not comment on whether the body cavity contains viscera packets. He likewise did not comment on whether amulets were found within the bandaging. He did remark that flowers were wrapped around the large toe of each foot, with single flowers placed on the left foot and wrapped around the right ankle.

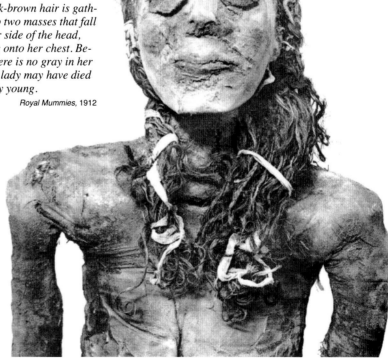

The face of Nesikhonsu's mummy was liberally sprinkled with powdered resin, & plates of resinous material were placed over the eyes & mouth & in the nostrils. Her own dark-brown hair is gathered into two masses that fall on either side of the head, reaching onto her chest. Because there is no gray in her hair, the lady may have died relatively young.

Royal Mummies, 1912

Compared to others of the Pinudjem family, the two-coffin set of Lady Nestanebti-shru was relatively crudely crafted (the innermost at left) & coated all over with bitumenous paint.

Cercueils, 1909

G. Elliot Smith regarded the mummy of Nestanebtishru (right) to be the best example of the embalmer's art to have survived from the Third Intermediate Period. Royal Mummies, 1912

The partially exposed head of Nestanebtishru, as published in Maspero's Les Momies royales *(1889).*

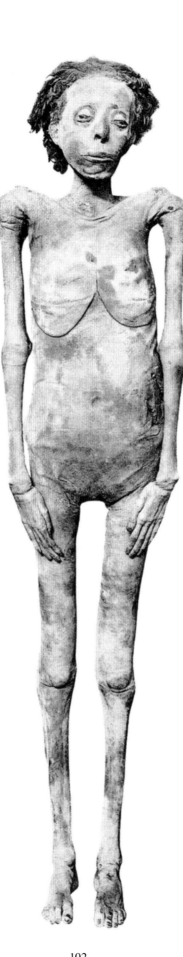

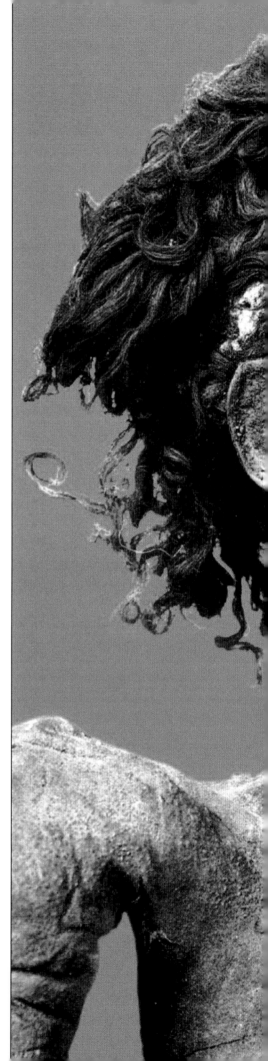

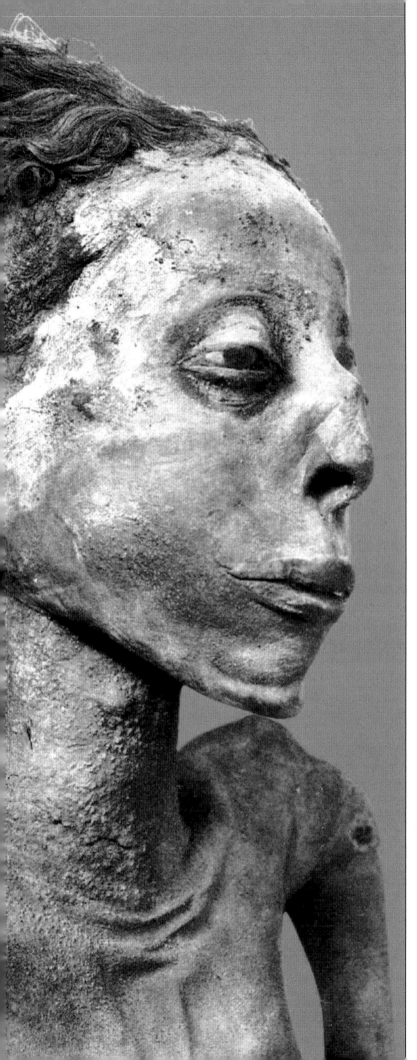

No. 61096
Nestanebtishru

21st Dynasty

Based on her coffin inscription, Gaston Maspero identified No. 61096 as Nestanebtishru, *"priestess of Amen, daughter of Nesikhonsu and probably Pinudjem II"* (*Les Momies royales*, 579-580). It has been further suggested that she was also likely the wife of High-Priest Djedptahiufankh (No. 61097). Inasmuch as her mummy was found intact, it is probable that the Pinudjem family tomb, TT320, was her original place of burial.

Unlike the other Twenty-first Dynasty coffins from the first Royal Cache, the two of Nestanebtishru were somewhat crudely crafted affairs, lacking refined detailing on the lids and coated entirely with black bitumenous paint, which more or less obscures the original low-relief decoration. They would seem to have been original to the lady, however, and not replacement coffins.

Maspero unwrapped the mummy on June 30, 1886, but only partially so, judging from Émile Brugsch's photograph of the lady's head which was published in *Les Momies Royales* (see opposite, bottom left). Again Elliot Smith does not comment on the presence of a linen-resin carapace encasing the body, but subsequent photographs of the mummy in his Catalogue Général volume (1912) show it to be completely denuded of bandaging, quite like that of Nesikhonsu (No. 61095).

Smith thought that Nestanebtishru's mummy *"is perhaps the best example of embalming that has been pre-served from the XXIst-XXIInd period. The face especially has been very successfully treated and the filling out of the cheeks and the artificial eyes of stone help in conveying a good idea of how this haughty, Bourbon-like lady must have appeared in the flesh"* (Smith, 110).

Only a moderate amount of packing material was introduced under the skin of the limbs, which are reason-ably well molded. The body cavity is very tightly stuffed with what Smith identified as *"exceptionally fine sawdust, or rather powdered wood, which still has a strong pungent aromatic odour"* (ibid). No packing was introduced into the large, flattened, pendulous breasts, however.

The fingernails and toenails are all *"neatly trimmed with a crescent edge. There are well-marked im-pressions upon the fingers and toes of the string which was tied around them to keep the nails in position during the embalming process"* (ibid).

The entire surface of the body appears to have been painted with a mixture of yellow ochre and gum, as was typical of female mummies of the Third Intermediate Period. In life the lady stood 1.620 m. (5 ft. 3.78 in.) tall.

Nestanebtishru's hair is her own, brown and wavy, without graying. Her protruding front teeth are al-most unworn. Thus, she may have died relatively young.

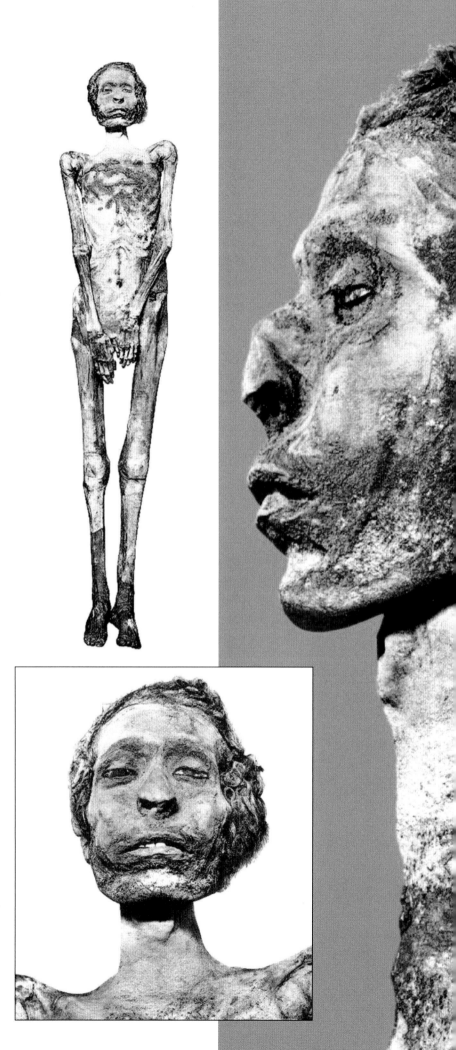

Except for one missing gilded hand on the outer-most coffin's lid (above, Cercueils, 1909), the funerary equipage of Djedptahiufankh was found in excellent condition. His mummy (right) was the only one of the Pinudjem family in TT320 which still retained several pieces of jewelry & numerous amulets of stone & faience. Royal Mummies, 1912

No. 61097
Djedptahiufankh

High-Priest (?)
21st-22nd Dynasty, c. 935 BC

Djedptahiufankh's connection to the Pinudjem family seems to be that he was married to the Lady Nestanebtishru. Inscriptions on his coffins identify him as a priest of Amen and holder of a rather peculiar title, *"Royal Son of Rameses."* Hieratic notations on his mummy wrappings can be dated to Years 5, 10 and 11 of Sheshonq I, meaning that Djedptahiufankh lived some half way through the first reign of the Twenty-second (or Libyan) Dynasty headquartered at Bubastis.

The undisturbed condition of his coffins and mummy suggest that he was buried directly in TT320, probably in Sheshonq I's eleventh or twelfth year of rule. Thus, he was undoubtedly the last of the Pinudjem-related individuals to be interred there; and it has been suggested that it was probably on the occasion of Djedptahiufankh's burial that the final reopening of TT320 took place and the deposit of the New Kingdom royal and associated mummies therein was affected.

Gaston Maspero partially unwrapped No. 61097 in 1886, and Elliot Smith completed the job on September 5, 1906, bringing to light a large number of stone amulets and other objects contained within the bandaging. Djedptahiufankh's fingers and toes also bore several band-like gold rings, which Smith thought had been employed to hold the nails in place during mummification. Maspero had likewise found items of jewelry on the mummy during his partial unwrapping.

The body had been treated in the manner common during the Third Intermediate Period, although packing of the limbs is minimal; the buttocks and anterior surface of the torso are untreated. The body cavity is stuffed with lichen, within which were found three bundles of the priest's mummified viscera (intestines, liver and kidneys). Only one of these (the intestines) was accompanied by a the figure of a funerary genie (an ape-headed Hapi).

Djedptahiufankh's mouth is packed with sawdust and artificial stone eyes are inserted behind the half-open eyelids. The priest's rather large aquiline nose has been flattened somewhat by tight bandaging. Both ears seem to have been pierced, but are thickly smeared with resin and mostly hidden under the mummy's hair. The moustache and beard had not been shaven for some days before death; these are reddish brown, the same color as the head hair. The latter, thickly plastered with resin, is longish, curled into pendant wisps, and without any trace of graying or thinning. This coupled with the unworn condition of the four teeth visible would suggest that Djedptahiufankh was relatively young at death.

The priest would have stood about 1.695 m. (5 ft. 6.73 in.) tall in life.

CHAPTER TWO

Catalogue
of the Mummies from
the Second Royal Cache, KV35

The happenchance discovery of the cache of royal and other associated mummies in the cliff tomb TT320 at Deir el Bahari South in 1881 revealed that a great many New Kingdom upper-echelon individuals had survived the deprecations of tomb robbers and the ravages of time, due to their desecrated remains having been rescued from their own plundered sepulchers by Third Intermediate Period Wasetan necropolis officials, restored as possible and rewrapped and recoffined, then hidden together for safekeeping in the family tomb of the Amen "priest-kings" of the Twenty-first Dynasty. But although the Royal Mummies of TT320 included several of the great rulers of the New Kingdom (Ahmose, Amenhotep I, Thutmose III, Seti I, Rameses II, Rameses III), numerous other kings, queens and known princes and princesses were not among them. Did Gaston Maspero and his colleagues in the Egyptian Antiquities Service even dare hope that another or other caches of mummified royalty might one day be revealed?

If so, their wait was not all that long, for eighteen years later, in 1898, Victor Loret — Maspero's successor as director-general of the Antiquities Service (three times removed) — just happened to personally discover the previously unknown Valley of the Kings burial place of Akheperure Amenhotep II, KV35, which was found to contain not only that plundered-and-dismantled tomb's royal owner — still resting within his sarcophagus — but the cached mummies (most of them recoffined) of eight other "missing" kings and an anonymous woman, plus four other unidentified bodies, denuded and without coffins.

Loret's success was short lived, however, as he was soon dismissed from the Antiquities Service. He returned home to France and, although he lived until 1946, he never wrote an official report on KV35 and its occupants — whether out of disappointment or pique is not recorded. Thus, the formal, scientific discussion of the Royal Mummies and others of the Second Cache was left to be done by G. Elliot Smith in his Catalogue Général volume, *The Royal Mummies* (Cairo, 1912).

Any number of New Kingdom rulers and family members are still unaccounted for. One can only wonder if yet a third cache of royalty awaits discovery in the Twenty-first Century.

Opposite, The roughly reshrouded mummy of King Siptah of the late 19th Dynasty, one of nine royal individuals found cached in a side chamber of KV35, the Tomb of Amenhotep II, in 1899.

Royal Mummies, 1912

No. 61069
Akheperure
Amenhotep II

18th Dynasty, Reigned c. 1427-1401 BC

When Thutmose III died after a long reign of more than half a century, he was succeeded by his son born to Meritre-Hatshepsut, his King's Great Wife. He had associated Akheperure Amenhotep II (*"Great Manifestations of Re, Amen is Pleased"*) with him in a coregency of some two-years duration. At his sole accession, the second Amenhotep was probably only eighteen years of age or so. He was apparently something of an athlete — if one is to believe his own claims — , taller than average for his family (5 ft. 6.5 in.) and robust. He had mastered the bow and was an accomplished charioteer. He loved lion hunting and pursued the beasts on foot rather than from his chariot. He boasted that he could outrow 200 men without stopping and could drink anyone under the table. He does not appear to have had inherited his father's intellectual capacity, however.

Within a few months of the great Thutmose III's death, the princes of Western Asia (Retenu) were in revolt, apparently to test the mettle of the new king in far away Kemet. Young Amenhotep II quickly marched the Egyptian army north and suppressed the uprisings, however, taking numerous prisoners and much booty. He likewise sailed south and demonstrated to the Nubians that they, too, would be brought to heel if they should forget their sworn allegiance to Kemet. A second Asiatic campaign in Year 7 was required to put down another revolt in the area, but the balance of Akheperure Amenhotep's twenty-six-year reign was relatively uneventful.

When he died, the king was interred in his sepulcher — today numbered 35 — in the royal necropolis at Waset (Thebes). Like most of the others there, the Tomb of Amenhotep II was robbed in antiquity and his mummy violated. But the latter was rescued during the Twenty-first Dynasty dismantling of the Valley of the Kings, rewrapped, recoffined and returned to the king's quartzite sarcophagus. There it reposed until found by Victor Loret in 1898. Al-

Opposite, Amenhotep II in his Festival Hall at Karnak. Author's photo *His mummy was initially left in the sarcophagus where in was found in his tomb, KV35, in 1898 (above,* archival photo*). It subsequently was ravage by modern tomb-robbers in 1902 & photographed by Howard Carter at the time G. Elliot Smith examined the mummy* in situ *in 1907 (right,* ASEA 3*).*

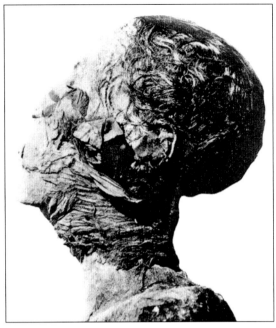

though initially left on display in KV35, Amenhotep II's mummy was taken by train to Cairo in 1931, to join the rest of the royal mummies housed in the Egyptian Museum there.

Elliot Smith conducted his 1907 examination of Amenhotep II while the mummy was still in its tomb. He noted physical similarities between the king and his son, Thutmose IV, except that he felt Amenhotep probably had the stronger "character" of the two. From the wear of his teeth and the gray in his hair, Smith estimated that Amenhotep II was likely between forty and fifty at death, according with the historical record. As in the cases of his father and grandfather, the king's skin was found to be studded over the whole body with small tubercles.

The mummy of Amenhotep II was not examined by CT-scanning of DNA analyis during either the Egyptian Mummy or Family of Tutankhamun projects.

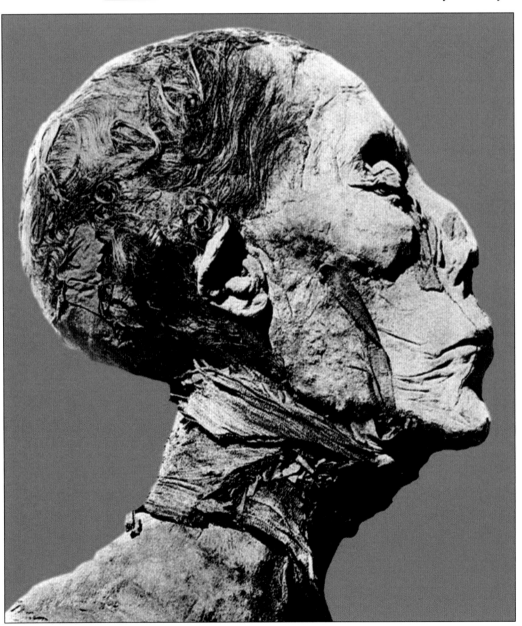

Amenhotep II's mummy has longish wavy brown hair interspersed with gray, & there is a large patch of baldness on the crown of the head. Although the king's teeth are worn, they are in a good state of preservation. In life Amenhotep's nose was prominent but slender; today it is somewhat flattened by the embalmers bandaging. Although the royal genitalia are flattened against the perineum & embedded in resin, it appears the king was circumcised.

Like Thutmoses II's & III's mummies, that of Amenhotep II exhibits numerous small tubercles on the skin, resulting from some disease or or else the effects of embalming salts. ASEA 3

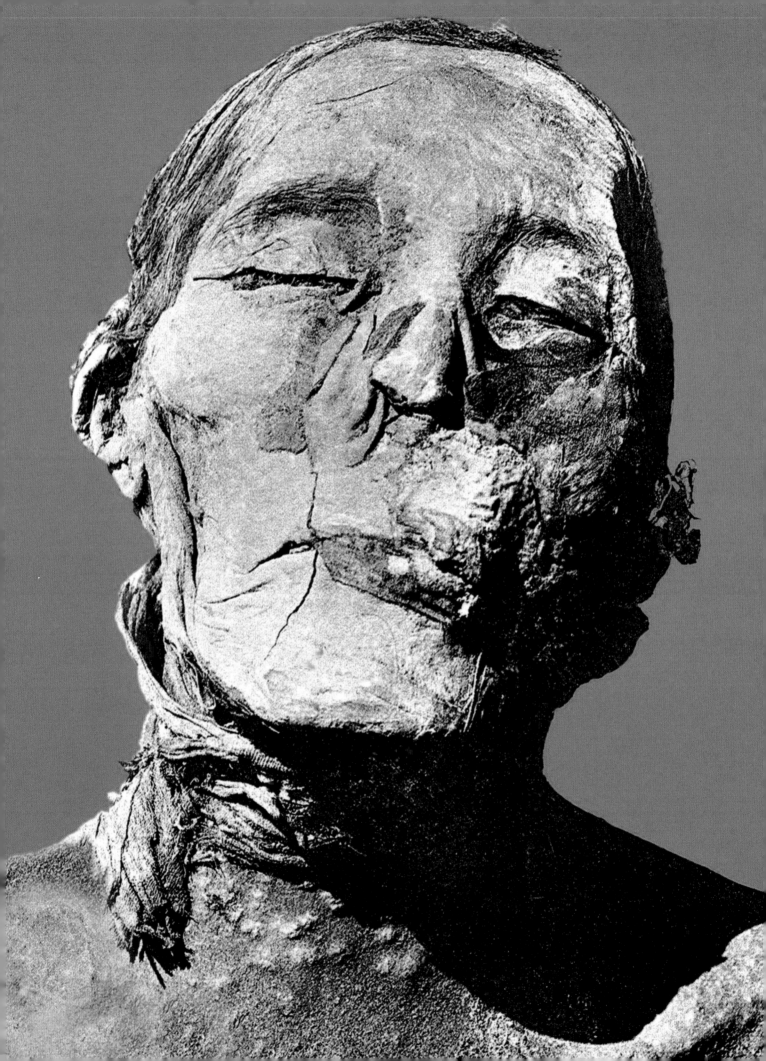

Above, Pigmented raised-relief depiction of Menkheperure Thutmose IV in his reconstructed courtyard at the Open Air Museum, Karnak. Author's photo
Opposite, Full frontal of the head of the Thutmose IV mummy. Note salt incrustations on the face & post-mortem damage to the neck.

Adapted from *Royal Mummies*, 1912

Black-granite pair-statue of Thutmose IV & his mother, Tiaa. Adapted from archival photo

No. 61073
Menkheperure
Thutmose IV

18th Dynasty, Reigned c. 1401-1391 BC

Apparently Prince Thutmose was not the first in line for the throne of his father, Amenhotep II. When he succeeded the latter, it may have been the result of some sort of palace intrigue, in which an elder brother was set aside to make way for Thutmose. At least the new king saw fit to "legitimatize" his claim to the crown by stating on the "Dream Stela" which he caused to be erected between the paws of the Great Sphinx at Giza that, while he slept in the monument's shadow after chariot racing nearby, the ancient colossus promised Prince Thutmose he would become king if he cleared drifts of sand from around the its base. So he did and so he would.

The fourth Thutmose (*"Born of Thoth,"* Djehutimese in Egyptian) took the throne name Menkheperure (*"Everlasting Manifestations of Re"*). A young man at his crowning, he seems to have been under the influence of his mother, Tiaa, with whom he had himself depicted in a black-granite pair-statue found in the Karnak cachette and now in the Cairo Egyptian Museum. Tiaa had been a secondary wife of Amenhotep II, giving further credence to the possibility of a usurpation by Thutmose IV.

Little of interest appears to have occurred during Menkheperure's decade on the throne. If military campaigns took place in Western Asia and Nubia during his reign, scant record of them remains. Diplomacy seems to have been favored by this king. His chief building activity was a large porticoed forecourt which he had raised in front of the Fourth Pylon at Ipet-Isut, the Mansion of Amen at Karnak. This was later dismantled by his son, to make room for the latter's own Third Pylon construction.

Thutmose's other major monument was his tomb in the Valley of the Kings, KV43, found in 1903 by Howard Carter in the employ of Theodore Davis. Although littered with funerary debris, the tomb was devoid of its owner, whose mummy, of course, had been found five years earlier, cached in the Tomb of Amenhotep II.

That same year, 1903, the remains of Thutmose IV were exposed in the Egyptian Museum by Maspero, Brugsch and Georges Daressy. Following its unwrapping, the mummy was then radiographed (x-rayed) by one Dr. Khayat. G. Elliot Smith later examined Thutmose IV for the purpose of writing his description for his *The Royal Mummies* volume of the Catalogue Général (1912).

Smith wrote of Thutmose IV that he was *"an extremely emaciated man"* whose *"head has a very effeminate appearance"* (Smith, 43), the first a peculiar observation, inasmuch as all New Kingdom mummies have the appearance of "extreme" emaciation, due to their very nature; and the second expressing a personal opinion bordering on prejudice toward the king's rather refined features.

The body had suffered postmortem injuries at the hands of tomb robbers, both feet being broken off, as well as the right leg at the knee joint; a severe abrasion on the neck probably occurred at the same time. The traditional position for kings is seen in the arms crossed over the chest with the hands flexed. The body is well preserved throughout,

including the genitalia (it appears Thutmose IV was circumcised). The mummy's skin is *"very dark and discoloured, so that it is not possible to form any accurate idea of its original colour"* (Smith, ibid.).

Smith estimated the age of the king at death at between twenty-five and twenty-eight years, although he admitted that Thutmose IV might have been even older. He wrote that *"Thoutmosis* [sic] *IV presents a striking resemblance to Amenothes* [sic] *II, but the latter had a more virile appearance and was considerably older"* (Smith, 45).

Elliot Smith thought the refined facial features of Thutmose IV "effeminate." The king's nose is relatively small, narrow & aquiline, the lips thin, the chin somewhat prominent. His eyebrows were moderately thick in life & met over the bridge of his nose. Although the mummy is very clean-shaven, Smith observed that the moustache was particularly dense, especially at the angles of the mouth. The hair of the head is full & wavy, with locks as much as 16 cm. (6.29 in.) long; it has a henna color, but microscopic examination shows it to have been dark brown in life. Thutmose's well-formed ears are pierced for earrings, the earliest example of this seen in a New Kingdom monarch. The king stood 1.646 m. (5 ft. 3.34 in.) tall in life.

The Family of Tutankhamun Project of 2007 did not CT-scan or DNA analyze the mummy of Thutmose IV, although he historically was the paternal great-grandfather of the boy-king. The mummies of Tutankahamen's great-grandparents, the commoners Yuya and Thuyu, were fully studied by the same Project, however.

Above, Thutmose IV's non-royal replacement coffin of 20th Dynasty date, its inked inscription identifying the king by both his nome & prenomen. Cercueils, 1909
Right, An artist's trial-sketch thought to depict Thutmose IV late in his life (bearing a strong resemblance to his mummy's profile), showing him as somewhat gaunt, suggesting perhaps that he died at an early age from a wasting illness; as a young king he had been sculpted as somewhat robust (see p. 112). Author's photo.

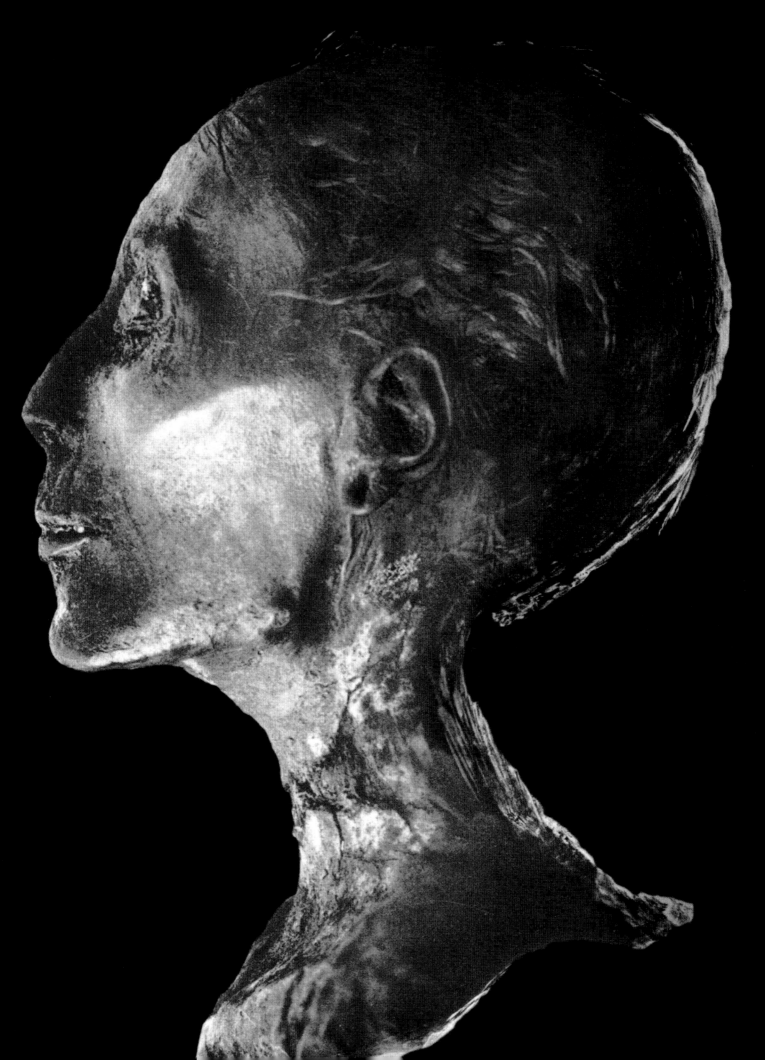

No. 61074
Nebmaatre
Amenhotep III (?)

18th Dynasty, Reigned c. 1391-1353 BC

Inarguably the third Amenhotep was one of the preeminent rulers of the New Kingdom, as well as of the entire pharaonic period. He is remembered not as a warrior-king, but rather as a builder on an extensive and colossal scale, and even as a prerevolutionary, inasmuch as it was his personal reelevation to prominence of the sun god Re, and his subsequent self-deification as a living god in his own right —which led ultimately (perhaps inevitably) to the religious revolution of his son and successor, Amenhotep IV/Akhenaten. Nebmaatre (*"Re Lord of Truth"*) Amenhotep-Heqawaset (*"Amen is Pleased, Ruler of Waset* [Thebes]*"*) enjoyed one of the longer reigns of the empire period (thirty-nine years) and celebrated three jubilees or *Heb-Seds*. When he died at about age fifty, he was interred in the large, well-decorated tomb (WV22) he had caused to be hewn in the western branch of the royal necropolis at Western Waset, breaking with the established tradition of his dynasty.

The identity of the badly damaged mummy found by Loret in KV35 — and inscribed on its coffin and shroud with the throne name of Amenhotep III — has been the subject of debate. This doubt is due to the manner of mummification, in which the limbs of the body have been stuffed with a resinous material, a practice not seen previously, nor again until the Twenty-first Dynasty (although the packing material used at that time was mud, sand, sawdust, etc., rather than resin). It is thought from late portrayals of him that the king was somewhat stout towards the end of his life, so this innovation was perhaps peculiar to only him.

Damage to the remains in question occurred in antiquity: the right leg is broken from the body; portions of both feet are missing, as is the entire front wall of the trunk; and the head is detached. All of the soft tissues of the head have disappeared, except for a portion of the scalp. If the individual represented is Amenhotep III, the king would have stood 1.561 m. (5 ft. 1 in.) tall, was almost completely bald in life and suffered from toothache caused by severe dental abcesses. Smith estimated his age at between forty and fifty, which would accord with the historical record, the king having reigned for one year shy of four decades, coming to the throne at the age of ten or twelve.

The Family of Tutankhamun Project included No. 61074 in its 2007 CT-scannings and DNA analyses and concluded that he was the genetic father of the skeletal remains from KV55 and so the grandfather of the boy-king. There was no such study of the Thutmose IV remains (No. 61073) to confirm 61074's own paternity, however.

Above, A smaller-than-life-size gypsum-plaster head found in a sculptor's workshop at El Amarna & today in the collection of the Berlin Egyptian Museum. It is probably made from a cast of a stone statue & although uninscribed is generally thought to depict the king towards the end of his life, when other sculptures from that period indicate he was decidedly overweight. Aidan Dodson photo

Opposite, An adapted National Geographic *photograph of the badly damaged mummified head of Amenhotep III, essentially reduced to a skull with bits of flesh remaining. The king's remains rest today in the Cairo Egyptian Museum.*

Photo © *National Geographic*

Right, Life-sized grandiorite head in the Cairo Egyptian Museum is uninscribed, but almost certainly depicts a realistically portrayed Amenhotep III during the last decade of his long reign. It may possibly belong to one of the pair of grandiorite life-sized headless statues of the corpulent king found at the site of his mortuary temple.

The wrapped mummy identified in the 21st Dynasty as that of Amenhotep III is seen resting in the crude coffin in which it was found. The latter also bore the names of Seti II & Rameses III.

Royal Mummies, 1912

118

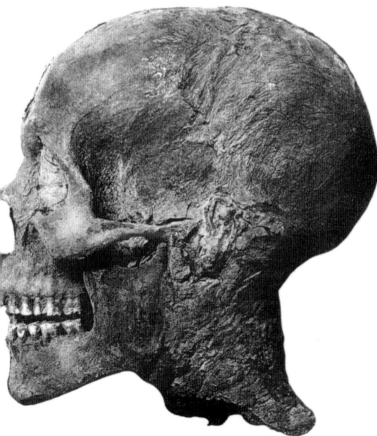

Above, Profile view of No. 61074, arguably the remains of Amenhotep III. It is one of the most damaged of all of the royal mummies, the frontal wall of the trunk being gone, one leg detached,
portions of both feet missing & the head broken off. As can readily be seen from the profile view of the latter at left — save for
some of the mostly bald scalp — all of the soft tissues have disappeared reducing the head to essentially a skull. Pads of gummy
cloth fill the eye orbits & the mouth is similarly stuffed. The individual whose remains these are suffered from massive dental tar-
tar & severe abscesses, & his upper incisors were lost prior to
death. Adapted from *Royal Mummies*, 1912

Opposite left, Profile view of the gypsum-plaster head from an El Amarna
sculptor's workshop thought to depict Amenhotep III in his last years, for
comparison with the skull. Berlin Ägyptisches Museum

No. 61079
Baenre-Merinetjeru
Merneptah

19th Dynasty, Reigned c. 1224-1214 BC

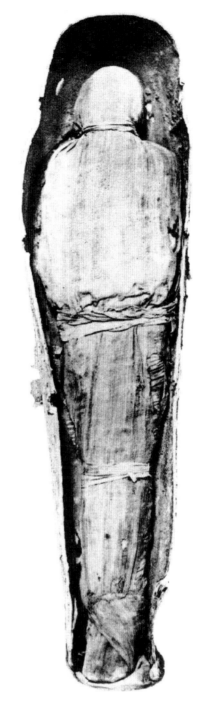

That Rameses II lived so long resulted in the ultimate termination of the Nineteenth Dynasty less than thirty years following his demise. Twelve crown-princes predeceased Rameses, his successor being the thirteenth son (by his second wife, Isetnofret). When Baenre-Merinetjeru Merneptah (*"Soul of Re, Beloved of the Gods," "Beloved of Ptah"*) came to the throne he was already an old man, perhaps even in his sixties. His own ten-year reign was highlighted by the need in Year 5 to repel, successfully, an invasion of the Delta by nomadic tribes of Libyans from the western desert. While he was at it, Merneptah successfully crushed a simultaneous rebellion in Nubia, as well.

Time not being on his side, the fourth ruler of the Nineteenth Dynasty resorted to quarrying the no-longer-functioning Memorial Temple of Amenhotep III, in order to acquire stone for his own memorial structure being raised nearby. He focused his building efforts on this monument and on his tomb, KV8, which he situated close to that of his father in the Valley of the Kings. The chief feature of this burial place was the presence therein, originally, of a set of nested huge stone sarcophagi with recumbent Osiride images of the king on their lids. One of these eventually was reused for the burial of Psusennes I at Tanis.

When the mummy of Merneptah was not among those discovered in the TT320 Royal Mummies Cache in 1881, biblical scholars were not surprised especially, inasmuch as in their view the king — traditional Pharaoh of the Hebrew Exodus — doubtless perished in the Red Sea and so simply was not to be found. That his remains eventually did turn up in 1898 in KV35 was not especially a disappointment to traditionalists, however, since extensive salty encrustations on the skin of the mummy were evidently — so the erroneous explanation went — the result of Merneptah's watery demise.

Elliot Smith unwrapped No. 61079 on July 8, 1907. The mummy's physical similarities to the remains of both Seti I and Rameses II left *little doubt as to the correctness of* [its] *identification,"* he thought (Smith, 65). The body proved to be that of a bald old man who had been obese in life, stood 1.714 m. (5 ft. 7 in.) tall, and suffered from dental problems, arthritis and arteriosclerosis.

The mummy had been treated roughly by tomb robbers and displays numerous postmortem wounds and fractures, including a large hole in the right side of the cranium. The end of the penis is also missing. Peculiarly, so is the

Opposite, Pigmented relief the King Merneptah in KV8's entryway. Author's photo *Above, The king's wrapped mummy as found in the basin of a replacement coffin inscribed for King Setnakht of the 20th Dynasty.* Royal Mummies, 1912 *Below, No. 61079 as displayed today in the Cairo Egyptian Museum.*

entire scrotum, the evidence of this castration (almost certainly postmortem) being covered with a layer of resin.

Merneptah's aquiline nose has been flattened by pressure from bandaging. His lobes are pierced for earrings. The body was arranged in the standard royal pose for the New Kingdom, the clenched hands probably once having held scepters — symbolically at least, if not in reality. Chemical tests of the "salty" deposits on the skin show these to be natron resulting from embalming. So much for drowning in the Red Sea!

No. 61079 was among the mummies CT-scanned and DNA-analyzed for the Egyptian Mummy Project. The study confirmed Elliot Smith's visual examination a century earlier. The CT-scan revealed that the hole at the back of the king's cranium had likely been made by the embalmers, in order to introduce (in lieu of the usual resin) fibrous embalming material (likely linen or other fabric) into the empty space — the brain having been removed by the transnasal method. The damage to the king's genitalia was confirmed to be postmortem. Cause of death could not be determined.

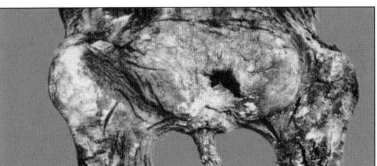

Postmortem damage to the mummy of Merneptah by those who robbed his tomb was extensive. Skin has been sliced from the right cheekbone by a sharp instrument, & there is a cut on the left side of the chin to the bone. There are gashes on the larynx & a deep axe-cut that has severed the right clavical, first rib & part of the sternum. The right arm is broken midway between the elbow & wrist, & almost all of the anterior abdominal wall has been chopped away. Photos adapted from *Royal Mummies*, 1912

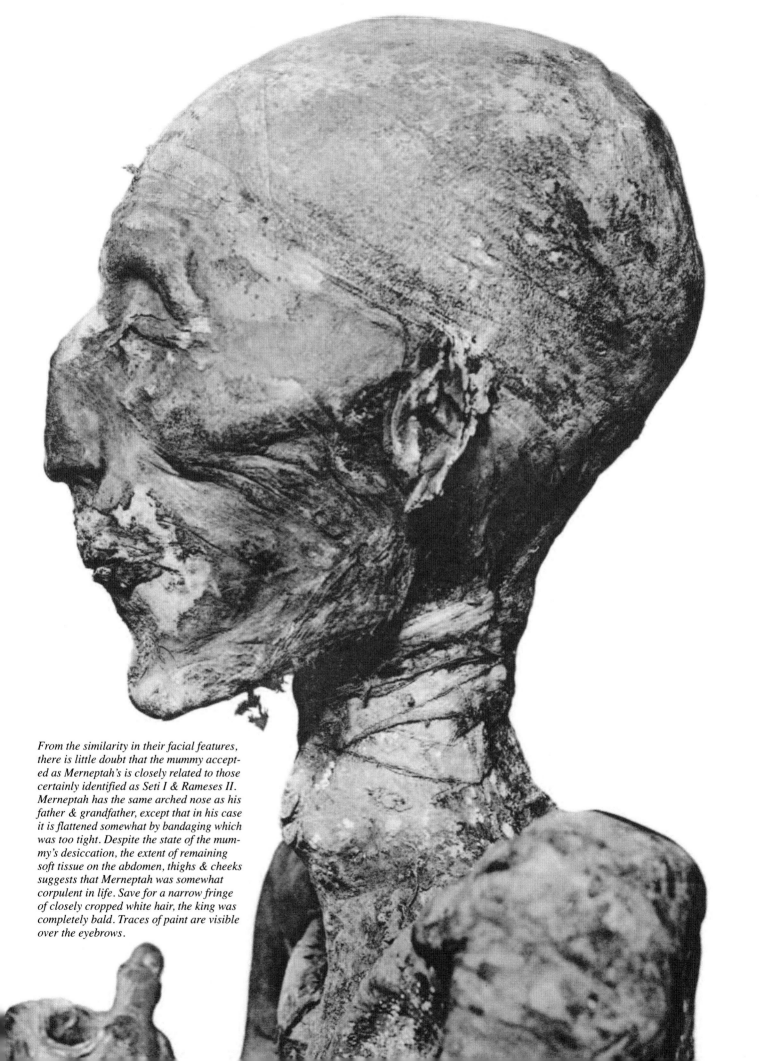

From the similarity in their facial features, there is little doubt that the mummy accepted as Merneptah's is closely related to those certainly identified as Seti I & Rameses II. Merneptah has the same arched nose as his father & grandfather, except that in his case it is flattened somewhat by bandaging which was too tight. Despite the state of the mummy's desiccation, the extent of remaining soft tissue on the abdomen, thighs & cheeks suggests that Merneptah was somewhat corpulent in life. Save for a narrow fringe of closely cropped white hair, the king was completely bald. Traces of paint are visible over the eyebrows.

No. 61081
Userkheperure-Setepenre Seti II (?)
19th Dynasty, Reigned c. 1214-1204 BC

When Merneptah died after only a decade on the throne, there appears to have been some confusion over the succession. By all rights the next ruler should have been a fully mature Crown-Prince Seti-Merneptah; but he seems to have been supplanted by an usurper, one Amenmesse (probably a lesser prince of the Ramesside family, even a younger son of Rameses II), who held the throne for four years before dying or being deposed. Seti-Merneptah then assumed his birthright, ruling for a decade as Userkheperure-Setepenre Seti II (*"Powerful Manifestations of Re, Chosen by Re," "Of Set"*). His queen was one Tausret, possibly a half-sister by a secondary wife of Merneptah.

Seti II's major surviving monument — aside from his tomb, KV15 — is a sandstone barque-chapel situated in the court between the First and Second pylons at Ipet-Isut (Karnak).

The mummy which royal necropolis priests of the Twenty-first Dynasty labeled as Seti II was denuded of its shrouds and bandages of exceptionally fine linen by Elliot Smith over several days, commencing September 3, 1905. It was discovered that the middle-aged individual in question was embalmed in a manner more akin to the Eighteenth Dynasty than the late Nineteenth, and that in his facial features (narrow, high-bridged aquiline nose, pronounced overbite, etc.) "Seti II" looked more Thutmosid than Ramesside. His head was smaller and he was also shorter than his putative father and grandfathers, being 1.640 m. (5 ft. 4.5 in.) tall, more in the range of the male rulers of the preceding dynasty.

Thus, it has been suggested that No. 61081 is not Seti II, but rather one of the earlier Thutmosid kings, perhaps the seemingly missing Thutmose I. (A point against such an identification is the fact that the lobes of "Seti II's" ears are pierced, a characteristic not seen in Thutmosid males until Thutmose IV.)

Whomever he was in life, No. 61081 was badly battered by tomb robbers before being rescued and rewrapped in the Twenty-first Dynasty. The mummy's head is detached, both arms are broken and the right forearm and hand are missing altogether. A large part of the anterior wall of the trunk is broken away (although found separately in the bandages) and there are numerous knife gashes on the body overall. The cranium displays a small hole on the left side. The whole of the scrotum and the greater part of the penis were broken off in antiquity and lost.

The face of No. 61081 is coated all over with a thick paste of resin, although the rest of the head was left untouched. This resinous "mask" — which does not obscure the facial features overly — has cracked and fallen away in places, however, revealing that the skin of the cheeks is quite smooth and unwrinkled. The closely cropped hair, is dark brown.

Above right, Relief depiction of Seti II on his barque shrine at Karnak. Author's photo *Above, The mummy of "Seti II," was found rewrapped in a quantity of exceptionally fine linen bandages, shrouds & shirting. Several small glazed amulets strung on cording were located on the body, especially the legs.* Royal Mummies, 1912

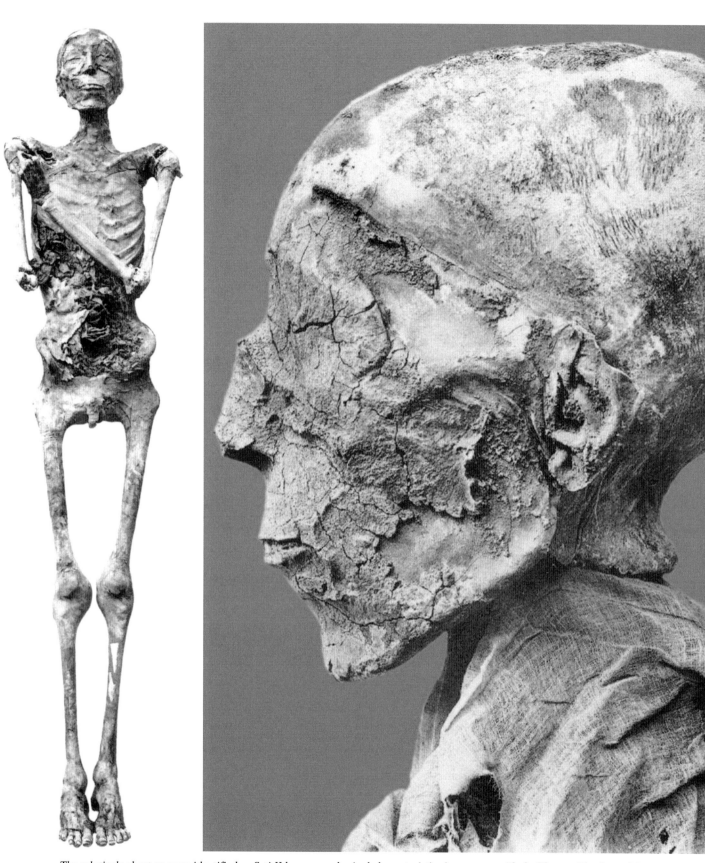

The relatively short mummy identified as Seti II has more physical characteristics in common with the Thutmosid rulers of the 18th Dynasty than with the 19th Dynasty Ramessides, suggesting that these remains may be the "missing" Thutmose I, or else Thutmose II. Mummification techniques employed with No. 61081 are also more typical of the embalming practices of the 18th Dynasty. That the mummy's ears are pierced would argue for a post-Thutmose IV dating, however. Adapted from *Royal Mummies,* 1912

No. 61080
Akhenre-Setepenre Siptah

19th Dynasty, Reigned c. 1204-1198 BC

Exactly who Seti II's successor was is debatable. Whether Akhenre-Setepenre Siptah (*"Beautiful for Re, Chosen by Re," "Son of Ptah"*) was the offspring of Seti and his sister-queen, Tausret (they apparently had a son named Rameses-Siptah), or possibly was the son of the usurper Amenmesse is not known. He came to the throne at the young age of twelve years or so and ruled for only six, most of which he was under the direct influence of Dowager-Queen Tausret and her confidante, Chancellor Bay. When he died, he was succeeded briefly by Tausret, who assumed kingly prerogatives. Siptah was buried in his unfinished but partially decorated large tomb, KV47, in the Valley of the Kings, discovered by Edward Ayrton for Theodore M. Davis in 1905.

The unwrapping of Siptah's mummy by anatomist G. Elliot Smith commenced on August 29, 1905, and took three days. The resin-smeared original bandaging still bore the imprints of long-stolen jewelry. The right arm of the mummy had been broken by tomb robbers, then splinted by the necropolis priests, and the right hand — also torn off in antiquity — was reattached with bandaging. The right cheek, lips and front teeth are broken away, despite the face having been thickly coated with a resinous paste. This serves to obscure most of the young king's features, athough Smith removed some of it to determine that the high-bridged nose — now flattened and distorted by the bandaging — was originally *"small, narrow, acquiline and graceful in form"* (Smith, 73). The king's hair is short, curly and reddish brown. Smith wrote, *"In the mummy of Siphtah* [sic] *several innovations in the technique of embalming make their appearance The cheeks are filled out with linen packing and the body cavity is stuffed with dried lichen"* (Smith, ibid.). He also noted that the embalming incision is sewn up with a narrow strip of linen, a technique first observed in the Eighteenth Dynasty mummy of royal mother-in-law Thuyu.

The most curious feature of the mummy

Pigmented raised-relief portrait of young King Siptah, carved at the entrance to his royal tomb, KV47.

of Siptah is that it displays the only physical deformity observed in the Royal Mummies, a severely clubbed left foot, which would have made the young king a virtual cripple in life, possibly unable to walk without the aid of a crutch, even bodily carried on occasion. It has been suggested that this deformed foot may be the consequence of poliomyelitis (although only one other possible example of this affliction is known from dynastic Egyt, and that from a relief depiction).

Siptah stood 1.638 m. (5 ft. 4.5 in.) tall in life.

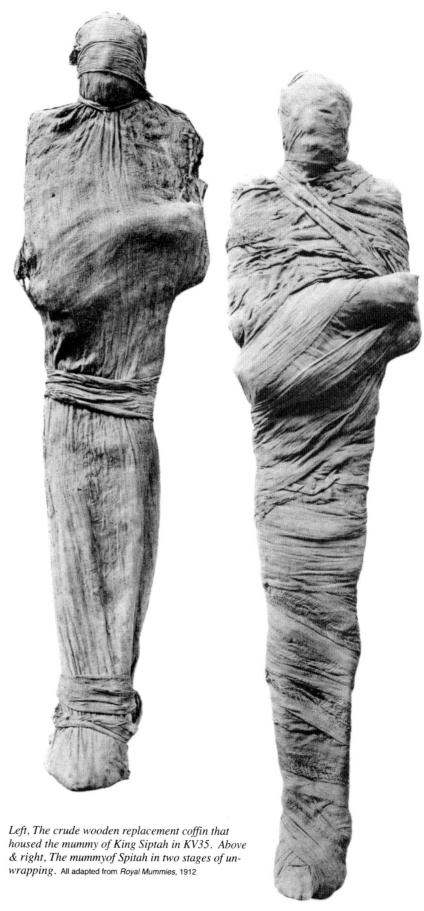

Left, The crude wooden replacement coffin that housed the mummy of King Siptah in KV35. Above & right, The mummyof Spitah in two stages of unwrapping. All adapted from Royal Mummies, 1912

127

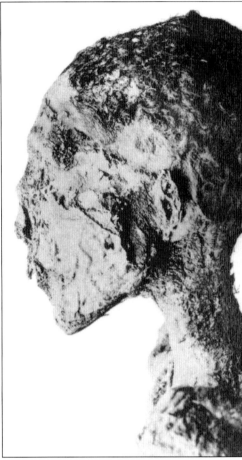

Left & above, The mostly unwrapped mummy identified by the 21st Dynasty necropolis priests as the next-to-last ruler of the 19th Dynasty, Akhenre-Setepenre Siptah. Most of the mummy's re-bandaging was of very high quality linen. The face of the boy-king (18 when he died) is "masked" by a coating of resinous paste. His hair is short, curly & reddish brown. Adapted from *Royal Mummies,* 1912

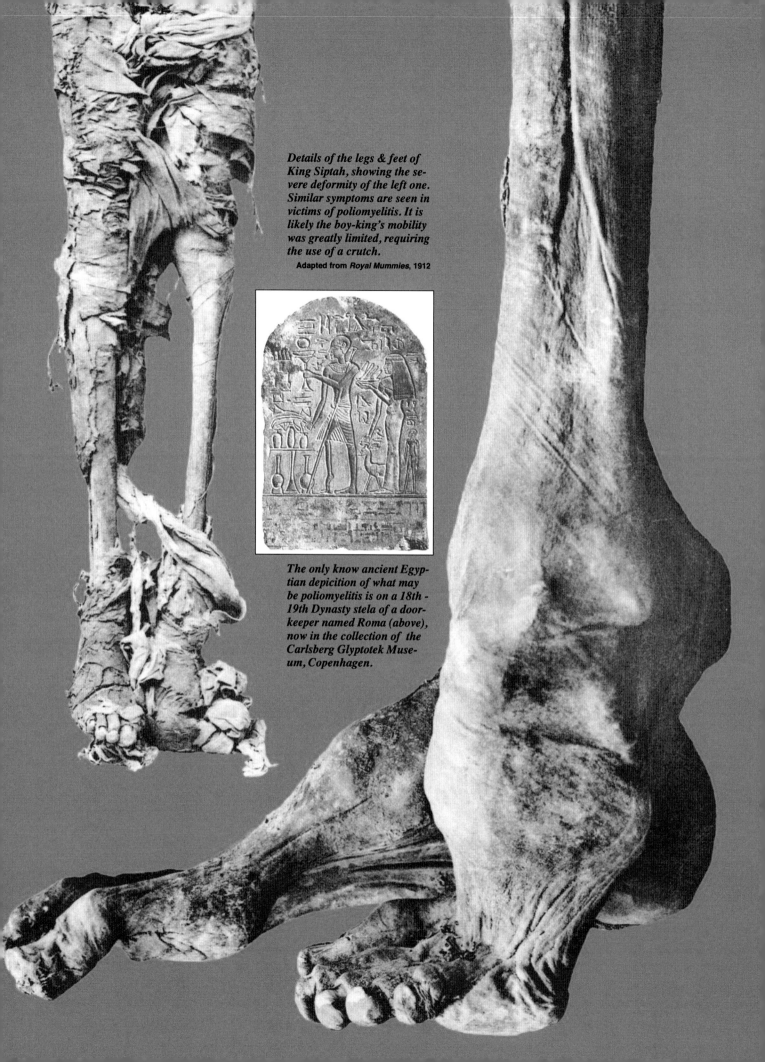

Details of the legs & feet of King Siptah, showing the severe deformity of the left one. Similar symptoms are seen in victims of poliomyelitis. It is likely the boy-king's mobility was greatly limited, requiring the use of a crutch.

Adapted from *Royal Mummies*, 1912

The only know ancient Egyptian depicition of what may be poliomyelitis is on a 18th - 19th Dynasty stela of a doorkeeper named Roma (above), now in the collection of the Carlsberg Glyptotek Museum, Copenhagen.

No. 61082
"Unknown Woman D"
Possibly
Sitre-Meriamen Tausret?
19th Dynasty, Reigned 1198-1196 BC

The brief two-year reign of Sitre-Meriamen Tausret-Setepenmut (*"Daughter of Re, Beloved of Amen," "Mighty Lady, Chosen of Mut"*) as female pharaoh marked the anticlimactic end of the previously glorious Nineteenth Dynasty. When the crippled boy-king Siptah died without issue at about age eighteen, his previous regent (and possibly his mother), Dowager-King's Wife Tausret, must have considered that she had no choice but to grasp the reigns of full power herself — in order to forestall, for however long, the end of the House of Rameses I as occupiers of the Horus Throne. She was no doubt encouraged in this by Chancellor Bay, a foreigner (Syrian) who was apparently the strongest influence at the court of Siptah, perhaps even the juvenile king's puppet master — and, some have suggested, the widowed Tausret's lover.

It has been offered that Tausret, the King's Great Wife of Seti II, was the daughter of King Merneptah by a lesser queen, and therefore the half-sister of her husband. A comparison of the facial profile of the mummy of Merneptah with that of the anonymous mummy (No. 61082), sometimes thought to be that of Tausret, suggests that identification may have some validity. Whatever her claim to the crown, the court and country was in no mood for a female ruler controlled by a foreigner with pretensions (to be king himself?); and civil war broke out, the opposition forces led by one Setnakht.

The latter's pedigree is not known, but it is highly likely that he was himself a descendent of the great Seti I and Rameses II (given his name, the Ramessides having a predisposition towards the god Set), who therefore may have had some legitimate claim on the crown. In any case, Tausret died in short order, or else was deposed; and Setnakht took the throne and thereby founded the Twentieth Dynasty, which would also prove to be Ramesside, if in name only. He took for himself Tausret's tomb, which was in the process of being hewn in the Valley of the Kings (KV14). Where the late queen-pharaoh was subsequently interred is not known, and the recognition of her mummy is limited to that of the "Unknown Woman D," found with several other rulers in Amenhotep II's tomb. Interestingly, she was resting there in the upturned lid of a cartonnage replacement coffin inscribed for Setnakht, whose own mummy has never been identified.

Unknown Woman D" was first unwrapped by G. Elliot Smith in 1905. The mummy is that of an elderly woman whose breasts have completely atrophied. In life she would have been approximately 1.589 m. (5 ft. 2.26 in.) tall. Her well-preserved hair is arranged in a series of peculiar "sausage" curls. The aquiline large nose has been flattened some by bandaging (like that of Merneptah). The only damage is a gaping hole in the anterior abdominal wall and missing toes.

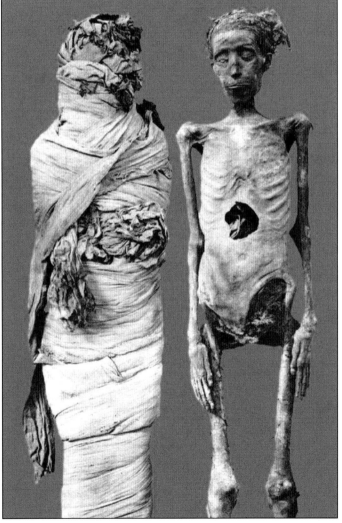

Above, The wrapped & unwrapped mummy of "Unknown Woman D," who possibly may be the 19th Dynasty female pharaoh Tausret. It was found resting in the coffin lid of Setnakht, Tausret's successor. Adapted from Royal Mummies, 1912 *Top, Relief from the Barque Shrine of Seti II at Karnak, thought to possibly depict Tausret as queen.* Author's photo

"Unknown Woman D"/Tausret is well preserved, except that the nose is flattened from overly tight bandaging & the cheeks are distorted by over-packing. A comparison in profile with the mummy of Merneptah might suggest his paternity.

Adapted from *Royal Mummies, 1912*

No. 61084
Heqamaatre
Rameses IV

20th Dynasty, Reigned c. 1163-1156 BC

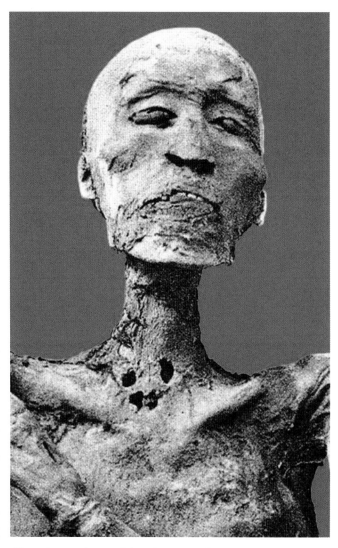

When Rameses III died by assassination, he was succeeded by his eldest son, Crown-Prince Rameses, who donned the Double Crown as Heqamaatre Rameses IV (*"Ruler of Justice Like Re, Born of Re"*). No doubt aspiring to his father's three-decade-long rule, he however sat on the throne for only some seven uneventful years, then was laid to rest in his unfinished tomb in the Valley of the Kings (KV2).

When his mummy was found in KV35 by Victor Loret in 1898, it was in a simple white-painted wooden anthropoid coffin of Twentieth Dynasty date inscribed with the fourth Rameses's prenomen and nomen cartouches. Elliot Smith unwrapped the king's remains on June 24, 1905, to discover that they had been completely denuded of their original bandaging in antiquity, then *"rewrapped"* by Twenty-first Dynasty necropolis priests, who merely threw a mass of rags around the body (these held in place by a few simple bandages) and enclosed the whole in a shroud — which also had the name of Rameses IV inked on it.

Rameses — whom Smith judged to be about fifty when he died — stood 1.604 m. (5 ft. 3.15 in.) tall and was all but completely bald (having only a narrow fringe of very closely cropped hair at the temples and on the occiput). The body is in a relatively good state of preservation, except that *"a great part of the skin of the forehead has been eaten by beetles or some other insects"* (Smith, 88), with further such damage at the front of the neck; while the skin of the torso and limbs is blackened, that of the face and scalp is of natural-looking light-brown color. Black paint has been applied in the area of the eyebrows, and a crescent-shaped band of black paint to the forehead. Continuing a tradition first seen in the mummy of Rameses III, artificial eyes have been inserted under the eyelids, in this case in the form of onions. The king's ears are small and shrunken, but Smith thought that two nodules on the right ear suggested that the latter had been pierced and the greatly stretched lobe *"torn right through"* (Smith, ibid.).

Rameses IV had been mummified in the traditional regal position, arms crossed on his thorax, hands unflexed. Nails on both hands are missing.

Above, Insects damaged the otherwise well-preserved mummy of Rameses IV (on the forehead & neck), probably while it lay in KV2 denuded of its bandaging by tomb robbers. The right foot has been broken off, no doubt by those same desecraters of the royal remains. The fingers of the crossed arms are extended. Adapted from *Royal Mummies,* 1912 *Below, The king's conserved mummy as it is displayed today in the Cairo Egyptian Museum. Opposite, Sunk-relief depiction of Rameses IV in the Temple of Khonsu at Karnak. Note the downturned mouth, also seen on the mummy itself.* Author's photo

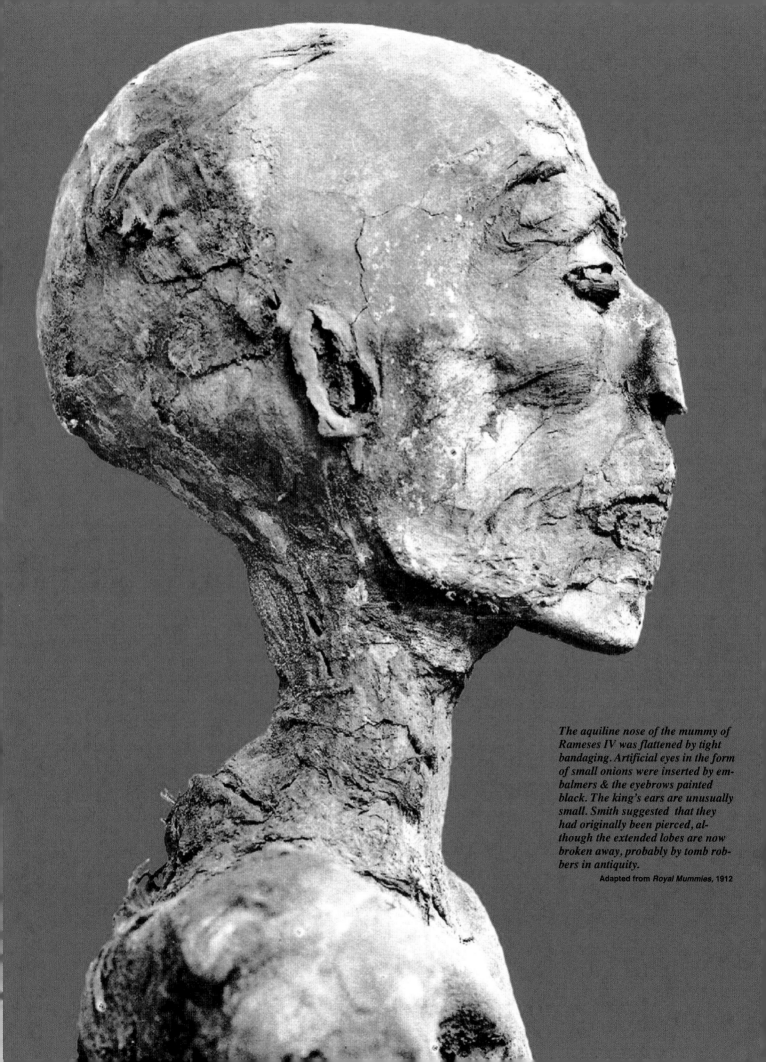

The aquiline nose of the mummy of
Rameses IV was flattened by tight
bandaging. Artificial eyes in the form
of small onions were inserted by embalmers & the eyebrows painted
black. The king's ears are unusually
small. Smith suggested that they
had originally been pierced, although the extended lobes are now
broken away, probably by tomb robbers in antiquity.

Adapted from *Royal Mummies*, 1912

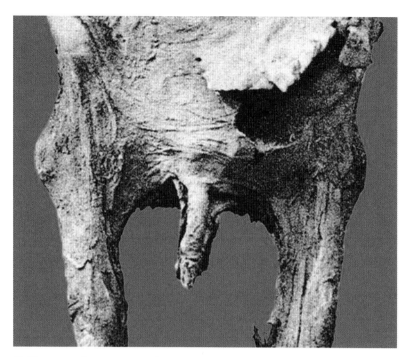

Unlike most other mummies of male royals, that of Rameses IV (above & left)) has the penis and scrotum intact, each having been wrapped separately; they are 9.1 cm and 7.6 cm long respectively. Smith concluded the the king had been circumcised. Adapted from *Royal Mummies*, 1912

As with the mummies of Merneptah, Seti II & Rameses V & VI, the skull of Rameses IV's mummy (above) exhibits a large hole in the upper-rear cranium. Maspero suggested these wounds were made by the embalmers to "let out evil spirits." The Egyptian Mummy Project determined in the case of Merneptah, however, the hole had been made in order to introduce fibrous material into the empty cranium, from which the brain had been removed in the traditional transnasal manner. Royal Mummies, 1912

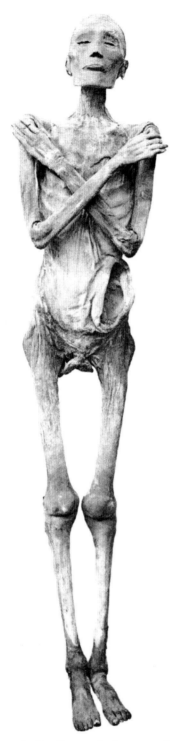

No. 61085

Usermaatre Rameses V
Amenhirkhopshef I

20th Dynasty, Reigned c. 1156-1151 BC

Scholars are in disagreement as to the identity of the fifth king calling himself Rameses. In one view he is a son of Rameses III, who usurped the throne following the death of his half-brother, Rameses IV, the crown by all rights belonging to another half-brother who was senior in age. After a short four-year reign consumed by civil war, according to this scenario, Rameses V was succeeded by the sixth Rameses, the elder half-brother in question. A second view, however, sees Usermaatre Rameses V Amenhirkhopshef I (*"Powerful Justice of Re, Re Fashioned Him, Amen is His Strength"*) as the son of Rameses IV, who died prematurely (and childless) from small pox, to be succeeded by his uncle, the sixth Rameses. Whichever the case, there is little evidence from the reign of Rameses V, and his sole architectural monument is his unfinished and only partially decorated tomb in the Valley of the Kings (KV9), where he apparently was interred. His desecrated mummy was collected by the Twenty-first Dynasty necropolis priests, rewrapped and cached in the Tomb of Amenhotep II; it was discovered there in 1898 and unwrapped on June 25, 1905, at the Egyptian Museum in Cairo.

Like the mummy of his immediate predecessor, that of Rameses V, it had been treated only half-heartedly by those who restored his remains: the upper part of the body, beneath the enveloping outer shroud, was found by Elliot Smith to be surrounded only by a loose mass of torn bandages and rags. The body itself was observed to be very well preserved, embalmed in the traditional regal position with arms folded across the thorax, like Rameses IV with the hands unflexed. The embalmer's incision is extraordinarily large and wide-gaping in Rameses V's case, the abdomen containing *"sawdust with some unrecognisable* [sic] *viscera lying loose (without wrappings) in it"* (Smith, 90). The mummy had suffered relatively little damage at the hands of tomb robbers, only the tips of the fingers of the left hand having been sliced off by a sharp instrument, as well as the skin of the left knuckles.

Smith thought Rameses V to be much younger than both his predecessor and successor, probably no more than twenty-five-years-old at death. In life the young king would have stood about 1.726 m. (5 ft. 8 in.) tall. He had a full head of closely cropped hair.

Above right, Small granodiorite statue of Rameses V in the Luxor Museum. Author's photo *Above, No. 61085, the mummy of Rameses V found in the KV35 Royal Mummies cachette in 1898. The penis & scrotum of the king were not banadaged separately; rather the former was pressed against the right thigh, the latter pushed back under the perineum. The large size of the scrotum suggests the king suffered from a hernia. Arms are crossed over the chest & the hands are extended. The emblamer's incision is unusually large and gaping.* Royal Mummies, 1912 *Opposite, Detail of Rameses V's face, as conserved & displayed today in the Cairo Egyptian Museum.*

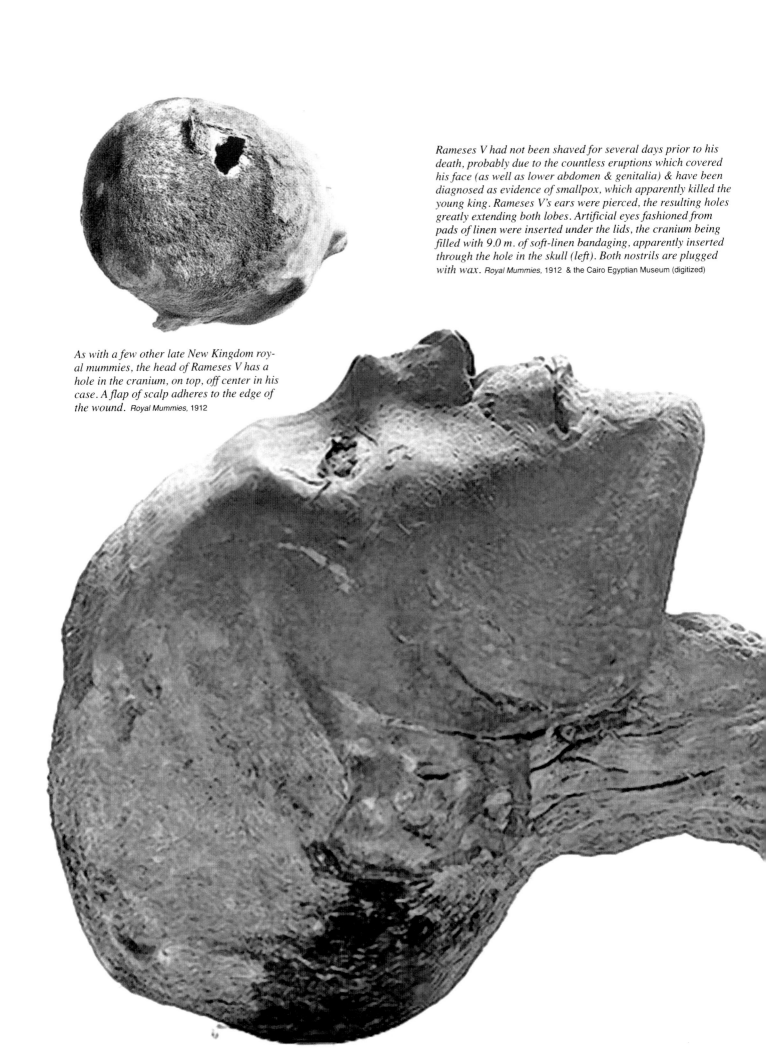

Rameses V had not been shaved for several days prior to his death, probably due to the countless eruptions which covered his face (as well as lower abdomen & genitalia) & have been diagnosed as evidence of smallpox, which apparently killed the young king. Rameses V's ears were pierced, the resulting holes greatly extending both lobes. Artificial eyes fashioned from pads of linen were inserted under the lids, the cranium being filled with 9.0 m. of soft-linen bandaging, apparently inserted through the hole in the skull (left). Both nostrils are plugged with wax. Royal Mummies, 1912 & the Cairo Egyptian Museum (digitized)

As with a few other late New Kingdom royal mummies, the head of Rameses V has a hole in the cranium, on top, off center in his case. A flap of scalp adheres to the edge of the wound. Royal Mummies, 1912

No. 61086
Nebmaatre-Meriamen Rameses VI Amenhirkhopshef II

20th Dynasty, Reigned c. 1151-1143 BC

Whatever his exact relationship was to the fifth Rameses (uncle or brother), Nebmaatre-Meriamen Rameses VI Amenhirkhopshef II (*"Re Lord of Truth, Beloved of Amen," "Born of Re, Amen is His Strength"*) almost certainly was one of the younger of the several sons of Rameses III. He was accused by early scholars of having usurped the monuments and statues of his two previous predecessors as a move to erase their memories; but more probably this was simply a matter of adding to his own monument count in the manner of the great Rameses II, at a minimum effort and cost.

While he was to reign only eight years, his time on the Horus Throne was longer than either of those predecessors. Those eight years were to prove uneventful, marked by an Egyptian pull-back from Palestine and abandonment of mines in the Sinai. When Rameses VI was laid to rest — succeeded by his son, Rameses VII — it was in the appropriated tomb of the fifth Rameses, although what became of the immediate interment of the latter is unknown. Now identified as the Tomb of Rameses VI, KV9 is one of the larger and most fully decorated of the late-Ramesside sepulchers in the Royal Valley.

The thieves who robbed KV9 in antiquity were particularly destructive of the mummy of the sixth Rameses. When his reshrouded mortal remains were unwrapped by G. Elliot Smith on July 8, 1905, they were found to have been hacked quite literally to pieces, with the severed and smashed head and miscellaneous body fragments tied to a rough piece of coffin board to give them some semblance of a mummy's form. Also discovered in the mass of rags enveloping the Rameses VI parts were the right hand of a woman and the mutilated right hand and forearm belonging to a man other than Rameses. Even the king's own body parts were not arranged in any correct order — the pelvis, for example, being positioned where the neck should have been.

Smith determined that the entire facial skeleton was broken off and lost, with only skin remaining. From these pieces, he was able to somewhat reassemble the head and face, as seen in Émile Brugsch's photograph for the Catalogue Général *Royal Mummies* volume, opposite.

Rameses VI was middle aged at the time of death.

Top left, Wooden ushabti of Rameses VI, from his Valley of the Kings tomb, KV9; it probably is closer to a portrait of the ruler than is usually seen in such funerary figures. Cairo Egyptian Museum *Above, The jumbled mass of disarticulated body parts that were roughly bound together on a piece of coffin board to represent the mummy of Rameses VI. Not even the mummy of Amenhotep III had been treated so viciously by ancient tomb robbers. Mummy parts not belonging to Rameses were found included as well. Opposite, Because the facial skeleton of Rameses VI's skull had been smashed & lost, with only sections of mummified skin remaining, G. Elliot Smith had to resort to reassembling the latter fragments in order to recreate some semblance of the king's shattered visage. Using a magnifying lens, the anatomist could detect a closely shaved beard & mustache. The part of the scalp which is visible is bald. The king's ears are pierced. His teeth are only slightly worn. Smith guessed Rameses VI to have been middle-aged at death, estimated his height at 1.714 m. (5 ft. 7.48 in.).* Royal Mummies, 1912

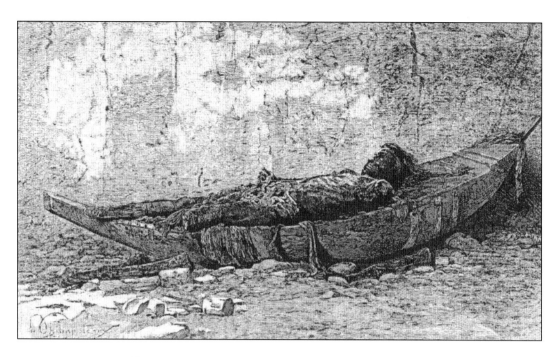

The Other Mummies from KV35

"Unknown Man on a Boat"

When in 1898 Director of Antiquities Victor Loret and his *reis* made their first penetration into the interior of the just-discovered Valley of the Kings tomb which would come to be identified as belonging to the Eighteenth Dynasty's Amenhotep II and subsequently numbered KV35, they were stunned to discover in the columned first large chamber a truly bizarre sight. Midway up against one long wall was a large painted-wood model Nile vessel (one of five to be found in the tomb), atop of which, supine was the badly damaged cadaver of an adult human male: the left arm had been torn off at the shoulder and was laying on the chamber floor close to and parallel with the boat (indicated on the photo opposite); the left hand was separated at the wrist and lay palm down under the curve of the hull; the right foot was also separated from the leg at the ankle and laying at an angle near the boat's prow. The left leg had been broken in two at the knee, the lower part also on the chamber floor, its foot partially detached. The right arm was in a pendant position, the hand with extended fingers resting on the right thigh.

Loret believed (and wrote in his brief account of KV35's discovery) that the man on the boat was a naturally desiccated corpse, the body of an ancient tomb-robber for some reason murdered by his cohorts, or else by necropolis police who had interrupted the robbery in progress. This despite the fact that the body was, indeed, a still-partially wrapped mummy, as would later be recognized. It was decided to leave the boat and its sorry burden *in situ,* so that it might be viewed by visitors to the tomb. And so it remained, covered by chicken wire, until 1901, when modern tomb-robbers broke into KV35 in search of something missed by the excavators— especially to be found on the mummy of Amenhotep II, which had been left undisturbed in his replacement cartonnage coffin resting within the huge stone sarcophagus (the lid of which had been removed, however). The painted model-boat had resale value, so the chicken-wire caging and the corpse within were removed from it and the human remains "torn apart," apparently purposefully. The boat was stolen and has never been identified in a private collection, subsequently. What became of the totally desecrated mummy was not recorded: either it was destroyed or else remains unknown in a Ministry for Antiquities Luxor-area storage magazine.

There, of course, has been speculation as to the identity of the Unknown Man on a Boat. Probably best guess is that he was Prince Webensenu, a son of Amenhotep II who predeceased him and whose interment in KV35 is indicated by the presence of the human-headed lid of one of his canopic vessels. The second suggested candidate is founder of the Twentieth Dynasty King Setnakht, whose cartonnage coffin-lid supported the mummy of KV35's "Unknown Woman D." Arguing against this identification is that the photograph of the remains on the boat suggests the man had a full head of longish dark hair, and Setnakht is thought to have been advanced in age when he took the throne.

Opposite, 1898 photograph by V. Loret of KV35's "Unknown Man on a Boat," today in the University of Milan Egyptological Archives. Above, Engraving from a photograph by Loret, which appeared in the French magazine L'Illustration.

Three Anonymous, Uncoffined Mummies
Found in KV35 Sideroom J-a

One of the surprises confronting Victor Loret when he first explored KV35 was the *"extraordinary spectacle"* of three mostly denuded, uncoffined mummies lying supine side by side on the floor of a sideroom of the royal tomb's second pillared chamber, the so-called "Chariot Hall." The feet of the parallel cadavers were towards the doorway to the smallish space, later designated J-a. To one side of these bodies was a jumbled quantity of miscellaneous debris left behind by tomb robbers, especially small mummiform coffins containing resin-coated funerary statuettes.

The human occupants, from right to left, were: 1) a mature woman of *"severe beauty"* with ragged bandaging covering her legs, a piece of ancient fabric draping her head (partially veiling the face), the left arm crossed over her chest, hand clenched; 2) a fully nude prepubescent male with a full sidelock on the right side of the head (*"magnificent goat-like black hair"*), arms pendant with hands covering the crotch, who Loret thought was probably about fifteen at death; and 3) an individual Loret presumed was male — chiefly because the head was shaved bald — from whose broken mouth protruded a rag, so that the deceased resembled, Loret wrote, *"a mirthful young cat about to swallow a morsel."* All three cadavers had suffered the same sorts of bodily damage by tomb robbers that Loret had noted on the "Unknown Man on a Boat": their thoraxes were broken open, limbs were torn off (except for the boy) and each had a hole on the top of the cranium.

As part of his clearing of KV35, Loret had padded planks made as supports for the uncoffined mummies, which then were placed in especially constructed individual packing cases. These were then removed from the tomb and carried to and placed aboard the Antiquities Service steamer waiting on the Nile. With all of the material cleared from the tomb loaded — including the nine crated Royal Mummies (less Amenhotep II, left behind in his cartonnage replacement coffin and sarcophagus) — but, before the steamer could get underway for Cairo, Loret received a telegram from the Ministry of Public Works, with orders for the ancient kings to be returned to the tomb where they had rested for some 2,500 years. The three J-a anonymous mummies were taken back into the sideroom and uncrated. Loret, however, laid them in the reverse order from how they had been found, the boy still in the middle, however. The space was blocked up and the trio resumed their eternal rest.

There, of course, was speculation among scholars and others as to the identity of these anonymous but presumably royal individuals. The mature female, who would be dubbed the "Elder Lady" was quickly thought to perhaps be Hatshepsut or Great Wife Tiye, even Nefertiti. The other female — it was determined by Royal Mummies anatomist G. Elliot Smith that Loret's "he" was, in fact, a "she" — was easily enough given the descriptive name "Younger Lady." Speculation as to who she was ranged from Tiye's eldest daughter, Sitamen, to Nefertiti herself. The boy — who Smith thought more likely only about eleven at death — has been frequently thought to be Prince Thutmose (V), Amenhotep III's crown-prince who died young; while other opinion sees him as an original occupant of KV35 rather than a refugee thereto, that is Prince Webensenu.

Opposite, Badly deteriorated glass-plate image of KV35 J-a with the uncoffined three mummies in situ. University of Milan Egyptological Archives

Above, The KV35 sideroom trio in situ, *as photographed by Victor Loret in 1898.* University of Milan Egyptological Archives *Right, Internet photo of the trio, showing the incorrect order which Loret returned the mummies to the tomb.*

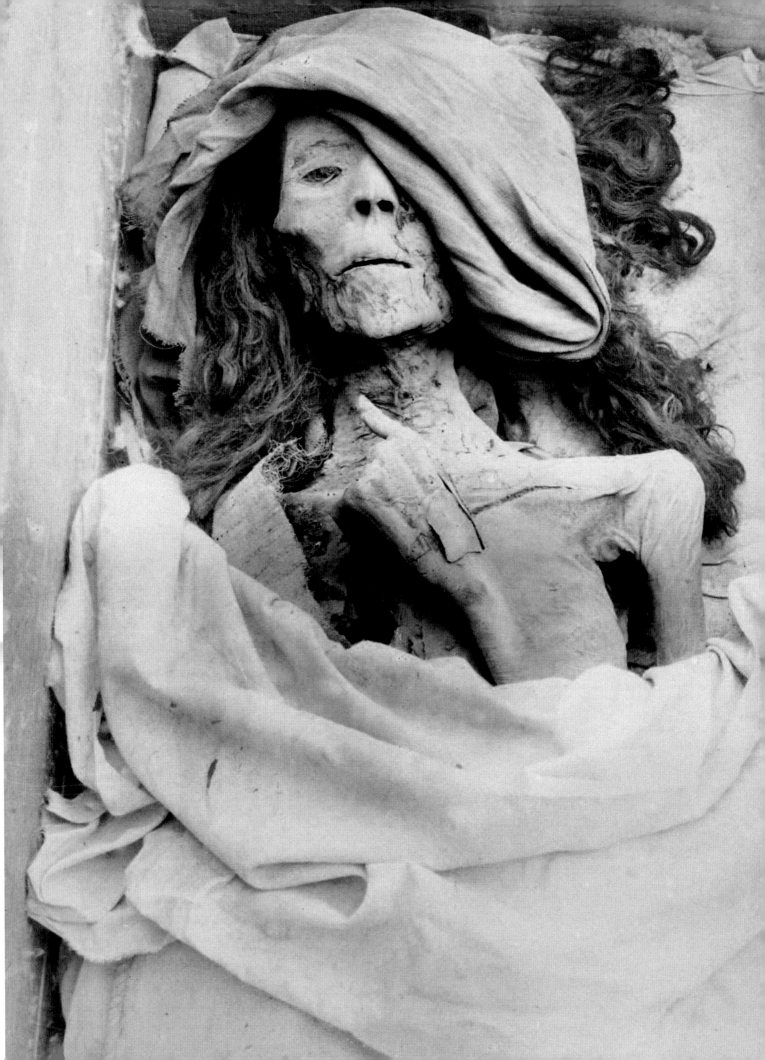

No. 61070
"The Elder Lady"

Identified as
Tiye

King's Great Wife/Dowager King's Great Wife/King's Mother
Reigns of Amenhotep III & Akhenaten
18th Dynasty, circa 1395-1340 BC

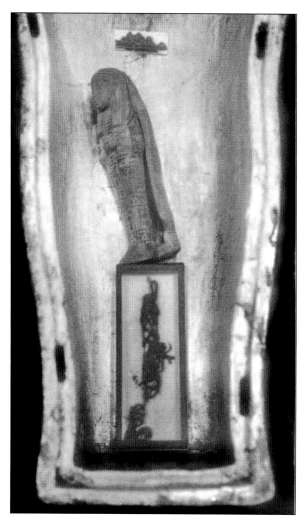

Certainly one of the most dynamic figures of the Eighteenth Dynasty, even of the New Kingdom, was the commoner King's Great Wife of Amenhotep III, a woman named Tiye who was the daughter of a family from the Middle Egyptian town of Akhmin that apparently had connections to the Thutmosids during the mid-part of the dynasty. Tiye was married to the juvenile Nebmaatre Amenhotep-Heqawaset in Year 2 of his reign, when she was probably no more than ten or twelve years of age. The marriage itself was announced on a commemorative scarab issued by the young king, in which Tiye's commoner parents, Yuya and Thuyu, were named.

In addition to being the high-profile consort of the third Amenhotep, Tiye was, as is well known, the mother of the heretic pharaoh, Akhenaten, into whose reign she lived, becoming a prominent figure at Akhetaten, her son's new capital, as well. Dying in perhaps Year 14 of that reign, Tiye was interred either in the Royal Tomb there or in a side-room suite off the burial chamber of her deceased husband in the Valley of the Kings. She possibly also resided temporarily in KV55, where her funerary tabernacle was found. Scholars are of divided opinion regarding this.

It was not until the 1970s that a scientific test was made comparing hair from a lock thought almost certainly to have been Queen Tiye's that was found preserved in a miniature coffin as a memento in the Tomb of Tutankhamen (KV62) with that from the head of the "Elder Lady" anonymous mummy found in KV35 in 1898. Results showed that No. 61070 was very likely Queen Tiye, or at least the same person who was the source of the KV62 lock. This conclusion was disputed, subsequently, by at least one scholar, although majority opinion still favored the Tiye identification.

In 1902 Elliot Smith examined the "Elder Lady" mummy (along

Opposite, Mummy of the KV35 "Elder Lady" (a.k.a. King's Great Wife Tiye), in 1898, resting in the packing case Victor Loret had made for her shipment to Cairo, with the ancient linen fabric still partially covering her head as found; however she was returned to the tomb's sidechamber J-a, where she would remain until 2007, when taken for CT-scanning & DNA-testing to the Cairo Egyptian Museum. Loret photo, University of Milan Egyptological Archives *Above left, Detail of a quartzite sunk-relief depiction of King's Great Wife Tiye in her prime.* Berlin Ägyptisches Museum *Above, Locks of hair & their miniature coffins identifying them as from Tiye, discovered in KV62 & today in the Cairo Egyptian Museum; in the 1970s they were compared to the hair of KV35EL, the match suggesting the strong probability that she as, in fact Tiye, which was confirmed by DNA-testing in 2007.* Author's photo

with her two companions) *in situ* in KV35. He described her as *"small,"* *"middle-aged,"* having *"pointed* [facial] *features"* and *"brown, wavy, lustrous hair"* with *"no grey"* in it (Smith, 38). While the right arm is placed vertically along the side with the open hand resting on the right thigh, the left arm rests diagonally across the torso, the left hand clenched — in what has come to be called a "queen's pose." The whole of the front of the abdomen and part of the thorax were broken away by tomb robbers. Strangely, the royal lady's ears are not pierced.

As part of the Family of Tutanhkamun Project, No. 61070 was removed from KV35 sideroom J-a in 2007 and taken to the Cairo Egyptian Museum, to be CT-scanned and DNA-tested. The results of the two-year study revealed that the "Elder Lady" genetically was the daughter of royal-inlaws, Yuya and Thuyu, whose mummies were also part of the Project. Thus her King's Great Wife Tiye identity was confirmed. The tests also showed that she was the mother by Amenhotep III of the anonymous individual represented by the skeletal remains from KV55, and also of the KV35 "Younger Lady," both of whom where determined to be the parents of King Tutankhamen.

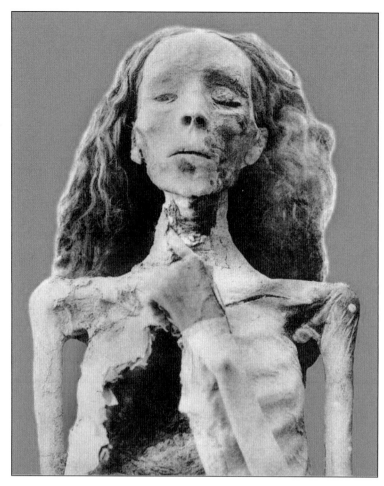

Opposite & right, KV35 "Elder Lady," photographed by Howard Carter in the tomb in 1902.
Adapted from *Royal Mummies,* 1912 *Below, Left side of the head of King's Great Wife Tiye, in the Cairo Egyptian Museum, 2010; note unpierced ear.*
Digitally adapted from uncredited Internet photo

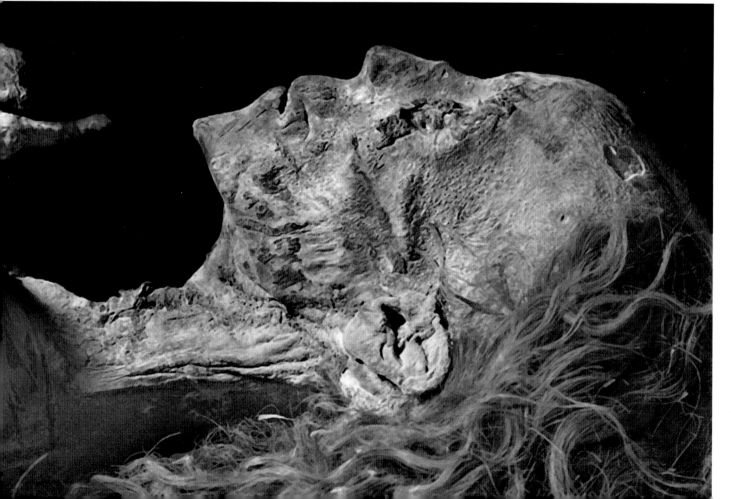

No. 61072
"The Younger Lady"

*Identified as Daughter
of Amenhotep III & Great Wife Tiye
& Mother of Tutankhaamen
Late 18th Dynasty*

Probably because of its completely denuded cranium, Victor Loret mistakenly took one of the three anonymous uncoffined mummies found in sideroom J-a off the burial chamber of Amenhotep II's tomb to be male, and described it as such. It was not until Elliot Smith conducted his *in situ* examination of these remains in 1902 that he discovered they belonged instead to a young female with a shaved head. Smith estimated the individual's age to be less than twenty-five years. He considered the embalming technique to belong to the middle part of the Eighteenth Dynasty, stating *"There can be no doubt that these individuals* [the three J-a mummies] *were contemporaries of* [Amenhotep II]... [with] *the obvious presumption...that they were royal personages and members of his family"* (Smith, 41). He saw in the young woman *"the projection of the...upper jaw* [overbite] *which is such a constant and distinctive trait of the royal family of the XVIII*th *Dynasty"* (Smith, Ibid.).

In the 1970s one of the KV35 companions of the "Younger Lady" was tentatively identified as likely Tiye, principal consort of Amenhotep III and mother of Akhenaten. Subsequently this writer has proposed elsewhere (*Kmt* 2:2, summer 1991, p. 72) that, given the apparent relationship between the three

Opposite, KV35's "Younger Lady," in a recent uncredited photo from the Internet. She is today housed in the Cairo Egyptian Musem. Digetelly adapted Internet photo *Below, Victor Loret's glass-plate photograph taken of No. 61072 as she laid in the crate he planned to convey her in from the tomb to Cairo in 1898. The rag protruding from her badly damaged mouth is still in place, as found.*

Milan University Egyptological Archives

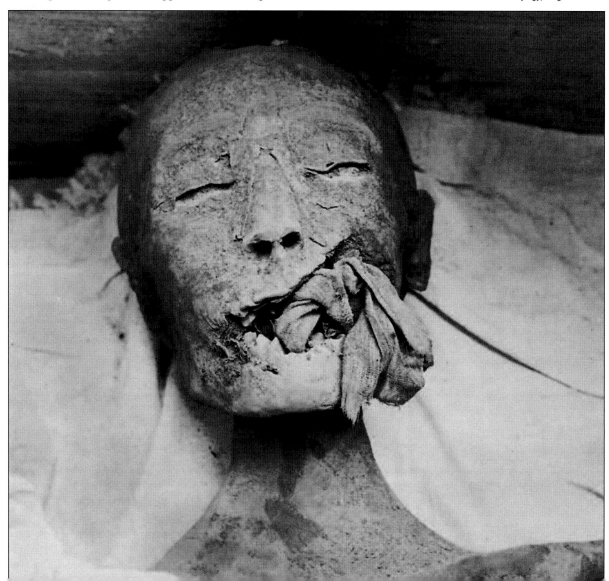

anonymous KV35 mummies (same period of mummification, similar condition of tomb-robber mutilation, lack of bandaging and coffins), the "Younger Lady" might very well be none other than Queen-Princess Sitamen, Tiye's eldest daughter by Amenhotep III, whom the latter took as his second King's Great Wife in conjunction with his first *Heb-Sed* in Year 30, and whom some scholars believe was interred in that king's tomb (WV22) in a specially prepared side-room suite.

Except for severe damage by tomb robbers (extended right arm torn off at the shoulder and right hand detached, anterior upper thorax broken away), No. 61072 is relatively well-preserved. Additionally, the left side of the mouth and cheek are totally gone, which Smith thought was a postmortem injury. She is 1.580 m. (5 ft. 2.2 in.) tall.

English Egyptologist Joanne Fletcher acquired permission in 2003 from the Egyptian Supreme Council for Antiquities (SCA) to have access — along with a team of ratiologists and other specialists — to KV35 J-a for the purpose of studying the three mummies there at close hand; her particular focus, however, was on "The Younger Lady," whom she was proposing as Nefertiti, principal spouse of the heretic pharaoh, Akhenaten. The results of her quick (and not exactly fully scientific) investigation were published in the June 8, 2003 edition of *The Sunday Times Magazine* of the *Times of London* newspaper — hardly a scholarly journal. Soon after, on August 17, a television documentary aired on the (American) Discovery Channel, titled "Nefertiti Resurrected," dealing with Fletcher's KV35 adventure and her identification of the famous Egyptian queen.

When the director of the SCA, Zahi Hawass, learned that the English Egyptologist had violated the conditions of being granted access to KV35 J-a and its resident mummies — which required that she first formally inform the SCA of her findings and then publish those in an accredited scholarly journal — he was outraged and banned her from working in Egypt in the future.

Only two years later, in 2005, Hawass began his own Family of Tutankhamun Project, and the two mummified ladies from KV35 were selected as subjects — along with eight other mummies, identified and anonymous — of the SCA-sanctioned study, using the latest techniques of CT-scanning and DNA-testing (which he had earlier opposed). They were removed from KV35 J-a and taken to the Cairo Egyptian Museum for the investigation.

The published results of the studies of KV35YL (*Scanning the Pharaohs*, 2015) showed that she was between twenty-five and thirty at death. There had been no brain removal. The arm with flexed hand found alongside the mummy by Loret belonged to another male individual. The massive wound to the lower left face most likely occurred either shortly before death or the was cause of death, as no boney fragments were found within the facial cavity, which would have been the case if the injury was a postmortem one by embalmers or tomb robbers. It was suggested that the fatal wound resulted from a blow to the face by a large, blunt instrument, possibly the hoof of an animal, such as a kicking horse.

The most significant find of the FTP was that DNA-testing showed KC35YL was genetically the daughter of Amenhotep III and Great Wife Tiye, and the mother of Tutankhamen, with the KV55 individual his father.; also that KV35YL and KV55 were full brother and sister. This relationship did not serve to give an "name" identity to "The Younger Lady," however, as Amenhotep III and Tiye had at least five attested daughters. It has been suggested by this writer (*Kmt*, 27:2, spring 2016) that instead she might be the granddaughter of Amenhotep and Tiye, so possibly Meritaten, eldest offspring of Akhenaten and Nefertiti, and King's Great Wife of KV55 (Smenkhkare).

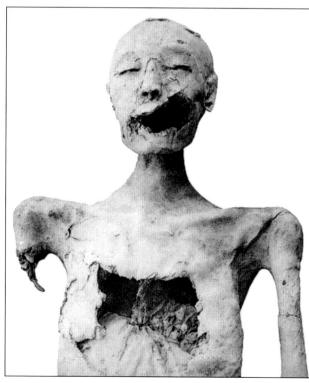 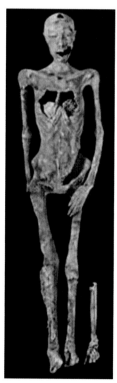

Opposite, Profile view of KV35 YL shows a cranium & jawline reminiscent of other members of the Amarna royal family, particularly KV55 & Tutankhamen. View at right shows the extent of her massive injuries, arm & thorax certainly post-mortem, but the facial wound probably premortem, so likely the cause of death. Adapted from Royal Mummies, 1912 *Far right, Full view of "The Younger Woman" & forearm (not hers) found with her.* SCA photo

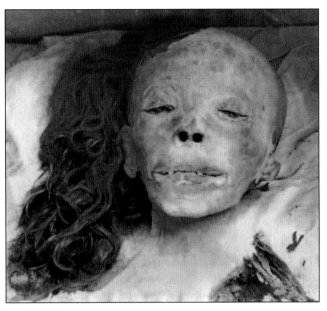

Detail of a stela in the Berlin Egyptian Museum depicting Crown-Prince Thutmose (V) as a servitor of the Apis Bull. A. Dodson photo

Victor Loret's glass-plate photograph of No. 69071 resting in a crate awaiting shipping from KV35 to Cairo. On orders of Egyptian authorities he was returned to the tomb's sideroom J-a. Milan University Egyptological Archives *Opposite, Howard Carter's full-frontal view of the Anonymous Boy taken* in situ *in KV35 J-a, when G. Elliot Smith examined the mummy.* Adapted from *Royal Mummies*, 1912 *Below, Uncredited Internet photo of No. 61071.*

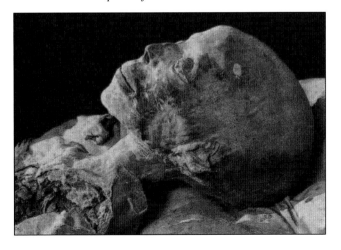

No. 61071
Anonymous Young Boy

Possibly Thutmose, Son of Amenhotep III & Tiye

Late 18th Dynasty

Victor Loret thought that the uncoffined, denuded young boy whose mummy was found — along with those of two anonymous women in like condition — in KV35 sideroom J-a was about fifteen years old; Elliot Smith, however, proposed in *The Royal Mummies* that he could not be less than eleven and probably a little older.

Smith thought it interesting that the youth, who wears the Horus side lock, is uncircumcised; this may suggest that that operation took place at puberty, which the boy had not yet reached by the time of his death. He would have stood 1.242 m. (4 ft. .1 in.) tall. His ears are pierced, which if he is a royal prince, as presumed, would probably date him to no earlier than Thutmose IV, the first Eighteenth Dynasty king with pierced ears. This writer has suggested (*Kmt* 2:2, summer 1991) that No. 61071 might possibly be Crown-Prince Thutmose, eldest son of Amenhotep III, who predeceased his father and could very well have been interred in the latter's tomb (WV22). Interestingly the boy's lack of eyebrows (shaved?) might accord with Prince Thutmose's attested role as chief prophet of the god Ptah at Mennufer (Memphis).

The boy's mummy is well preserved. Damage by tomb robbers consists of a large gash in the left side of the neck reaching the upper thorax, creating a more-or-less triangular gaping hole; there is also a large hole in the cranium on the top right side (seen also in his two female J-a companions). One of the mummy's toes is missing and may be represented by a corresponding digit found in another sideroom of the Amenhotep II tomb.

Although Elliot Smith was inclined to identify No. 61071 as a prince of Amenhotep II (and he labeled the mummy as "? Prince Ouabkhonsenou" [Webensenu] in his *The Royal Mummies* Catalogue Général volume), it is interesting to note that he draws a comparison of the boy's face to the statue of the god Khonsu found in the Karnak cachette. This work is identified today as bearing the facial features of King Tutankhamen, in whose reign the statue was carved. Smith described the young mummy's cranium as a wide long oval (brachycephalism), a characteristic, he noted, of the Khonsu statue — and which is also seen in the cranium of Tutankhamen's mummy. Perhaps this skull shape is circumstantial physical evidence for seeing an identification of No. 61071 as Crown-Prince Thutmose — who would have been Tutankhamen's uncle, if so.

Although Zahi Hawass and DNA experts examined the boy's mummy *in situ* in KV35 (as evidenced by a photograph in the September 2010 issue of *National Geographic*), no results of this have been published (nothing in that regard was included in Hawass's *Scanning the Pharaohs*, 2015), or whether No.61071 has been taken to the Cairo Egyptian Museum, subsequently. The mummy of Amenhotep II (No. 61069) apparently has never been subjected to DNA-testing, so a comparison with the boy's DNA is not possible to prove or disprove the proposed Prince Webensenu identity.

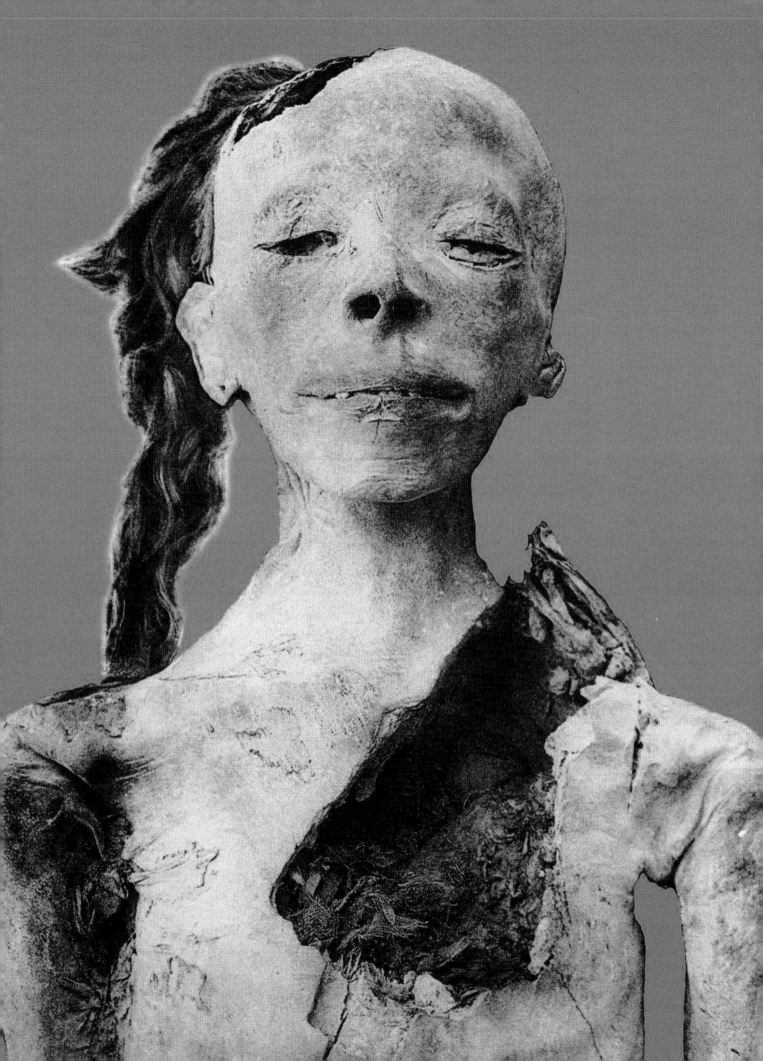

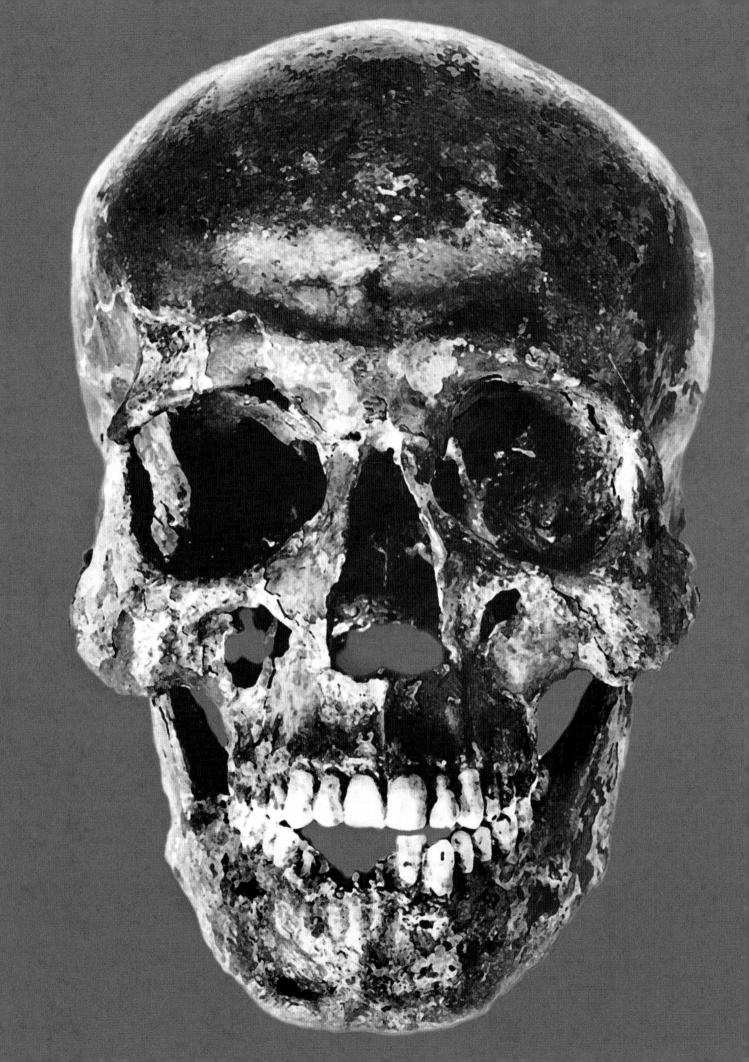

Whose Bones Were Found in KV55?

K ing's Valley Tomb 55, discovered in early January 1907 by English archaeologist Edward R. Ayrton, excavating for American treasure-seeker Theodore M. Davis, remains well over 100 years later one of the most confounding finds of all Egyptian archaeology, not only due to its rushed and slipshod clearance (even by the standards of the day), but also for the enduring mystery of who exactly was found interred there. The fully story of KV55 is told in the third volume of this series — *Tombs. Treasures. Mummies. The Tomb of Yuya & Thuyu (KV46) & The Amarna Cache (KV55)* — so need not be repeated here.

Partially protruding from an anciently mutilated and environmentally damaged *rishi*-style anthropoid royal-status coffin not originally its own, the excavators discovered a decapitated "mummy," which had been partially thrust out of the coffin when the low lion-bier supporting the coffin collapsed, probably due to water-induced decay and the coffin lid being struck (and split lengthwise) by a dislodged sizeable limestone chunk fallen from the chamber's high ceiling. The protruding head of the individual subsequently may have been struck by another falling stone, causing damage and separating it from the jutting body by several inches. When found the head had a gold-foil vulture-pectoral wrapped around it, which was initially mistaken for a "queen's crown."

After the coffin lid had been removed from the single-chamber tomb in three sections, it came time — on January 25, 1907 — to examine the "mummy" still resting in what remained of the coffin basin (the wood of which was also greatly decayed by water which had seeped into the space over the millennia). Eight persons were present at the reveal, including an invited American painter, Joseph Lindon Smith, who was selected to do the "dismemberment" of the remains, because he had the "*delicate hands of an artist.*"

Opposite, The Author's computerized rendering of the skull from KV55. The missing mandible incisors were destroyed when T. Davis touched them 1907. The damaged areas have been restored. Right, 1907 photo of the KV-55 coffin in situ, *protruding "mummy" indicated: head on the left, body covered with loose gold sheets on the right.* Adapted from The Tomb of Queen Tiyi

Detail of the head of the KV55 occupant, from the general view of the coffin taken in 1907. The gold-foil vulture pectoral which Maspero mistakenly thought was a queen's vulture crown is recognizable. The head had been detached from the "mummy's" body by a rock fallen from the tomb's high ceiling. Adapted from *The Tomb of Queen Tiyi*

After several uninscribed sheets of heavy gold-foil were removed from the corpse (described at the time as the size of "foolscap," so approximately 13x16 inches, which were believed by the excavators to have fallen from the interior of the coffin lid, although even today their function within the coffin has not been determined), the smallish body concealed by a dark-colored shroud was revealed. It proved to not be bandaged in the conventional manner for mummies, but rather — in the words of Antiquities Director Gaston Maspero, who was present — *"was somewhat scantily swathed in two or three wrappings of linen, fine in texture but very worn."* Maspero additionally remarked on the condition of the corpse that it was *"nothing more than a residue of fibrous bones and disconnected limbs, to which little dried flesh still adherred in places."*

In other words the individual occupying the rotting coffin was really more of a skeleton than a mummy, per se. It has to be wondered if the individual had, in fact, ever been fully mummified after death, but rather only naturally desiccated within a loose shrouding. The left arm was described as clearly bent and resting on the chest (rib cage); the right arm extended along the corpse's side, the hand on the right thigh. The only apparent decoration of the remains were six broad bracelets of very thin gold-foil, three on upper left arm, three on the right wrist. (The status of these today is unknown.)

Smith next turned his attention to the subject's skull, which rested approximately a foot from the coffin basin. The gold-foil vulture "crown" was removed and Smith later recalled that the skull *"was badly damaged* (specifically the right cheek bone by the falling stone which had broken the head from the

158

body) *but there were two rows of good teeth in a jaw fairly well preserved."* Maspero wrote enough flesh remained on the skull so that the *"features had suffered compairitively little and, in spite of the flattening of the nose, might still be clearly recognized."* And he thought the face was that of *"Khouniatonou."* (Akhenaten). Excavator Davis next impulsively touched the skull's teeth and two of the lower incisors *"fell into dust, thereby showing that the mummy could not be preserved."* These observations concluded, the skull and collected pieces of broken bone from the right cheek and eye-orbit area were placed into a basket provided by the archaeologist Ayrton.

With the several witnesses still looking on, Smith then returned to the corpse itself. He felt the *"mummy cloth around the neck,"* searching for a possible broad-collar necklace; but when he *"touched the surface of the mummy...it crumbled into ashes and sifted down through* [the] *bones. So it was with the entire body until nothing remained except a pile of dust and disconnected bones with a few shreds of dried skin adhering to them."* Smith characterized the shroud cloth and flesh as having *"the consistency of the ash of a cigar."* Davis wrote that it was he who *"attempted to lift a bit of the wrapping... [which] came off in a black mass, exposing the ribs."*

A simple gold-bead broad collar was, indeed, revealed by this activity; and Smith proceeded to recover its many pieces, some of which had fallen through the rib cage into the bottom of the coffin basin. Reaching under the skeletal rib cage to retrieve these, the artist discovered that water had accumulated there, enough to wet his hands. Thus, the presence of long-term moisture helps to explain the ruined state of both the coffin basin and its occupant.

At this point in the KV55 activity, former Inspector of Antiquities for Upper Egypt James Quibell entered the chamber. Looking at the jumble of disjointed skeleton in the coffin basin, he suggested that perhaps there was a surgeon among the tourists that day in the Valley of the Kings who could offer a professional opinion as to the sex of the KV55 individual. He left the tomb to go seeking such a person and returned shortly with someone who had identified himself as an obstetrician. After looking at the pelvic bones he summarily pronounced, *"without doubt this is the skeleton of a woman."*

Davis was estatic, of course, believing — as he would publish in *The Tomb of Queen Tîyi* in 1910 — that he had found the final resting place and sorry remains of the great principal spouse of Amenhotep III and mother of the Heretic. Maspero, however, cautioned him against reaching premature conclusions.

Smith remembered that he placed the rest of the disarticulated bones of the skeleton in the basket holding the skull and fragments of it. Antiquities inspector for Upper Egypt Arthur Weigall (Quibell's succesor in that position), one of those present that day, took charge of the collection, later soaking the bones in parafin wax — *"to prevent their breakage"* — and sending the sealed basket to the Cairo Egyptian Museum, for professional assessment there by G. Elliot Smith, the Australian anatomist who was just then examining the Royal Mummies recovered from the TT320 and KV35 caches for the Museum's Catalogue Général.

The basket received from Luxor was opened by Elliot Smith in late February 1907, wherein he found the parafin-soaked skeletal bones and skull. Although he would not precisely record so, apparently the basket also included bits of decayed mummy wrappings and a few scraps of human tissue, the latter perhaps having fallen from the skull, which had had enough dried flesh adhering to it when found to have a recognizable face. There were also gold-foil ribbons or bands, which had encircled the KV55 individual, but strangely had gone unremarked upon by any of the witnesses present, when they wrote accounts about the *in situ* destructive examination of the KV55 "mummy" one month earlier. These phantom bands would later be stolen from Smith's Museum storeroom, without have been photographed or otherwise formally recorded.

Upon examination Smith immediately saw that the remains from the basket were those of a male, not the famous queen Davis had hoped for. Perhaps understandably prejudiced by Antiquities Director Maspero, who was his employer, afterall, Smith would write in his *The Royal Mummies* (1912) that the skeleton was that of Khouniatonou, as Akhenaten was still being called at the time. Smith however found that, in his assessment, the bones were those of a male not very much more than thirty years of age, based on fusing (or lack thereof) of the cranial sutures and several bone epiphyses, which, arguably, would be too young for the Heretic. He hedged his bet by pointing out that time range when epiphyses consolidate ranges somewhat and that the individual under consideration might, in instances of some of the lack of ossifications, be as young as twenty at death. He also stated that the skull showed evidence — in the varying bone thicknesses of the cranium — that KV55 suffered from the condition of hydrocephalus (literally water on the brain), which he felt accorded with the historical depictions of "Khouniatonou." This diagnosis was subsequently discounted by everyone else who would examine the skull, however. Smith's *Royal Mummies* account of No. 61075 (the number the bones were assigned in the Cairo Museum catalogue) consists of a lengthy, very detailed description of most of the individual bones.

In 1919, at the request of then-Cairo Museum director James Quibell, the KV55 remains were reexamined by Dr. Douglas Derry, Smith's successor as the Museum's mummy-anatomist. Derry found no signs of hydrocephalus and concluded that the male individual represented by the skull and bones had been no more than twenty-three at death — quite clearly far too young for him to have been Akhenaten (unless the Heretic began his religious revolution at age six!). Derry would help "dismantle" the mummy of Tutankhamen in 1926 and subsequently make several observations regarding close similarities between the skulls of the indisputably identified boy-king and the KV55 individual, reaching the conclusion that the two were closely related, brothers or father and son.

By this time there was a new royal-male individual minimally attested among the players on the Amarna stage, an ephemeral coregent and/or successor of Akhenaten named Smenkhkare (or fully Ankhkheperure Neferneferuaten Smenkhkare Djoserkheperu). Although his parentage was unknown, it was speculated that he was a younger third son of Amenhotep III and Tiye, so Akhenaten's brother. Thus, here was a candidate who would

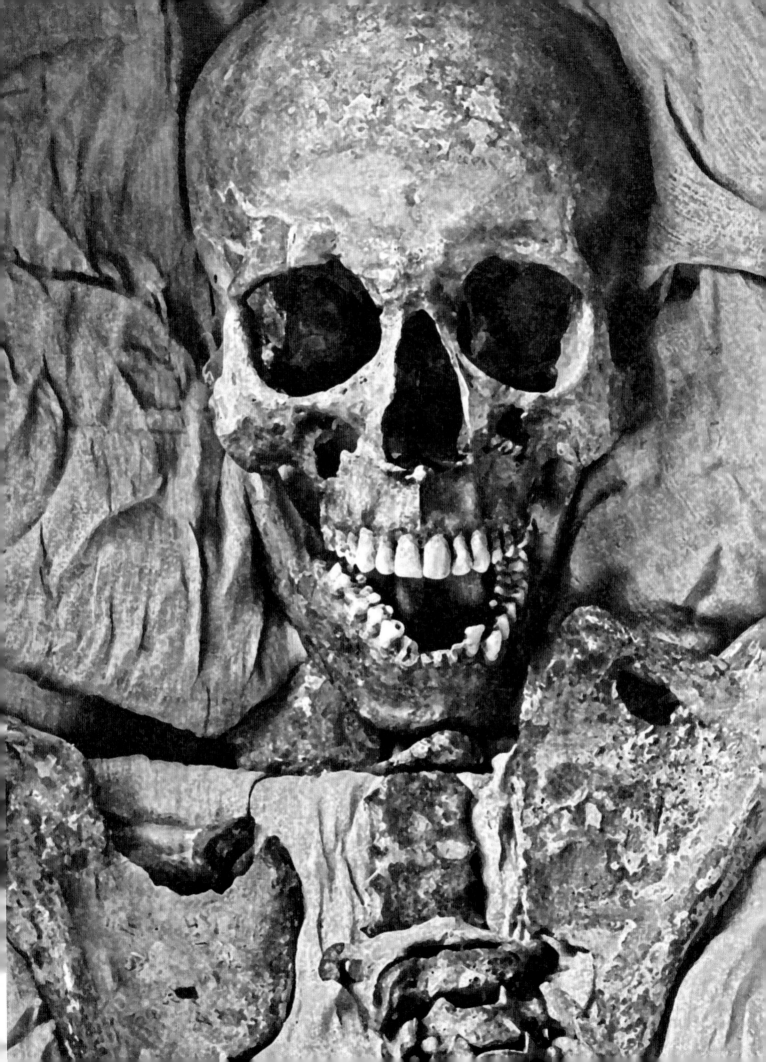

seemingly nicely fit the age perameters argued for the KV55 individual: no less than eighteen and no more than thirty.

The debated bones and skull were officially examined a third time, in 1963, by University of Liverpool professor of anatomy R.G. Harrison. He formally published his findings in *The Journal of Egyptian Archaeology* in 1966. Harrison was generally in agreement with Derry, discovering no evidence for hydrocephalus or other abnormalities. He was quite certain that the male person in question could not have been more than twenty-three at death, was even likely as young as nineteen or twenty. Based upon a forensic reconstruction of the face of No. 61075 which he commissioned — looking unlike Akhenaten but suggestive of the face of Tutankhamen's second or middle coffin — Harrison was convinced that the refugee from KV55 was Smenkhkare.

Nearly forty years later, in January 2000, the bones in question were examined yet again, this time by Dr. Joyce Filer, a British Egyptologist and physical anthropologist, who was also an assistant curator at the British Museum. She published her findings in the March/April 2002 issue of the American magazine *Archaeology,* essentially concurring with Prof. Harrison regarding the male person's anatomy/pathology and age at death, which she estimated at eighteen to twenty-five, but favoring the lower possibility. Filer did not go so far as to identify No. 61075, but was convinced that, due to her determined age-range, he could not possibly be Akhenaten.

Finally (at least for now), the Egyptian Supreme Council for Antiquities, under the direction of Zahi Hawass, undertook the Family of King Tutankhamun Project, a two-year-long study (September 2005 - October 2009; see Addendum Seven, pp. 198-215) of the known late-Eighteenth Dynasty royal remains, to determine through CT-scanning and DNA-testing their familial relationships. This commenced chronologically with the firmly identified mummies of Yuya and Thuyu (found together in their largely intact tomb, KV46), known parents of King's Great Wife Tiye; but, clearly an oversight, it did not include from the same generation Thutmose IV, father of Amenhotep III, Tiye's husband, the identity of whose mummy (from KV35) had been questioned in any case. Unquestionable Tutankhamen was included, of course, as were the KV55 bones and two anonymous adult-females also found in KV35 ("Elder Lady" and "Younger Lady"), but apparently not the prepubescent boy discovered lying between them, suggesting a probable relationship to the two women. Also studied and tested were the two fetal mummies found in KV62 (so presumed offspring of Tutankhamen) and the partial mummies (one headless) of two anonymous-but-possibly-royal females discovered in KV21.

When the results of the FKTP were announced on February 17, 2010, at a Cairo press conference and simultaneously in the *Journal of the American Medical Association* ("Ancestry and Pathology of King Tutankhamun's Family"), there was much criticism of the Project's methodologies and lack of corroborrating "blind" tests. The study announced that the bones from KV55 were "almost certainly" Akhenaten's and that he was indisputably the father of Tutankhamen, parented with KV35YL, who was his full sister. It was also decided that KV55 may have lived to be as old as sixty-five — which means Akhenaten would have been born before his mother, Tiye! This absolute certainy was not the result of sophisticated technological determinations, it turned out, but based only on the personal visual observations of a single radiologist from Cairo University, thus nothing different from the previous opinions of Smith, Derry, Harrison and Filer. Zahi Hawass had wanted KV55 to be Akhenaten, and so he was declared to be. Hawass later said that a Smenkhkare identification was not considered because *"not enough is known about him."* Well, as one Egyptological professional has said to this writer, *"There is science and then there is Egyptian science."*

So, the question posed by the title of this addendum goes unanswered.

Opposite, The KV55 "mummy" as displayed today in the Cairo Egyptian Museum. Computerized adaptation from an uncredited Internet photo

Right: Which One? Plaster studies of two unnamed kings from an El Amarna sculptor's workshop thought to depict Akhenaten (l.) & Smenkhkare, the candidates for the KV55 bones. Adapted Berlin Ägyptisches Museum photos

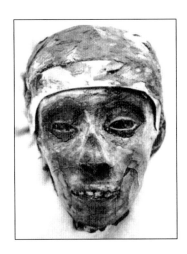

ADDENDUM TWO

Abusing Pharaoh
Mistreatment of the Mummy
of Tutankhamen
in Antiquity & Modern Times

Almost everyone who in their youth discovered and devoured all three volumes of Howard Carter's *The Tomb of Tut·ankh·Amen* probably also pondered the full-face and left-profile double portrait therein of the head of the boy-king's mummy (Plate XXXI of Volume II), attempting as they did to reconcile the desiccated and crackled empty-eyed husk in the two photographs with the remarkably handsome features of the youthful ruler in life, especially as idealized on the golden inner coffin, the famous gold funerary mask and numerous large and small representations of him from the tomb and elsewhere.

Looking at these two official images of Tutankhamen's mummified face published by Carter, one had no reason to suspect that the cotton batting framing the young king's mortal features in the Harry Burton photographs carefully masked a hard fact: this head was not attached to the mummy's body. Tutankhamen had been decapitated — by none other than his modern-day discoverer and a certain Dr. Douglas Derry, who assisted in the November 1925 complete dismemberment of the royal remains — in the course of the official scientific "dismantlement" of the all-but-intact Tomb 62 in the Valley of the Kings, discovered three years before.

The general world public in the mid 1920s had no reason to question the state of Tutankhamen's pathetic near-skeletal mummy, as seen in the official Burton full-figure photograph taken prior to the boy-king's October 1926 reinterment in KV62 — wherein the young ruler lies supine upon a shallow wooden tray filled with fine-grained sand, arms folded across the mid torso, stripped quite unregally naked, save for remnants of a crumpled bead collar on his narrow chest and what remained of a beaded skull-cap.

Opposite, The face of Tutankhamen's mummy today, after nearly a century of modern abuse. Notice in particular the punched-in eyesockets & absence of ears. Computerized uncredited photo from the Internet

Top, The mummy's portrait taken by Harry Burton in 1926. Cotton batting disguises the fact that the head had been decapitated. The open eyes are still present, long eyelashes visible.

Above, Harry Burton's photograph of the forearms of the mummy of Tutankhamen prior to their detachment in order to facilitate removal of the several (11) bracelets which adorned them. The hands were subsequently detached from the forearms, one of which Burton photographed (below) resting on a cotton-padded cardboard tray, gold finger-sheaths & rings not yet removed.

Few who saw this photograph at the time probably bothered to notice that the white sand in the tray — in which the mummy was partially submerged — mostly camouflaged the fact that Tutakhamen's head and limbs were detached from his trunk. Cosmetic retouching by Carter also hid the reality that the king's severed hands and feet had been reattached with resin to his wrists and ankles.

Sad though he was in this final official view, the last male of the Eighteenth Dynasty Thutmosid bloodline was seemingly *"reverently"* rewrapped[1] and returned to his outermost gilded-wood coffin. This was then placed again in the great rose-quartzite sarcophagus left *in situ* in his modestly scaled sepulcher — still being emptied by Carter of its staggeringly rich treasure. There King Tutankhamen was to remain undisturbed for another forty-two years.

In 1968 the occupied sarcophagus in the Valley of the Kings Tomb 62 was freed of its modern plate-glass covering and the first gilded coffin of Tutankhamen was reopened — under the gaze of onlooking tourists who just happened to be visiting the tomb at that moment — to reveal the boy-king's pathetic mummy inside. A British expedition headed by R.G. Harrison, professor of Anatomy at the University of Liverpool, had been given permission by Egyptian Antiquities authorities to conduct the disinterment for the purpose of taking x-rays of the royal remains, which had not been done during the initial examination of Tutankhamen's mummy by Carter and Derry in 1925. Harrison's purpose in x-raying the mummy was to attempt to determine a cause for the young ruler's premature death. He (and his team and official Egyptian observers present) made a rather startling discovery.

First, the royal remains had been "rewrapped" only somewhat haphazardly, despite Carter's diary entry that this had been done *"reverently"*; and the mummy still lay on the sand tray employed to disguise its true state in Tutankh-

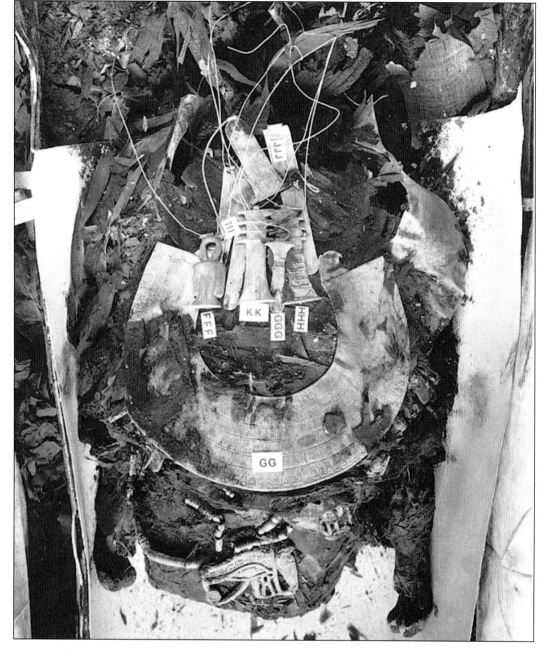

Burton's photograph of the decapitated, amulet-laden torso of Tutankhamen, bisected from the lower limbs at the iliac crest of the pelvis & lying on a sheet of heavy paper positioned lower in the solid-gold inner coffin (at the curve of the hips, it would appear). Although the forearms with the many bracelets have been removed, the upper arms (reduced to mere bones) are still in place.

amen's official post-"autopsy" full-length portrait recorded by the photographer Burton in 1926. Secondly, it was quickly evident to all present — from the disarticulated condition of the mummy on the tray — that the boy-king had been decapitated and further divided into several parts: his arms removed at the shoulders, separated at the elbows and hands severed; his legs separated at the hip and knee joints, the feet severed; and his torso cut from the pelvis at the iliac crest. Harrison's subsequent x-ray of the torso revealed yet a further, truly puzzling fact: the sternum and frontal rib-cage were missing, the remaining ribs clearly having been sawed through, presumably by the embalmers![2] This condition had escaped Dr. Derry's observation in 1925, inasmuch as the mummy's chest was thickly covered with hardened resin forming a carapace, which was further imbedded all over with pieces of a thoroughly fragmented bead collar, which Carter did not attempt

to remove — it having no intrinsic value justifying the effort it would have taken.

World press reaction to the decapitated state of "King Tut" was predictably strident, Carter being accused by Kamal al Malakh, archaeological editor of the Cairo daily *Al Ahram*, of *"having cut off the king's head and packed it with other remains in a cheap sugar box."*[3] Malakh was an official observer of the Harrison examination, although how he confused Carter's sand tray with a *"cheap sugar box"* is not clear, unless perhaps he thought the white sand in the wooden tray to be sugar.

Following Professor Harrison's examination of the nearly skeletal remains, and his x-raying of the head and trunk, Tutakhamen's fragmented corpse — without any attempt at rewrapping by the British team — was reinterred a second time in his original outer coffin, still resting somewhat disassembled on

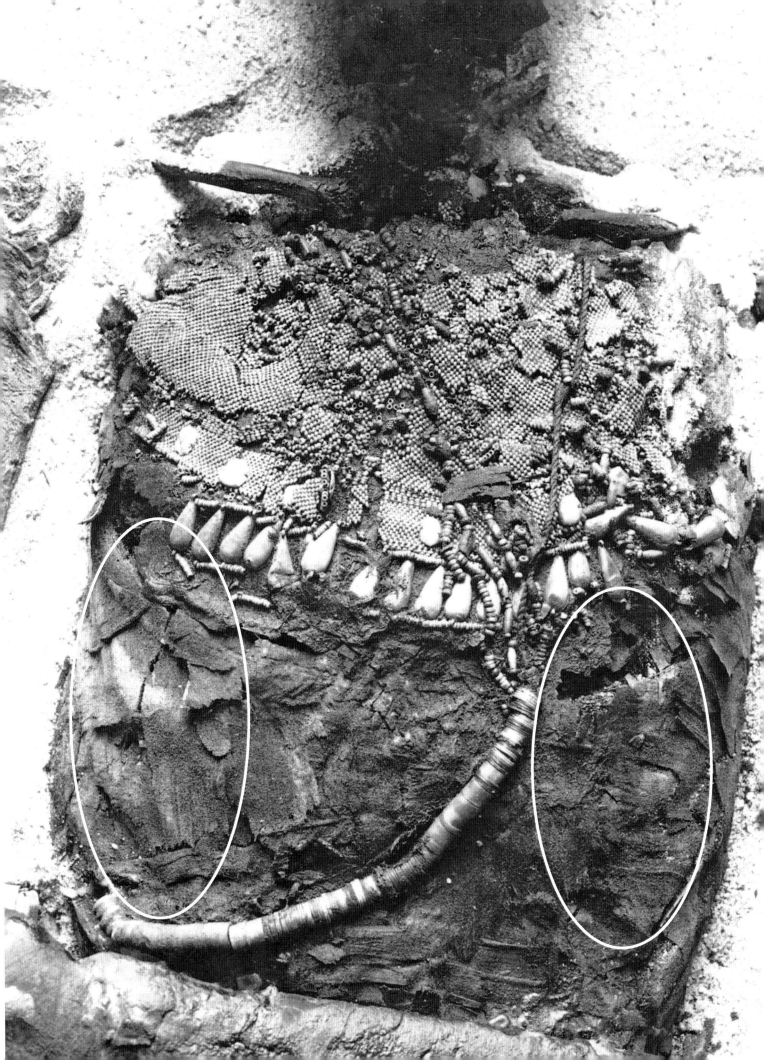

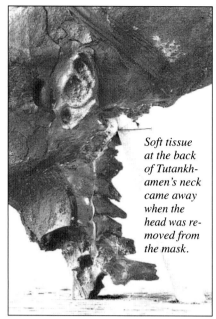

Soft tissue at the back of Tutankhamen's neck came away when the head was removed from the mask.

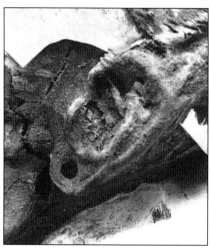

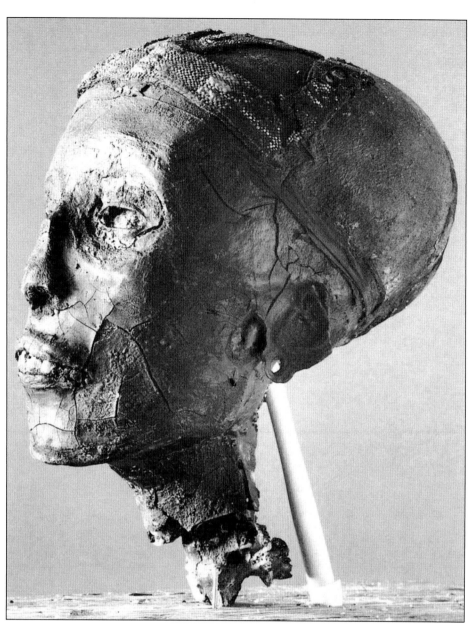

Opposite, Detail photo by Burton of the thorax of the mummy of Tutankhamen, taken after the king's reassembled remains had been positioned on the sand tray provided by Howard Carter. Note the burning in of the area of the neck at the top of the image, possibly done by the photographer Burton to hide the fact of the head's decapitation. The fragmented bead collar — which Carter chose not to remove — is pressed into a thick carapace of resin that covers the king's chest. This peculiar condition was not discovered until an x-ray was taken of the torso in 1968 by a British team examining the mummy, which revealed that the frontal rib-cage & sternum of the mummy are missing. However, the ribs are still present in 1926, as indicated on the photo, as well.

Above right, One of several views of Tutankhamen's decapitated head taken by Burton. It is propped up on a wooden dowel held in place by nails. Note the broken ear & large cheek-lesion.

Above left, top, Detail of another of Burton's "head shots" showing the exposed vertebrae of the neck, the soft tissue being lost when the head was extracted from the funerary mask using "hot knives"; bottom, The king's undamaged ear, the top portion of which was already broken away in Burton's later photos. This possibly would have inadvertently occurred when the sheet-gold temple band was removed.

Carter's sand tray; and the sarcophagus plate-glass cover was replaced. There — hidden from the prying eyes of countless thousands of tourists who, season after season, pilgrimaged to his famous burial site, as if to some saint's shrine — the sad earthly remains of the last Thutmosid male rested, until officially visited a decade later, in 1978, and disinterred a third time, the head being x-rayed yet again by an American team led by University of Michigan professor of Orthodontics James E. Harris.

In 1972 the Griffith Institute of the Ashmolean Museum, Oxford (recipient of Howard Carter's personal papers, notes and sketches, and of one set of Harry Burton's 1,400 glass-plate negatives recording the Tomb 62 clearance and objects), published the fifth slim monograph in its "Tut'Ankhamun Tomb Series," *The Human Remains from the Tomb of Tut'Ankhamun* by F. Filce Leek. Leek, a British dentist, had been a member of the Harrison investigating team in 1968, assisting with the x-raying. His terse study includes extracts from Carter's diary, Dr. Derry's manuscript of his anatomical report on the royal mummy (annotated with Leek's commentary) and, most significantly, numerous plates from Burton's photographic record of the remains, includ-

Damage to the Mummy of Tutankhamen at Its 1926 "Unwrapping"

Loss of parts of both ears (when brow band removed?)

Both upper arms originally left attached to trunk, but later removed, as evidenced by 1926 sand-tray photograph.

Thorax bisected from lower body at the iliac crest of pelvis.

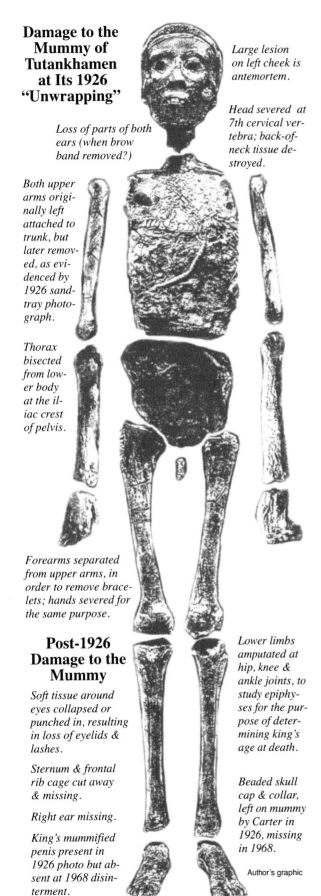

Large lesion on left cheek is antemortem.

Head severed at 7th cervical vertebra; back-of-neck tissue destroyed.

Forearms separated from upper arms, in order to remove bracelets; hands severed for the same purpose.

Post-1926 Damage to the Mummy

Soft tissue around eyes collapsed or punched in, resulting in loss of eyelids & lashes.

Sternum & frontal rib cage cut away & missing.

Right ear missing.

King's mummified penis present in 1926 photo but absent at 1968 disinterment.

Lower limbs amputated at hip, knee & ankle joints, to study epiphyses for the purpose of determining king's age at death.

Beaded skull cap & collar, left on mummy by Carter in 1926, missing in 1968.

Author's graphic

ding fourteen previously unpublished views of the severed head and other anatomical details of the body, as first revealed and when later disarticulated.[4] (A cropped, retouched view of the bodiless head was published in 1963, but more on that below.)

These scientific "record shots" prove to any of the interested public who saw them in Leek's volume that, indeed, the mummy of young "Tut" had been thoroughly taken apart by Carter and Derry in 1925. The only New Kingdom ruler to have been found undisturbed in his coffins, Tutankhamen's is also the only royal mummy to have suffered so severely in the name of modern science, official "greed" and morbid curiosity.

The indifferent (some might even say sacrilegious) treatment of Tutankhamen's mortal remains went unremarked in the many popular book-length accounts of the discovery and clearance of his tomb, which were prompted by the traveling exhibition of choice KV62 treasures in Europe, the United States and Canada throughout the 1970s. It was not until 1990 that Carter's and Derry's deeds were attacked in print again, this time at length and with specifics by a retired French physician, Dr. Maurice Bucaille, in his book, *Mummies of the Pharaohs; Modern Medical Investigations.* Dr. Bucaille not only detailed the Carter-Derry dismemberment of the king's mummy, he also attacked the blind eye cast for over seventy years by world Egyptologists and others in the know towards the treatment of the royal corpse, even charging efforts of an outright coverup on the part of renowned French Egyptologist and author (*Tutankhamen, Life and Death of a Pharaoh,* 1963), Mme. Christiane Desroches-Noblecourt.

Bucaille charged that, because Carter realized his treatment of the royal mummy would be discovered by the public eventually (there were Burton's incriminating photographs, after all), the English archaeologist, "*...exaggerated the damage to the outermost wrappings* [of the mummy] *by asserting in all of his writings that the wrappings and, by a false extension, the mummy itself had spontaneously suffered from the attack of fatty acids supposedly contained in the ointments poured onto the wrappings* [in antiquity]....*"* [5] The French physician proposed, instead, that the spontaneous combustion which allegedly carbonized the mummy and its bandages was caused not by the unguents liberally applied in the ancient funerary rites, but rather because Carter had exposed Tutankhamen's unwrapped corpse directly to the Egyptian sun for several hours on two consecutive days (November 1st and 2nd, 1925), when the temperature reached 65° Centigrade (149° Fahrenheit), in an unsuccessful attempt to melt the pitch-like material cementing the body and gold funerary mask to the bottom of the solid-gold innermost coffin.[6]

Bucaille wrote, "*There can be little doubt that serious damage was caused to the mummy by subjecting it to such intense heat, as was seen when the wrappings were removed. It is now a well-known fact that heat causes mummified tissue to burst.*" [7] He went on to show how Carter and Derry — forced to "unwrap" Tutankhamen within the close confines of his nested second and third coffins — found it expedient to separate the charred and cracked pelvis and lower limbs from the body's trunk at

Opposite, The carbonized mummy of Tutankhamen as it appeared when disinterred in 1978, for the purpose of x-raying the head a second time. It lies on the sand tray provided by Howard Carter, with protective padding left by the British mission which examined & x-rayed the remains a decade earlier. Note that the disarticulated arms were not repositioned across the torso in 1968. Note also that the penis would seem to be absent. Inset, opposite, The decapitated head of Tutankhamen held aloft in 1978. Damage to the eye sockets is clearly visible, soft tissue around the eyes now gone. Private photos

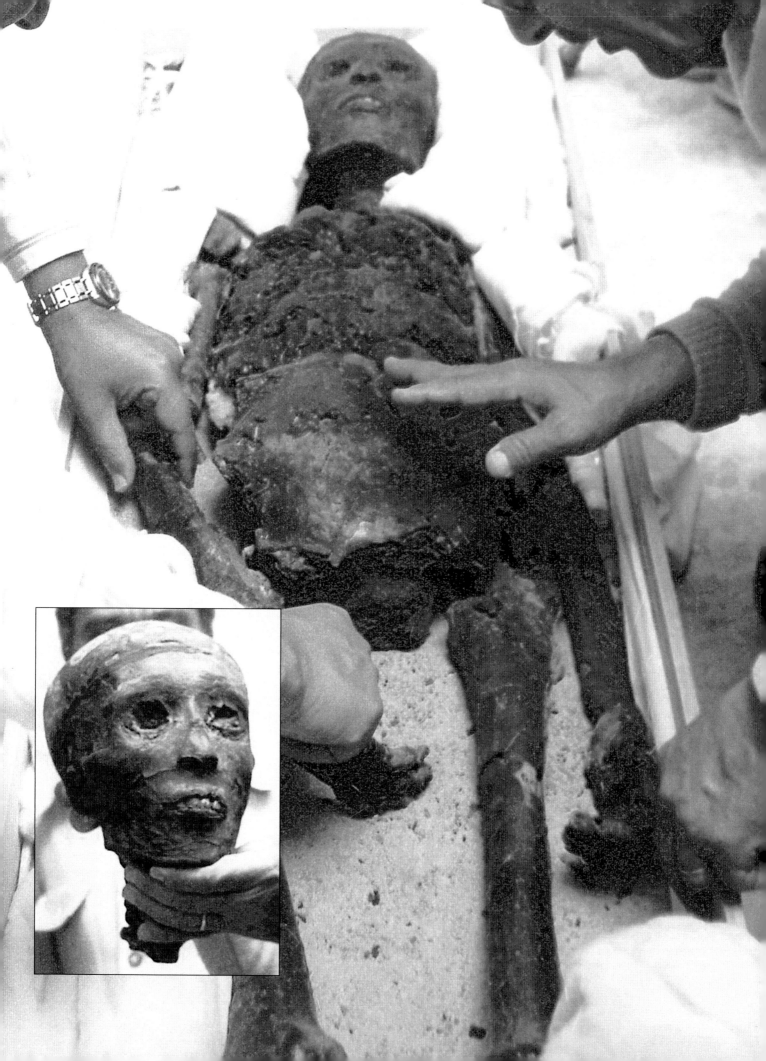

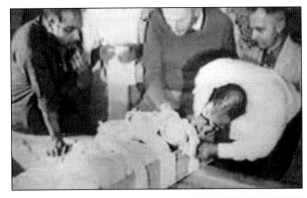

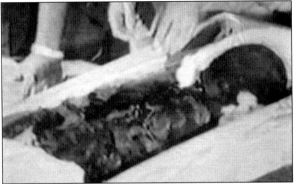

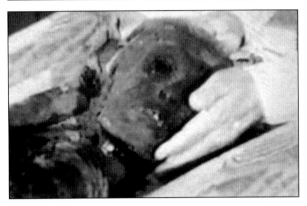

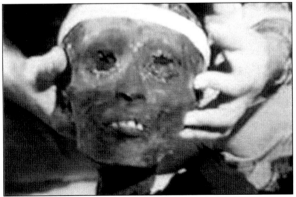

Stills from the film footage of the official 1968 first disinterment of the mummy of Tutankhamen, under the direction of University of Liverpool Anatomy professor R.G. Harrison. Left, from the top: The sand tray just removed from the coffin/ sarcophagus with jumbled cotton batting covering the upper part of the mummy (Harrison is in the red sweater); The upper part of the mummy after the cotton batting has been removed (note head turned to one side, the condition of the chest & absence of the bead collar); The king's detached head being lifted from the sand tray; Close-up of the head after it has been x-rayed, the white band being a tape measure (note the empty eye sockets). 1992 A&E Documentary, "The Face of Tutankhamun"

the iliac crest and to remove the latter from the coffin so that the thorax could be more easily cleared of the numerous funerary objects and jewelry covering it in multiple layers. To further facilitate this stripping of the now-bisected corpse, the forearms were then detached (the many bracelets encircling each forearm, eleven in all[8] — could not have been slipped off otherwise). Because the back of the king's cranium was stuck fast to the inside of the golden funerary mask, archaeologist and anatomist next severed the head at the seventh cervical vertebra, leaving it inside the mask when the trunk (with the upper arms still attached) was freed from the cementing pitch on its backside by the application of *"hot knives."* This same hot-knife treatment was used again to free the boy-king's head from the pitch adhering it to the backside of the mask. In the process the nape of the mummy's neck was pulled away, revealing the cervical vertebrae. What ultimately became of this royal tissue is not recorded by Carter/ Derry (nor, in fact, subsequently commented on by Dr. Bucaille).[9]

In his cataloguing of the physical indignities to which Tutankhamen's mummy was subjected during the 1925 "unwrapping" procedure,[10] Maurice Bucaille overlooked the apparent damage to the king's ears resulting from its handling by Carter and Derry. In the left-profile view of the head published in Carter's *The Tomb of Tut·ankh·Amen*, it is apparent that the pierced left ear is fully intact. In later views by Burton (where the head clearly is totally separated from the body and held upright by a dowel strut and nails driven into a wooden plank), the top half of the same ear is obviously missing. Did it, perhaps, come away accidentally when the gold brow band surrounding the head was removed? And, if so, was this small bit of Tutankhamen simply tossed out with the mummy-wrappings refuse? (Or possibly pocketed as a bizarre souvenir?) The right ear in Burton's photos seems inexplicably mostly gone (the top portion and lobe are missing); and when the king's severed head was photographed in 1978, this right ear appeared to be gone altogether.

In his controversial 1978 exposé, *Tutankhamun, The Untold Story*, the late Thomas Hoving waxed over Carter's reaction to the young king's countenance, when this was finally revealed: *"To Howard Carter, the royal visage was placid, the features well-formed. The King must have been handsome beyond belief. As he held the head in his hands, Carter was suddenly transported to the time when the young, vibrant king still lived. He was profoundly shaken by the experience."*[11] Since Carter himself did not write that he was "transported" or "profoundly shaken" on beholding the royal visage, one wonders how Hoving determined this. (But then, the the former director of the Metropolitan Museum of Art was totally mistaken when he informed his readers that *"the body* [of Tutankhamun] *was naked but for three decorations: the toes were encased in gold sheaths, as were the fingers and the King's penis."* Why did Carter not mention or catalogue this gold penis-sheath? And where is it today, if it existed at all in 1925? Another "souvenir," perhaps?)

For Maurice Bucaille, Thomas Hoving was but one of many knowledgeable commentators *"in Egyptological circles"* who have glossed over the evident Carter/Derry abuse of Tutankhamen's corpse. The Frenchman reserved a special resentment towards his fellow compatriot, Egyptologist Desroches-Noblecourt, however, blaming her for having advanced Carter's *"false thesis"* regarding the so-called ointment-ruined mummy *"in a spectacular manner."*[12] Since Desroches-Noblecourt had full access to the Griffith Institute materials concerning the mummy's examination (including Burton's tell-tale photographs) when she was researching her own work on Tutankhamen, Bucaille was persuaded that she knew very well *"that Carter had blatantly lied"*[13] about his slicing

170

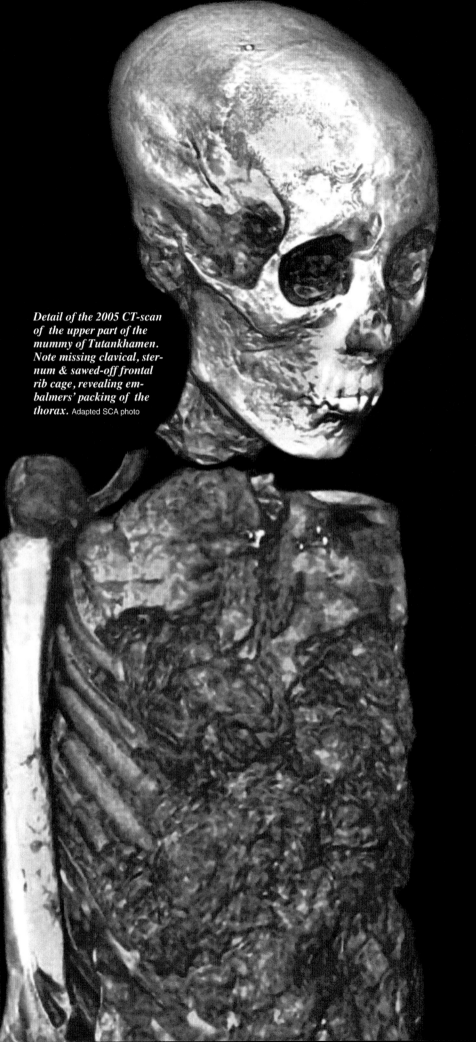

Detail of the 2005 CT-scan of the upper part of the mummy of Tutankhamen. Note missing clavical, sternum & sawed-off frontal rib cage, revealing embalmers' packing of the thorax. Adapted SCA photo

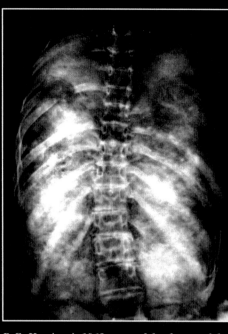

R.G. Harrison's 1968 x-ray of the thorax of the Tutankhamen mummy, showing the absence of clavicals, sternum & frontal rib-cage. Evident spinal curvature is probably situational rather than congenital. Archival photo

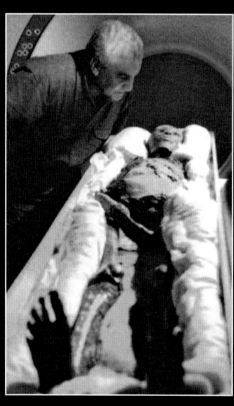

Zahi Hawass & the mummy of Tutankhamen at the time of its CT-scanning in 2005. SCA photo

up of the boy-king's remains. Bucaille was particularly incensed by the *"reproduction of the head of the pharaoh, carefully faked in her book,"* [14] inasmuch as Figure 134 in *Tutankhamen, Life and Death of a Pharaoh* is cleverly cropped to hide the fact of decapitation and the dowel propping up the head in Burton's original photo has been airbrushed out of existence.

Returning now to the official British reexamination of the Tutankhamen mummy in 1968, R.G. Harrison's x-rays of the head and thorax revealed that the young king had, in fact, been treated somewhat unkindly by his ancient embalmers. (Carter and Derry had earlier noted that Tutankhamen's scalp was most peculiarly shaven, covered with a white "fatty" substance overlaid by a beaded skull cap.) The broad, flat-topped, longish skull was found to be empty (the brains having been removed in the embalming process, as was normal procedure), except for two thick deposits of opaque material, probably solidified liquid resin which had almost certainly been introduced into the skull cavity through the same nasal passage via which the brains had been extracted. One of these deposits is at the back of the cranium, as would have naturally occurred with the king's corpse lying supine at the time of the resin's injection. The other deposit is at the top of the skull, however, causing Leek to speculate in his treatise on the royal remains that the king had been suspended upside down when this resinous liquid was introduced.[15] It has been suggested to this writer that such a deposit at the top of the skull also might have resulted from the head (with the body supine) being forced extremely backward over the edge of the embalmers' work table during the introduction procedure, and kept in that position long enough for the liquid resin to have solidified. In either case, a strange way to treat a god-king, even a teenage dead one!

Because the Harrison/Leek radiograph of Tutankhamen's skull was of somewhat inferior quality — especially in displaying the young ruler's dentition — American orthodontist and Royal Mummies expert James E. Harris (coauthor of *X-Raying the Pharaohs* and *An X-Ray Atlas of the Royal Mummies*) was granted permission by the Egyptian Antiquities authorities to disinter the boy-king for yet a third time, in 1978. Photographs taken during this one-day activity (with Egyptian officials and other observers in attendance) show still further damage to the battered last Thutmosid: the king's eye sockets had collapsed (or been pushed in?), so that the once partially open lids (with long lashes originally still visible) were now gone; and, as mentioned above, the right ear was entirely absent, likewise the penis. Also, the remains generally seemed even blacker, more charred looking (Derry's report described the mummy's skin as grayish in color[17]).

Carbonized, denuded, dismembered and emasculated, Tutankhamen continued resting within his outer (first) gilded-wood coffin, under a dusty sheet of thick plate-glass covering his open quartzite sarcophagus, uncounted curious tourists peering down from the Antechamber doorway, until January 5, 2005, when the chief of Egypt's Antiquities, Dr. Zahi Hawass, arrived with his Egyptian team and a trailer housing a CT-scanner. Hawass had been directing the Egyptian Mummy Project, a study of the mummies kept at the Cairo Egyptian Museum; and this had segued into the Family of King Tutankhamun Project, an investigation into who was who among the royal mummies of the late Eighteenth Dynasty, which would use CT-scanning and DNA-test-ing to unravel relationships between them. Tutankhamen himself, of course, was the key figure of unquestioned identity and absolute provenance, so the first of some dozen mummified remains to be be studied.

So the dismembered pathetic charred husk of the long-dead king was removed once again on its sand tray from the coffin and sarcophagus, and carried to the trailer parked outside of his tomb. CT-scanning is a relatively quick process, and in just thirty minutes some 1,700 images had been generated. Tutankhamen was returned to his sarcophagus and coffin, the glass-plate protection was replaced, the tomb closed; and Hawass and company went back to Cairo, to study and ponder the results.

When these were finally announced — along with all the findings of the Family of King Tutankhamun Project (seeing Addendum Seven, following) — at a Cairo press conference on February 17, 2010, coinciding with a full formal report published in the *Journal of the American Medical Association* on the same day,[18] it was revealed that the boy-king had been something of a physical wreck at the end of his short life. He suffered from a congenitally "clubbed" left foot (arch higher than normal, causing the king to walk on the side of the member, probably supported by a staff), a mildly cleft pallet and he had undergone multiple bouts of malaria. Plus, Tutankhamen apparently had died prematurely from the consequences of fracturing his left femur and resultant fatal infection, possibly because of falling from his moving chariot. The "wound" at the base of his skull and bone chips in the cranial cavity — seen in the Harrison x-ray, which had led to speculation that he had been murdered by a blow there— was explained as caused during the embalming process.[19]

The full analyses of the Tutankhamen remains were included in Hawass's (coauthored with Cairo University radiology professor Sahar N. Saleem) 2015 publication, *Scanning the Pharaohs: CT Imaging of the New Kingdom Royal Mummies*. Therein Hawass is especially critical of Carter's initial handling of the mummy. He blames the English archaeologist for the situation of the missing sternum and sawed-off frontal chest-wall (rib cage). He states matter-of-factly (p. 95) that Carter removed the beaded collar from the mummy's chest, extracting the sternum and ribs in the process, without subsequently mentioning this fact in his notes.

This harsh conclusion completely ignores (at least it is not cited in Hawass's *Scanning the Pharaohs* notes or bibliography) an article by this writer, coauthored with Drs. Salima Ikram and Janice Kamrin, published in the spring 2007 edition of *Kmt, A Modern Journal of Ancient Egypt* (18:1), titled "Tutankhamen's Missing Ribs," in which we specifically addressed that situation in some careful detail.[20]

We pointed out that the absent chest-parts were first documented by Harrison's x-ray in 1968. In filmed commentary on his examination of the king's mummy, Harrison had avoided mentioning the highly unusual thorax-situation, opting instead to address the normality of the unions of the king's vertebrae (if allowing that there was some abnormal curvature of the spine). Later, in 1978, Harris had nothing to say either, being only really interested in the boy-king's skull and dentition. We also noted Hawass's "Carter Did It" pronouncement, despite the excavator's diary record to the contrary and Burton's final portraits of the reassembled mummy on the sand tray in 1926. We thought it highly unlikely that Carter had changed his mind at the very last minute and decided to remove, after all, the bead collar (Carter Catalogue 256 ttt) and associated gold-bead girdle (Carter 256 sss), which he had earler regarded of so little intrinsic value as to take the time and trouble extracting them from the resin carapace by which they were attached to the mummy's chest. The same could be said, we thought, about the beaded-linen skullcap (Carter 256 qrt) which is present in Burton's sand-tray photo but gone in the Harrison disinterment film-footage and subsequently.

We allowed that while Carter and his team were guilty of quite literally taking Tutankhamen apart, in order to remove him from the funerary mask and innermost gold coffin — but secondarily to recover the extensive quantity of amulets and jewelry adorning the mummy — they were also very thorough in their written description of the corpse and so certainly would have noted the absence of ribs and sternum, if these had been discovered missing during the dismantlement. Dr. Derry's anatomical report on the mummy, in fact, specifically mentions: *"The left forearm lay above it* [the right forearm] *over the lower ribs."*[21]

The authors also pointed out that the mummy's head had suffered physical damage sometime between 1926 and and 1968. In Harrison's film it is held up for the movie camera (with a measing tape around the cranium) and very clearly the eye sockets — intact, even with lids and eyelashes in 1926 — are empty holes. The ears are also totally missing, although partially present in Burton's several photos of the mummy's decapitated head.

Additionally, in the 1926 sand-tray image of the reassembled Tutankhamen, the king's forearms are folded across the abdomen, as they had been positioned when found. In the Harrison footage — when the somewhat disarrayed cotton batting with which Carter had covered the sand tray is pulled away — the arms are fully extended along the body's sides and legs, obviously moved there by someone (they remained in that position during Hawass's CT-scanning).

Finally, there was the question of Tutankhamen's penis, we pointed out. It is indisbutably present in the 1926 sand-tray record, and definitely gone in a candid photo of the mummy taken during Harris's 1978 disinterment for x-raying purposes. Whether it was still present during the 1968 filming, it is not possible to say; and Harrison does not comment one way or the other. Interestingly during Hawass's 2005 CT-scanning, an independent object was recorded in the sand tray which is the right size and shape to be a detached mummified penis. But, how, we wondered, did it become detached in the first place?

All of this negative evidence pointed circumstatially to the strong possibility, we expressed, that the Tutankhamen mummy had been unofficially and clandestinely disinterred between 1926 and 1968, with the resulting theft of the bead collar and girdle, as well as the skullcap, the physical damage to the remains taking place at that time. We reported that a senior British Egyptologist (now deceased) had pointed out that the likely time-frame for this robbery to have occurred was during the Second World War (1939-1945), when security in the Valley of the Kings may have been understandably lax (since tourism was nil).

Such a disinterment, we wrote, would have been done

in all likelihood for the sole purpose of stealing the "jewelry" Carter had purposely left on the boy-king when he was re-interred in 1926. The culprits (assuming there was more than one) would have discovered, we posited, that the bead collar could not simply be lifted off the mummy, so a hack saw was produced to do the deed, cutting through the ribs. The king's ears were further damaged and his eyes punched in while removing the beaded skullcap (unless the thieves were a superstitious lot, and Tutankhamen was purposely "blinded" to the theft about to occur).

Why Zahi Hawass chose to not acknowledge our scenario explaining Tutankhamen's missing ribs, only he knows.

Notes

1. An extract from Howard Carter's diary for October 23, 1926 — published in F. Filce Leek, *The Human Remains from the Tomb of Tut'ankhamun* (Oxford, 1972), 9 — reads *"The first outermost coffin containing the King's Mummy, finally rewrapped, was lowered into the sarcophagus this morning."* An earlier entry for November 18, 1925, in the same diary (as published by Leek, p. 8) states, *"After photographic records are made of the King's remains, these will be reverently rewrapped and returned to the sarcophagus."* So seems to have been Carter's first intention; the expedient fact was something else, however. The dismembered state of Tutankhamen's corpse would have made a truly mummiform rewrapping all but impossible. Film footage of the 1968 disinterment shows the mummy to have been loosely covered with wide strips of white fabric, although these appear to be somewhat disheveled. No effort was made to replace these bandages when the mummy was subsequently reinterred; in fact, when examined again a decade later, the mummy's arms were found to be laying alongside the body rather than crossed at the waist, as when discovered.
2. C. Nicholas Reeves, *The Complete Tutankhamun* (London & New York, 1990), 118.
3. As reported by Reuters wire service, 1968.
4. Leek, plates VII-X, XII-XVIII.
5. Maurice Bucaille, *Mummies of the Pharaohs, Modern Medical Investigations* (New York, 1990), 43.
6. Leek, 5; Bucaille, 37. Bucaille dates this to October 31, 1925.
7. Bucaille, 37.
8. Carter, *The Tomb of Tut·ankh·Amen*, Vol. II (New York, 1927), 129.
9. Bucaille, 38-39.
10. In the caption to Figure 54 of *Mummies of the Pharaohs*, Dr. Bucaille identifies the king's disarticulated right hand (with the thumb detached) as Tutankhamen's left foot *"after removal of the sandals."* See plate XVI-XVII in Leek.
11. Thomas Hoving, *Tutankhamun, The Untold Story* (New York, 1978), 362. Filce Leek took another view of Carter's concern for the mortal husk of the young king. He wrote in *The Human Remains*, *"...from the diary as a whole, it is easy to follow Carter's devouring passion for all the many treasures and artifacts found in the tomb and within the sarcophagus. It is also possible to feel his lack of interest in the human remains, except as regards the king's facial resemblance to previous rulers, and his probable age at the time of his death,"* 9.
12. Bucaille, 43. 13. Ibid., 14. 14. Ibid.
15. Leek, 17; J.R. Harris, general editor of the Griffith monograph series, interjects as a footnote that *"the head alone was held vertically and upside down, by forcing it back into this position while keeping the body supine."*
16. Reeves, 118.
17. Leek, 11, 14.
18. *Journal of the American Medical Association*, Vol. 303, No. 7.
19. Bob Brier, *The Murder of Tutakhamen: A True Story* (New York, 1998).
20. D. Forbes, S. Ikram & J. Kamrin, "Tutankhamen's Missing Ribs," *Kmt* 18:1 (spring 2007), 50-56.
21. Leek, 12.

ADDENDUM THREE

Re-imagining Tutankhamen

Three Forensic Reconstructions
of How He May Have Looked in Life

As part of the Family of King Tutankhamen Project, three teams of physical anthropologists and forensic sculptors were commissioned by the Supreme Council for Antiquities (SCA) and *National Geographic* magazine to create full-scale bust reconstructions of Nebkheperure Tutankhamen's appearance in life, using the CT-scans that were made of his mummy to fabricate acrylic skulls from which to work. The teams were from Egypt, France and the United States. The Egyptians and French were aware of whose skull was being used for their reconstructions, while the Americans worked blindly, not informed of who they were attempting to depict, or even the individual's sex.

The French result is the most believable — in part because it is finished with realistic glass eyes, bristles of shaved head-hair and full skin-and-lip coloring, plus brows and eye cosmetics. The Egyptian bust is not colorized and seems like an unembellished mannequin, the smallish eyes blank and expressionless. Surprisingly the American "blind" result is quite similar to the French one, although also not colorized and detailed. The American "Tut" has a receding weak chin and overbite, as does the French version, although its nose is a bit shorter. The Egyptian effort suggests a robust individual with a thick, short neck.

Frankly none of the trio bears much — if any — resemblance to the many existing ancient depictions of Tutankhamen (whose representations, both three- and two-dimensional, are generally quite similar and easily enough recognized, in most cases), ranging from the two realistic granite near-life-sized statues from Karnak to the clearly idealized gold funerary mask which covered the king's head in death. Winifred Brunton's gouche-on-ivory modern portrait (above) is, of course, highly romanticized.

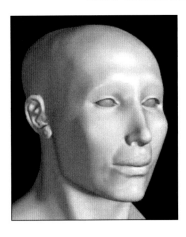

Left, The Egyptian forensic reconstruction of how Tutankhamen may have looked in life. Right, The French (l.) & American (r.) versions. Note the lack of pierced ear in the American "blind" reconstruction. Opposite, The fully rendered French bust, the most life-like.
All Photoshop adaptations of images published on the Internet

The Re-Search for Hatshepsut's Mummy
Or Royal Mummies Musical Chairs Yet Again

On June 27, 2007, at a press conference held in the Cairo Egyptian Museum, Egypt's then-Antiquities chief, Zahi Hawass, announced to the world that he had made the definitive — "100 percent certain" — identification of the "missing" mummy of the famous Eighteenth Dynasty female pharaoh Maatkare Hatshepsut. Although he had earlier dismissed the mummy then labeled KV60-A as too tall and obese to be the presumably petite ancient ruler (judging by surviving portrait statues and relief depictions from early in her twenty-year reign), he said that he had been proven wrong by "scientific" evidence.

This was a broken molar discovered in a small wood-and-ivory coffer inscribed with Hatshepsut's nomen and prenomen cartouches, which was found in the Royal Mummies Cache in 1881, containing a mummified liver or spleen (which was uncertain). This tooth, it turns out "perfectly matched" a gaping hole in the upper jaw of the mummy, observed in a CT-scan that had been made of the KV60-A individual in a new laboratory built in the Egyptian Museum basement and paid for by the Discovery Channel, which was producing a television documentary on Hatshepsut. A portion of a broken root remaining in the skull matched the break of a missing root on the molar — in the opinion of an Egyptian dentist called in for a professional assessment.

The molar itself remains imbedded in a quantity of hardened resin at the bottom of the coffer, so it could be studied (and measured) only via the CT-scan. Likewise, it was not possible to open KV60-A's mouth to directly observe the molar hole and root fragment. Nonetheless it was concluded that the "perfect match" of broken root in the mummy and the molar with missing root in the coffer labeled with Hatshepsut's cartouches was certain proof of KV60-A's identity as the female king — a 180-degree flip-flop by Hawass.

In the summer 2006 issue of the journal *Kmt* (17:2), the SCA chief had speculated that another female mummy discovered in KV60 by Howard Carter in 1902 (now identified as KV60-B) and taken to the Cairo Egyptian Museum in 1906 (probably by Edward Ayrton, who may have rediscovered the reburied tomb) *very well* may be *the mummy of Hatshepsut.*" In this article ("Quest for the Mummy of Hatshepsut: Could She Be the Lady in the Attic of the Egyptian Museum, Cairo?") it was posited that KV60-A (then still in the tomb) could not be Hatshepsut because *"This woman was elderly at death and had been very fat in life, with huge pendulous breasts; and the position of her arm* [crossed over her chest] *is not convincing evidence of royalty."*

KV60-B, on the other hand, is the mummy of a short elderly lady (less than five feet tall), *"well mummified and wrapped with fine linen, fingers bandaged individually.... She has long wavy white hair remaining on her head."* Because of the mummy's short stature, Hawass stated, *"... the coffin is... some seven feet... long, suggesting that it was not originally intended for this person."* The author continued, *"I think the face is quite royal and believe that anyone who sees it will have the same reaction."* He concluded, *"The mummy with the huge breasts still in KV60 is probably the wet-nurse, the original occupant of the coffin in Cairo."*

That was 2006. But one year later KV60-A was "100 percent" the mummy of Hatshepsut. The Discovery Channel was producing its Hatshepsut documentary and looking for "secrets" regarding the supposedly "missing" female pharaoh's ear-

Opposite, Detail of a life-sized seated portrait statue in limestone of 18th Dynasty female pharaoh Hatshepsut, found in a quarry near her mortuary temple at Deir el Bahari on the Luxor west bank. It is thought to date from early in her reign, when she was still having herself depicted as a petite female, wearing the kingly Nemes *headcovering. It is today in the collection of the Metropolitan Museum, New York.*

The small wood-&-ivory coffer found in TT230 containing a mummified liver or spleen & bearing the cartouches of Hatshepsut has been shown by CT-scan to also contain a human molar. Author's photo

thly remains to give a "hook" to their TV program. Thus Discovery offered to pay for the building of a CT-scan and DNA lab in the basement of the Cairo Museum, so that Egyptians themselves could conduct examinations of the possible candidates for Hatshepsut's mummy. This was an offer that could hardly be refused, even though Hawass had earlier repeatedly expressed strong reservations about subjecting Egypt's Royal Mummies to DNA testing.

It will be remembered that, under his direction, in January 2005, the mummy of Tutankhamen was CT-scanned, resulting in a determination that the boy-king had died from possible complications of a fractured femur rather than from an assassin's blow to the back of the head, as had been speculated on the basis of x-rays taken in the 1960s and '70s. Thus, the SCA chief was open to Discovery's desire that the likely "Hatshepsut" mummies be CT-scanned, with a little DNA testing thrown in for good measure — inasmuch as the latter would be conducted by Egyptians rather than by foreign investigators working in non-"mummy laboratories" outside of Egypt itself.

The only obvious candidates for this CT-scanning and DNA testing were, of course, the two female mummies found in KV60, one already in the Cairo Museum and the other still in the Valley of the Kings tomb, resting in a new simple wooden coffin provided by American archaeologist Dr. Donald P. Ryan, following his 1989 rediscovery of KV60. This individual had been seen in 2005, during the filming of another television documentary. So, the mummy — now being referred to as KV60-A (and the mummy in the Museum attic as KV60-B) — was transferred to Cairo, where it could be subjected to the CT-scanning and DNA testing.

It was decided to DNA test the uncontested mummy of Ahmes-Nefertari for comparison with KV60-A. But there is a problem as to whether she would have been a blood relative, inasmuch as there has long been a question regarding the origin of Hatshepsut's father, Thutmose I. The best-case scenario for a lineal connection between Ahmes-Nefertari and the female pharaoh would be if the latter's father was a collateral member of the House of Tao, not in line of succession, but selected to follow the childless Amenhotep I on the throne, because he was the nearest living male-relative with male children. There has been speculation that such a connection would exist if Thutmose was the offspring of Ahmose-Sipari, an elder son of Ahmose I who predeceased him. This would make Thutmose I a grandson of Ahmes-Nefertari, the latter then being Hatshepsut's great-grandmother.

There is, however, a slim possibility that Ahmes-Nefertari was her grandmother, if Hatshepsut's own mother, Queen Ahmes, was a sister of Amenhotep I, thus the daughter of Ahmes-Nefertari. The problem lies with the fact that Ahmes bore only a single title (besides King's Great Wife of Thutmose I): King's Sister; she, however, was not referred to (in surviving records) as King's Daughter, so some scholars have posited that the king referred to was actually her husband, Thutmose I.

Thus, a mitochondrial connection between Hatshepsut and Ahmes-Nefertari is iffy at best, the latter being the female pharaoh's great-grandmother, grandmother or no direct blood-relation at all.

CT-scans of KV60-A produced some very interesting results, regarding the elderly woman's poor health at the time of her death. Besides being morbidly obese, she suffered from several badly abcessed teeth, one of her upper secondary-molars was even missing — although it appeared that one root of same remained imbedded in the skull. More significantly, KV60-A (who was probably in her fifties at death) probably suffered from diabetes and a cancer in her pelvis, which had spread throughout her bones and would have caused her agonizing pain.

But Hawass recognized that something else mummified was possibly connected to Hatshepsut: the previously mentioned small wood-and-ivory coffer — inscribed with Hatshepsut's prenomen and nomen cartouches — found in the Royal Mummies Cache, TT320, containing

SCA photo of the two female mummies found in Valley of the Kings Tomb 60, one of whom is very likely the female pharaoh Hatshepsut. KV60-A is on the right, KV60-B on the left.

a preserved human viscus (exactly which is not certain). He decided to CT-scan the coffer and its contents and — truly a surprise! — discovered that embedded in a quantity of hardened resinous material at the bottom of the container was what appeared to be a human molar. And, just coincidentally, this tooth in the coffer — viewed only in the 3-D CT-scans — proved to have a broken-off root, which turned out to be a "millimeters-perfect match," according to the Egyptian dentist enlisted for a professional opinion, to the upper-molar root still imbedded in KV60-A.

Voila! Although in most courts of law, the apparent physical connection between a human molar with a broken root discovered in a box clearly engraved with the throne name of Hatshepsut seemingly being from a mummy found in her supposed wet-nurse's tomb (with an upper-molar root remaining in its mouth) would be considered circumstantial evidence at best — let alone that this seeming connection proved "100-percent" conclusively that said mummy KV60-A was, indeed, Hatshepsut. Nonetheless, Hawass was personally convinced that he had been

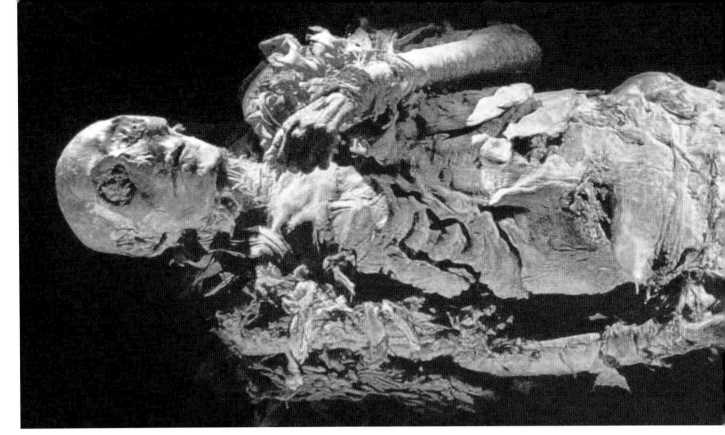

Above, Anonymous mummy KV60-A, found uncoffined on the floor of King's Valley Tomb 60, simple burial place of Sitre-In, attested nurse of Hatshepsut. SCA photo *Left, Plan of KV60.* Author's graphic *Below, Burial chamber of KV60 as refound in 1989, KV60-A* in situ. Donald P. Ryan photo

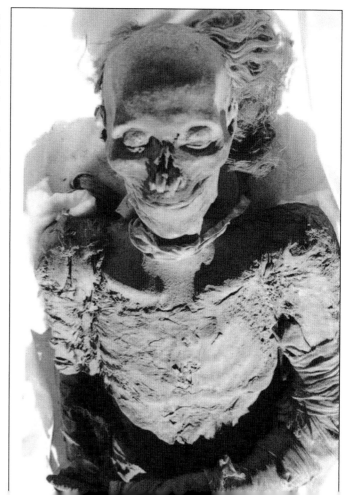

Left, Adzed coffin basin from KV60 with name of nurse In-Sitre still readable, which housed unwrapped anonymous mummy KV60-B, below, when relocated in the Cairo Egyptian Museum attic in 2005.

wrong in dismissing out of hand KV60-A as Nurse In-Sitre ("Fish, Daughter of Re"), chiefly based on his visual observation of her gross obesity and pendulous breasts. Although DNA testing of tissue samples from KV60-A and Ahmes-Nefertari were still underway, with "preliminary" results only "promising," it was decided that that the "scientific proof" of the tooth was enough to announce to the world that the mummy of Hatshepsut had been positively identified, *"the greatest discovery since the Tomb of Tutankhamun"*!

Thus, at the press conference held in the Cairo Museum on June 27, 2007, the SCA chief pronounced his 100-percent certainty that the obese elderly woman found in KV60 is Hatshepsut. And, of course, the media took this news of "certainty" at face value and had a field day for a brief week or so about the finding of the "lost" female pharaoh. And the Discovery Channel had its "hook" for the "Search for Egypt's Lost Queen" documentary, which was edited to include the unexpected tooth-and-mummy identification.

Egyptologists, never known for jumping on bandwagons, when asked for a reaction to this Discovery "discovery," opted to wait until all of the DNA "evidence" was in and could be analyzed by "independent researchers." One was quoted as saying, *"You have to be so careful in reaching conclusions from such data."* Meanwhile, the Little Old Lady in the Attic of the Cairo Museum (KV60-B) seems to have gone all-but-forgotten in the post-Discovery hoopla.

Because this particular student of Hatshepsut and her times was hoping that petite KV60-B would turn out to be the female pharaoh, I decided to play devil's advocate on her behalf, by raising several questions regarding the conclusion of "certain" identity based on what appears to be, at best in my view, only circumstantial evidence.

THE TOMB & MUMMIES

Both KV60-A and -B were found by Howard Carter in the spring of 1903 in a small, roughly hewn two-chamber uninscribed tomb in the Valley of the Kings, positioned close by KV20, the long-known Tomb of Hatshepsut (although it has been argued — not very convincingly, in this researcher's view — that it was actually the *"no one seeing, no one hearing"* Tomb of Thutmose I, appropriated by the female pharaoh for her own burial alongside her father). Carter was of the opinion that the two unwrapped elderly female mummies (one, A, lying directly on the floor in the largest of the two chambers; the other, B, resting in a thoroughly adzed coffin basin in the same space) were possibly a pair of nurses somehow connected to Thutmose IV, whose tomb was just up the VOK slope. In any case, the thoroughly robbed two-chamber tomb (later dubbed KV60 in the Valley numbering sequence) was reburied by Carter — who just then had bigger fish to fry in KV43 (Thutmose IV).

It seems that only three years later KV60 was "found" again, this time by Edward Ayrton, working for American tomb-hunter Theodore M. Davis. Thoroughly robbed tombs and denuded anonymous mummies weren't of any interest to the latter, so KV60 was buried again and "lost." In 1906 the coffin basin from the tomb and its little-old-lady mummy occupant were taken to Cairo (presumably by Ayrton, but exactly whom is apparently unrecorded) and put in storage in the Egyptian Museum third-floor attic. It likely was at this time that an "In" ("Fish") was noted on the coffin-basin and equated with Hatshepsut's nurse, In-Sitre, a personage known chiefly from a fragmentary statue of her found at Hatshepsut's Deir el Bahari mortuary temple. Thus KV60 came to be identified as the Tomb of In-Sitre, who likely would have been interred with close proximity to her mistress.

At the suggestion of the late independent-researcher Elizabeth Thomas, who spent many years studying "hands on" the royal necropoleis of western Luxor, Donald Ryan relocated KV60 in the long entry approach to KV19 (cut in the late Twentieth Dynasty for Prince Montuhirkhopshef, a son of Rameses IX). The elderly female mummy still resting on the tomb's floor proved to have been very obese in life, with large pendulous breasts. Thomas had suggested to Ryan that this individual might be none other than Hatshepsut herself (allowing, it would seem, that the mummy in Cairo was Nurse In-Sitre, inasmuch as she had been found in a coffin basin with the "In" part of that name remaining on it). Ryan posited this possibility in his article on the KV60 rediscovery in the "Hatshepsut Special" premiere issue of the quarterly journal *Kmt* (1:1, spring 1990).

Unable to interest the EAO (Egyptian Antiquities Organization, predecessor of the SCA) in sending a representative from Cairo to take a look at the KV60 mummy, Ryan had a simple plank-wood coffin made for her; and she was left resting in the tomb, along with boxed funerary debris gathered up during Ryan's clearance (including a very fragmentary wooden face-piece from a coffin, with a notch under the chin, suggesting the earlier presence of a false beard). And once again the stairway entry to KV60 was filled in and the tomb left undisturbed until it was opened one more time for the purpose of a TV documentary on Thutmose III, when the recoffined "obese" mummy was officially seen for the first time (by Hawass).

So that, briefly, is the modern history of KV60. But its identification as the Tomb of In-Sitre is purely circumstantial, based on the coffin basin's fragmentary "In" name and the tomb's close proximity to the Tomb of Hatshepsut. It can not be said with absolute certainty, therefore, that the two mummies are either In-Sitre herself or Hatshepsut. It is not beyond the realm of possibility that they were wholly intrusive, placed there during the official dismantlement of the Royal Valley in the Twenty-first Dynasty, thus making KV60 a mummy mini-cache.

THE COFFER, VISCUS & TOOTH

As already noted, among the non-mummy materials found in TT320, the Royal Mummies Cache, in 1881 was a small-but-tallish wooden coffer with trim and a knob of ivory. Inside the little box — but protruding from it, lifting the lid — was a preserved mass of something organic which was thought at the time by Gaston Maspero to be a mummified liver or spleen. Interestingly, the coffer front end, under the ivory knob, bore the prenomen and nomen cartouches of Maatkare Hatshepsut (with the Amen-epithet portion of the nomen seemingly erased). Because the mummy of God's Wife of Amen Maatkare — a daughter of Priest-King Pinudjem I — was among the TT320 occupants, Maspero suggested that a coffer apparently belonging to the Eighteenth Dynasty female pharaoh had been appropriated for use as a canopic container for the Twenty-first Dynasty God's Wife, owing to their shared Maatkare name. This seems not only very odd but, well, highly unlikely.

Later commentary posited that the mummified viscus belonged, in fact, to Hatshepsut herself, the only part of the female pharaoh to have been "rescued" by the necropolis priests in the Twenty-first Dynasty, when they dismantled KV20. If noticed, it went uncommented on that the bottom interior of the "Hatshepsut" coffer contained a quanity of hardened resin. Whether the viscus was embedded in this or sits atop it is not clear from what had been published. Drip stains on the front, sides and back of the coffer suggest that the resin might have been introduced as some sort of anointing ritual (albeit executed rather sloppily, probably hastily).

In any case — without questioning the Hatshepsut identification with the coffer viscus — it was decided by Hawass to have the box CT-scanned (which implies that the viscus *is* embedded in the resin, so it can not be simply lifted out for physical examination). This resulted in the revelation of what would seem to be a broken molar submerged in the resin and so never noticed previously. And the rest, as said, is "100-percent" certainty.

But, it has to be asked, what are the viscus (liver? intestines?) and broken tooth doing in the small wood-and-ivory coffer with Hatshepsut's prenomen, an object which seems more like a simple jewelry box than a makeshift canopic vessel? On his personal Internet website, Hawass wrote, *"We know from other 'embalming caches' that anything associated with a body or its mummification became ritually charged, and had to be buried properly. Therefore, it seemed that, during the mummification of Hatshepsut, the embalmers put into the box anything that came loose from the body during the mummification process."*

Whoa! In the first place, anyone who has ever had a molar extracted by a dentist knows very well that these large teeth with long roots don't just "come loose." Therefore it is highly unlikely that the molar simply fell out of KV60-A's mouth post-mortem. Because the CT-scan shows that the elderly woman suffered from several abcessed teeth, it is more probable that the molar was pulled while KV60-A was still living (one root broken off and remaining in the skull during the process), and that it was retained for whatever reason, probably in the coffer where it is now.

Secondly, a mummified viscus is not exactly a by-product of the mummification process, rather a purposeful result of same, requiring its special "canopic" container. When he cleared KV20 in 1903-1904, Carter found that Hatshepsut's canopic vessels were missing from her (lidless) quartzite canopic chest still in the tomb. There is no record of these having ever been found. Thus, it is reasonable to suggest that the viscus in the coffer may have been separated from its original container and ended up conveniently stashed in the not-quite-large-enough TT320 coffer.

But does this necessarily mean the viscus belongs to the female pharaoh? It would seem that there are no present plans to DNA test the organ to determine that it, in fact, came from KV60-A. Thus, its association with Hatshepsut (or at least KV60-A) is, at best, only circumstantial — as is the presence of the partial tooth in the coffer with her name on it.

A SCENARIO

I have difficulty getting my mind wrapped around the possibility that the delicate, even pretty, Maatkare Hatshepsut of the Metropolitan Museum portrait statues — as well as the many relief images on the Red Chapel and the depictions on her fallen obelisk at Karnak — was, in fact, a raw-boned, big-breasted woman with a heavy jaw and very fat at the end of her life. Thus, I'm just not persuaded that KV60-A *is* Hatshepsut and under-five-foot-tall, petite, flat-chested KV-60-B *is* Nurse In-Sitre, after all. For the purpose of the following scenario, I am arguing the opposite identifications.

Riddled with painful cancer and possessing a mouthful of badly abcessed teeth, elderly Nurse In-Sitre submitted to having one of her offending molars pulled near the end of her life. The shock of this necessarily violent (especially in the days before anesthesia) procedure, and the consequent loss of blood, may very well have contributed to her demise. For whatever reason, the extracted molar (one root of which had broken off and remained in In-Sitre's mouth) was retained and ended up placed in a jewelry coffer belonging to her mistress, Hatshepsut (perhaps kept by the female ruler as a peculiar physical memento of her late, life-long friend — *à la* the lock of hair in KV62?).

So, Nurse In-Sitre died following her dental work, probably sooner rather than later, perhaps from resulting massive loss of blood, was mummified (the embalmers had to tuck her excess skin under her, she had been so fat in life) and was put to rest in a gilded-all-over coffin in the small tomb that Hatshepsut had cut for her nearby the Female Horus's own kingly sepulcher.

Not so many years later, Hatshepsut, too, was dead and put to her rest in the yet-unfinished chamber she had earlier had the mummy of her beloved father, Akheperkare Djehutymes

(Thutmose I), transferred to from his own tomb (KV38) — even giving up her original quartzite sarcophagus for his reinterment, having a new one made for herself. Very likely a great quanity of funerary furnishings and personal belongings went into the tomb with Osiris Hatshepsut — including a small wood-and-ivory jewelry coffer.

A long while later, towards the end of his sole reign, Hatshepsut's former coregent, Menkheperre Djehutymes (Thutmose III), made the decision to set things right with Maat and erase all evidence of his aunt/stepmother's co-kingship — revise history, as it were. As part of this symbolic/political program, he had the mummy of his grandfather, Akheperkare Djehutymes, returned to that ruler's original tomb.

Furthermore, he ordered Hatshepsut herself taken out of her kingly burial place — inasmuch as she was no longer a king — and reinterred in the nearby tomb of Nurse In-Sitre (KV60), the location of which was still remembered. Due to the weight involved and the long upward haul out, only Hatshepsut's inner coffin (like her father she would have had at least two) and canopic jars would likely have been moved, the remainder of the grave furnishings and personal possessions left behind. It is not inconceivable that one (or more) of her viscera packages accidentally became separated from its (their) jar(s) in the rush to depart the foul air of bowels-deep KV20, fallen to the floor, unnoticed in the dark, and abandoned.

Once in KV60 it was decided to place the coffined Hatshepsut and her canopics in the small side room off the corridor of the tomb. One last act by the king's agents before departing — perhaps having specific instructions to do so — was the pulling off of the kingly false beard and uraeus that adorned the face piece of Hatshepsut's innermost coffin (perhaps a false beard and cobra would also have been removed from the outer coffin left in KV20). KV60's entry stairwell was reburied and the tomb forgotten.

That is until some 350 years later, when it was accidentally discovered by the royal-necropolis workmen cutting the approach to the Tomb of Montuhirkhopshef (KV19). They entered the previously unviolated sepulcher and, at their leisure, proceeded to thoroughly loot it over time. The coffins were emptied of their occupants and meticulously adzed to remove all gilding and any inlays. Hatshepsut's coffin and the lid of In-Sitre's were essentially destroyed in the process. The two mummies were likewise stripped of their bandaging, so that jewelry placed on the deceased could be removed. Whatever funerary furnishings that had been interred with the old nurse were carried away, or judged of no value and smashed to smithereens. Hatshepsut's canopic jars were carried off for recycling (their contents dumped beyond the tomb and lost forever).

For a period the workmen used KV60 as a storeroom (as evidenced by the broken Twentieth Dynasty pottery found within by the modern excavators). Then, when work on Montuhirkopshef's (unfinished) tomb abruptly came to an end, KV60 was reburied once more, not to be found again until nearly 3,000 years later.

A final act of one of the departing workmen (a scribe?) was the placing of Hatshepsut's denuded small mummy in the empty coffin basin that had contained Nurse In — perhaps out of pious reverence, the female pharaoh's identity having been recognized earlier from the cartouches on her now-destroyed coffins. In-Sitre, however, was left ignobly on the floor.

Several generations later, during the official dismantling of the royal necropoleis burials and the rescuing of the remains of the New Kingdom rulers, their family members and close retainers, the priests conducting those operations located and entered the Tomb of Hatshepsut (KV20), presumably looking for her mummy and any recyclables. They found a great deal of the latter, left behind 400 years earlier by Thutmose III's agents; but both quartzite sarcophagi in the tomb were empty, as was a matching canopic chest inscribed for Maatkare Hatshepsut. Clearly the burial had been selectively "robbed" in the past. One of the priests noticed an innocuous small bundle on the antechamber floor and recognized it for a mummified viscus. He and his fellow dismantlers concluded that this preserved organ was all that remained of Maatkare Hatshepsut. A small, plain wooden jewelry coffer at hand proved a convenient (if really too small) container; and the viscus was conveyed, ultimately, to the Royal Mummies cache — after the female pharaoh's "lost" organ was anointed with a quantity of resin, no one having noticed the broken tooth in the bottom of the coffer.

Fiction? Certainly. But farfetched? Not if at some future time DNA testing shows that the TT320 viscus belongs, in fact, to KV60-B!

It should be noted that in his 2015 publication *CT Scanning the Pharaohs*, Zahi Hawass has persisted in his stubborn view that he, indeed, "found" the mummy of Hatshepsut in 2005. He reported therein that dental experts had assured him upper molars sometimes have fused roots, so appear as only two instead of three, which he attributed to the situation with the tooth in the box. Apparently a decade later and the "promising" DNA results of comparisons between KV60-A and Ahmes-Nefertari have not been resolved with any positive proof that the former is in any definite way related to the latter — or if so, it has not been made public.

And KV60-B has not, apparently, been further DNA-compared with the male Thutmosoid relatives of Hatshepsut (Thutmoses II and III), so, effectively remains in limbo, Hawass's In-Sitre.

This writer was greatly disappointed to discover during his most-recent (and very probably last) visit to the Cairo Egyptian Museum, that the ladies from KV60 were being displayed in one of the two Royal Mummies Rooms, but quite literally only a few inches off the floor, so that visitors looked down on them. Hardly I thought a display worthy of the dignity of one of the first great women of history, allowing that either KV60-A or -B is the Female Horus Maatkare Hatshepsut!

KV60-B, Eliminated by a Broken Tooth?

The female mummy found resting in a coffin basin in KV60 in 1902 and four years later removed to the third floor of the Egyptian Museum in Cairo for storage (and subsequently all but forgotten), came to the attention of Dr. Zahi Hawass's Egyptian Mummy Project after this writer, in early 2006, was asked by one of his assistants if I had any suggestions as to which "missing" known mummies should be relocated and examined for the EMP. My suggestions were missing Pinudjem I from TT320, the part-Nubian Maiherpri — found in his tomb, KV36, in 1898, and subsequently examined and photographed for inclusion in a Catalogue Général volume, and presumably still in his coffin in the Museum's display of objects from the tomb — and also the individual from KV60, thought to possibly be the royal nurse In-Sitre, purportedly to be found in her coffin basin in the Museum's "attic." Maiherpri was subsequently examined in 2010 for another study; but, not long after my suggestions, Hawass announced that *he* had "discovered" the attic mummy and was persuaded it was none other than Hatshepsut herself! He wrote an article to that effect ("Quest for the Mummy of Hatshepsut," *Kmt* 17:2, summer 2006).

The mummy indeed seemed to fit the qualifications for such an identification. She was an elderly woman, short, petite, with atrophied small breasts, and a face and cranium which appeared, visually, Thutmosid in type (despite the missing nose), with prominent cheekbones and the overall heart-shape seen in early sculptures of the female pharaoh. KV60-B (as she came to be labeled, to differentiate her from the other female mummy discovered in KV60) had been well mummified in the manner of the early 18th Dynasty, with one arm pendant by her side, the other resting across her midsection, the fingers of that hand clenched. The remaining linen is of the high quality which would be expected for a royal mummification.

Hawass had KV60-B CT-scanned, but seemed to have quickly lost interest in her Hatshepsut candidacy when a broken molar was seen in a CT-scan of the "Hatshepsut" coffer from TT320; and the CT-scanned tallish, obese, robust KV60-A mummy was found to have a missing molar, and thus was proclaimed by Hawass to be "scientifically proven" as Hatshepsut — despite her having no apparent physical resemblance to the historical individual and having the pendulous breasts one might expect of an elderly wet-nurse. Mitochondrial DNA comparisons between Queen Ahmes-Nefertari (Hatshepsut's great grandmother?) and KV60-A were apparently never published; whether KV60-B was likewise directly compared to Ahmes-Nefertari is unknown.

An interesting anomoly of the KV60-B mummy is what would appear to be eruptions on the skin in the immediate vicinity of the left shoulder (opposite & detail left). Similar maculae are to be seen on the torsos of Thutmoses II & III & Amenhotep II, & speculated to be possibly a congenital skin disorder (if not the result of the same mummification process over three generations). If this condition was noted during the EMP examination of KV60-B, it was never formally commented on, to my knowledge. **DCF**

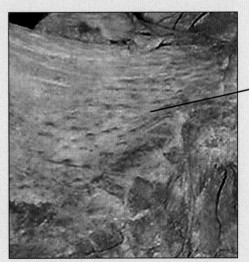

Photo: Salima Ikram

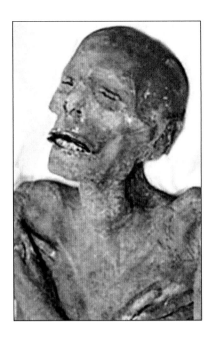

Opposite, A relief depiction of Rameses I from his small chapel at Abydos, now in the collection of the Metropolitan Museum of Art, New York City. Author's photo *Above, Lid of the 21st Dynasty replacement coffin of Rameses I found in empty in TT320, its basin broken into pieces.* Cerceuils *Top, The Niagara Falls mummy tentatively identified today as that of Rameses I & displayed in the Luxor Museum.* Internet photo

Overleaf, The mummy displayed in the Luxor Museum and labeled as "Rameses I ?" George B. Johnson photo

ADDENDUM FIVE

The Mummy of Rameses I Found?
Or Not

There has been uncertainty about the mortal remains of Rameses I, from the discovery of TT320 in 1881 down to the present day. Was the founder of the Nineteenth Dynasty rescued from his Valley of the Kings tomb (KV16) by necropolis priests in the Twenty-first Dynasty, placed temporarily in the tomb of his son and successor, Seti I, (KV17) and finally re-interred in the Royal Mummies Cache, to perhaps be removed from there prior to its official rediscovery and recovery of the occupants and their surviving miscellaneous funerary equipage?

Among the objects cleared from TT320 in 1881 was a Twenty-first Dynasty polychrome-wood coffin lid and broken fragments of its basin which had belonged originally to a woman whose name had been erased in antiquity and replaced by the prenomen of Rameses I (Menpehtire). Apparently close by these coffin parts lay a naked male cadaver, described by Gaston Maspero in his *Momies Royales* as *"...a very well-built man with short hair and robust limbs; his entire skin black, the features somewhat damaged, but otherwise well preserved."* However, in the same volume, the director of the Antiquities Service describes those remains as: *"No. 6. A mummy, or rather cadaver, stripped of its bandages and rolled in a mat — the one I believe to be Rameses I."*

Thus it would, from that evidence, appear that Menpehtire Rameses (rescued and re-coffined) had, indeed, been placed in the Royal Cache, but then was secondarily replundered, after having been turned out of his subsequently destroyed replacement coffin. If the Royal Cache had not been entered before the Abd Rassuls, then they must have been the parties guilty of the further desecration of Rameses I and his secondary coffin (perhaps the king's mummy, when rescued from KV16 had not been rebandaged but merely wrapped in a reed mat). The question remains: what became of this denuded male mummy, which apparently was not assigned a Cairo Museum catalogue number and was not described by Elliot Smith in his Catalogue Général volume, *The Royal Mummies*. In fact, Smith, when dealing with mummy No. 61056 (unwrapped by Maspero in 1886), thought that it was the one which had been identified by Maspero as Rameses I; but which turned out, however, to be an anonymous female (Unknown Woman B), now generally thought to possibly be King's Great Wife Tetisheri of the late Seventeenth Dynasty (see p. 19). So does Maspero's *"very well-built man"* languish anonymously on a shelf in the Cairo Egyptian Museum, like Pinudjem I perhaps unrecognized by the Egyptian Mummy Project?

Or is the "real" Rameses I mummy on display in a special small gallery of the Luxor

Museum, alongside the remains of Ahmose I, "The Liberator" and putative founder of the Eighteenth Dynasty? This individual, cautiously labeled as "Rameses I ?," was repatriated to Egypt in 2003, by the Michael C. Carlos Museum at Emory University in Atlanta, Georgia — with considerable media fanfare and a television documentary (Nova, "The Royal Mummy Who Would be King"). The Carlos had purchased the mummy in 1999 from Toronto businessman Bill Jamieson, who had acquired it when the Niagara Falls Museum de-acquisitioned its mummy collection. The curator of Ancient Art at the Atlanta museum, Peter Lacovara, had raised the $2 million asking price for the Niagara mummies, having been persuaded that the principal one of them

them (NFM.M5) was the otherwise-missing first Rameses. Several New Kingdom rulers were still unaccounted for (Thutmose I, Akhenaten, Aye, Horemheb, Rameses I, Setnahkt, and Rameses VII, VIII, X and XI) and Niagara NFM.M5 did indeed look royal, especially with its arms crossed over the chest and the toes widely separated, as if once adorned with gold toe-sheaths. Mummification of the well-preserved cadaver was consistent with that seen in the later Eighteenth and the Nineteenth dynasties. And the physique, large skull and strong jaw of the individual were quite similar to those of the known Ramesside kings. In fact, earlier, an identification of the mummy with Rameses I had been suggested by Egyptologist Gayle Gibson of the Royal Ontario Mu-

seum and Egyptologist Aidan Dodson of Bristol University — who felt NFM.M5 also bore a strong resemblence in profile to Rameses V and could possibly be the missing Rameses VII.

Lacovara commissioned a series of tests of the Carlos's new acquisition, including x-rays and CT-scans, which provided further likelihood of a royal mummy of later New Kingdom date. Satisfied with a Rameses I identification, the Carlos curator decided that the king should be resting in Cairo rather than Atlanta, and so made arrangements with the Egyptian Supreme Council for Antiquities (SCA) for return of the wayward royal remains.

But how did "Rameses I?" end up in Niagara Falls, Canada, in the first place? The museum there opened in 1827, as a tourist attraction of natural-history and enthographic curiosities (such as a five-legged pig and two-headed calf). In 1861 the Niagara Falls Museum acquired five Egyptian mummies and their coffins from a Canadian doctor, James S. Douglas, who had purchased them while wintering on the Nile in 1859-1860. Four further mummies and coffins were added to the Niagara collection in 1878, when a Colonel H. Wood closed his own curiosities museum in Philadelphia. Those four mummies had a checkered history in the United States, and even may have been owned once by Joseph Smith, Jr., founder of Mormonism. It is unclear from Museum records, however, exactly which of the Niagara Falls mummies were acquired by Douglas and which had been owned by Wood.

A fragment of the wooden coffin basin found in TT320 which had apparently originally contained the mummy of Rameses I recovered from the tomb of his son, Seti I, KV17, by 21st Dynasty necropolis priests. The lid of this replacement coffin was intact but the basin had been smashed to pieces, likely by the Abd Rassul brothers. Momies Royales, 1889

English independent researcher and student of the Royal Mummies Dylan Bickerstaffe has pointed out that the dates of acquisition in Egypt of both the Douglas and Wood mummies (1859-1860 and 1817-1820, respectively) do not accord with the possibility of Niagara Man ("Rameses I?") having come from the Royal Mummies Cache (TT320), inasmuch as that was not discovered until 1871, as claimed by the Brothers Abd Rassul, who had found it quite by accident then. There is the possibility that the brothers were dissimilating about the actual time of their discovery, allowing for them to have removed a mummy from the cache as early as 1859, which they then sold in Luxor to Dr. Douglas through an intermediary agent, British Consul Mustapha Aga Aya.

The problem, however, with such an early discovery of TT320 is that objects (papyri, ushabtis, etc.) purloined from the cache-tomb by the Luxor West Bank *fellahin* family did not begin appearing on the illicit-antiquities market in Egypt until the mid-1870s — which had alerted Antiquities Service authorities in Cairo that a previously unknown Twenty-first Dynasty "royal" burial had been found in the Luxor area, prompting an investigation of the Rassuls, the confession of the eldest brother, Mohamed, and the ultimate "official" discovery of the Royal Cache by the Service in 1881. It is highly improbable that the looters would have removed a single mummy from TT320 in 1850-1860, sold it via Ayat and then bided their time for some fifteen years to further profit from their good fortune of having made such a potentially rich find.

Thus, it seems highly unlikely that NFM.M5 (a.k.a "Rameses I?") originated in the Royal Mummies Cache so never

occupied the empty and broken "Rameses I" coffin found there. Disallowing an identification of NFM.M5 with the first Rameses, Bickerstaffe then examined other possiblities. Because of the late-Eighteenth/Nineteenth Dynasty mummification technique, the unaccounted for Aye and Horemheb were considered as candidates. However those kings quickly were ruled out because a Carbon-14 testing of the mummy in question (conducted by the Carlos Museum) had produced dates with a range from the very end of the Twentieth Dynasty to the end of the Twenty-second Dynasty, most likely some midpoint thereof, e.g., 900-840 BC. This also eliminated the possibility that the Niagara mummy was of Ptolemaic date, when the Osirian crossed-arms pose is seen in non-royal remains. No royal mummies from the Twenty-second Dynasty are known (other than some skeletal remains from the royal tombs at Tanis); the governance of Egypt was in the Delta at that time, in any case, so it is highly unlikely that a Takelot, Sheshonk or Osorkon would have been interred at Waset (Thebes/Luxor).

NFM.M5 was originally displayed in the Niagara Falls Museum with a label reading "Septhnestp, Wife of Amenhotep IV." Bickerstaffe felt this was just too unlikely to have been made up in the Nineteenth Century and concluded that the original hieroglyphs had been SePTHeNeSTP; so he tried juggling the prenomens and nomens of the later Twentieth Dynasty rulers to see if he could come up with something similar. He settled on Menmaatre SETEPENPTAH Khamewase Mereramen Rameses Netjerhequainu — in other words, Rameses XI!

But the whole question of whether the Michael C. Carlos Museum's gift to Egypt was, as thought at the time, likely the missing mummy of Rameses I could have been resolved rather quickly had the 2005-2011 Egyptian Mummy Project (see Addendum Six, following) compared the DNA of so-called "Rameses I" with that of the king's known son, Seti I, and grandson, Rameses II. It has to be wondered why this was not done (or if it was, why the results were not published in the formal report of the EMP, *Scanning the Pharaohs: CT Imaging of the New Kingdom Royal Mummies*, which does treat extensively Seti I, Rameses II and Merneptah in Chapter 9). Perhaps it was simply a matter of logistics, with "Rameses I?" having been on display in the Luxor Museum since 2004 and the EMP focused on mummies in the Egyptian Museum (except Tutankhamen, of course).

Bibliography

Dylan Bickerstaffe, "Examining the Mystery of the Niagara Falls Mummy," *Kmt* 17:4, winter 2006-2007, 26-34

— *An Ancient Egyptian Case Book*, Chapter 5, "Can the Niagara Falls Mummy Really be Ramesses I?" (Canopus Press, 2014), 103-124

Dennis C. Forbes, *Tombs.Treasures.Mummies.*, Book One, *The Royal Mummies Caches (TT320 & KV35)*(Weaverville, NC 2015)

Gayle Gibson, "Names Matter: The Unfinished History of the Niagara Falls Mummies," *Kmt* 11:4 winter 2000-2001, 18-29

Gaston Maspero, *Les Momies Royales de Deir el-Bahari* (Cairo, 1889)

ADDENDUM SIX

EMP:
The Egyptian Mummy Project

Cairo's Egyptian Museum is arguably the largest repository of preserved human remains in the world. Housed there are not only the dozens of historically important persons recovered from the two Royal Mummies Caches (TT320 and KV35), but those of scores of named commoners and even anonymous individuals as well, ranging the spectrum of ancient Egypt's over 3,000-year history. Perhaps surprisingly, except for the Catalogue Général volume *The Royal Mummies* (1912), there was really no inventory of the Museum's uncounted mummy holdings. Some were stored in the attic of the 1902 Tahrir Square building, many others in the basement; and still others rested in coffins displayed in the institution's numerous galleries, but which had not been opened in dozens of years, a large number of those coffins having been placed on display in the early years of the Twentieth Century.

Of course the Royal Mummies had been of special interest since a dozen or so of them were made available for public viewing (at an additional fee from Museum admission) in a second-floor space called simply Room 52. Prior to that they had been housed in a Cairo mausoleum originally built for Egyptian nationalist leader Saad Zaghlul. But in 1981 Egyptian President Anwar Sadat closed the Museum's Room 52 to the public, on the grounds that it was disrespectful of the deceased ancient kings for them to be stared at by modern commoners. However, in early 1994, a select dozen of the better-preserved royal occupants of TT320 and KV35 were once again on view, in the Royal Mummies Hall, a specially designed contemporary gallery space; and they rested within new, environmentally controlled display cases. In 2007 a second Royal Mummies Hall (adjoining the first) opened at the Museum, with an additional nine individuals from the Royal Caches on view in an identical environment and display cases.

Above, View of the first Royal Mummies Gallery of the Cairo Egyptian Museum, with the 19th Dynasty mummy of Rameses II (foreground) as the centerpiece.

Cairo Egyptian Museum

General view of the first or original Royal Mummies Gallery at the Cairo Egyptian Museum, where select mummies from the Royal Cache, TT320, are on view. These include Seqenenre Tao II, Amenhotep I, Meryetamen, so-called Thutmose I, Thutmose II, Thutmose III, Amenhotep II, Thutmose IV, Seti I, Rameses II & Seti II. Displayed in the second Royal Mummies Hall are: Rameses III, Rameses IV, Rameses V, Rameses IX, Nodjmet, Pinudjem II, Istemkheb, Henttawy & Maatkare.

Cairo Egyptian Museum

This renewed interest in the Royal Mummies resulted in the formation of the Egyptian Mummy Project (EMP) in 2004, the brainchild of then-director of the Supreme Council for Antiquities Zahi Hawass. The discovery at the end of the Twentieth Century at Bahariya Oasis of a cemetery of an estimated 10,000 Graeco-Roman mummies (234 of which had been excavated by 1999) inspired him to establish a SCA program for studying Egyptian mummies generally, using the latest non-intrusive technology — including CT-scanning in addition to x-raying, plus DNA analyses — to investigate Egyptian mummies generally, in order to gain new insights into how the ancient Nile Dwellers lived and died, including building a data base of statistics regarding their physical ailments and dental health.

Hawass's ambitious plan was to inventory, document, examine externally and non-intrusively interally every mummy extant throughout Egypt — in museums, storage magazines and *in situ* — spanning a timeframe from the Pre-Dynastic Period to the end of the Roman era. Skeletal remains showing no evidence of mummification were not included in the Project. The CT-scans would serve as virtual images of the mummies, providing information on their conditions valuable to their conservation, restoration and ultimate protection.

The obvious place to start the Project was the Cairo Egyptian Museum's vast warehouse of mummified humans (animals were not a part of the study, although a future expansion of the Project to include them, as well, was planned). It was quickly discovered that, aside from the Royal Mummies, a great number of the Museum's mummy population had never been formally registered and many even were without identification tags. The exact location of certain other important mummies in the Museum was not recorded or even known.

This writer was contacted by one of the EMP team inquiring if there were any particular mummies I personally thought should be looked for. I suggested the never-published (in *The Royal Mummies*, 1912) remains of Pinudjem I from TT320, which seemingly had gone missing; an also-unpublished male mummy found uncoffined in the same Royal Cache; the female mummy from KV60 — possibly Hatshepsut's — which reputedly was in the Museum attic (last viewed by a researcher in the 1970s); and the mummy of mid-Eighteenth Dynasty royal fanbearer Maiherpri, which had not been seen since initally examined, photographed and described in print by Georges Daressy in 1901.

To solve the problem of lack of identification of many of the Museum's mummy population, an EMP "subproject" created radio-frequency indentifcation tags (microchips), which were placed within mummy wrappings, under the supervision of Museum conservationists. Using a detecting device, these small-disk IDs could be linked immediately to the Project's data base.

When the Cairo Museum staff working with the EMP had located all of the human remains housed at the Tahrir facility (every coffin opened and over 300 mummies found, including royalty, nobility and commoners), the next step in the Project was to subject these individually to CT-scanning (computerized axial-tomography). This was done using a high-resolution Siemens Somatom Emotion 6 scanner, which had been donated *gratis* to the Supreme Council for Antiquities by the German high-tech company Siemens and the American National Geographic Society — the NGS helping to fund the Project, with Siemens covering costs of maintenance of the scanning machine. This unit was mounted inside a self-contained, air-conditioned trailer, which permitted its transporation to any part of the country the EMP required. It arrived at the Cairo Museum in November 2004. The mummies were taken to the scanner-trailer parked next to the Museum one at a time, where each full-body scan took less than two minutes.

It was at this point that the EMP went off the rails, so to speak — or at least shifted its focus. Zahi Hawass first became fascinated with identifying the mummy of Queen/King Hatshepsut (between the two female mummies found

Another view of the Cairo Egyptian Museum original Royal Mummies Hall, opened to the public in 1994. The environmentally controlled case in the foreground houses the mummy of Thutmose II. Cairo Egyptian Museum

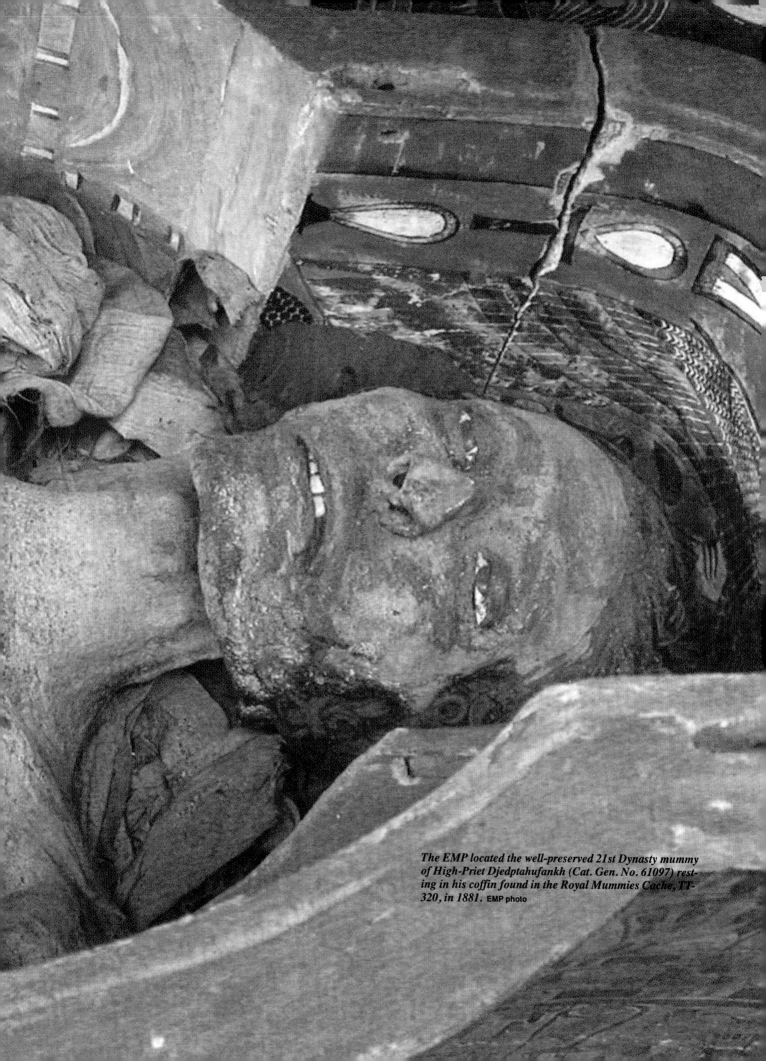

The EMP located the well-preserved 21st Dynasty mummy of High-Priest Djedptahufankh (Cat. Gen. No. 61097) resting in his coffin found in the Royal Mummies Cache, TT-320, in 1881. EMP photo

It was at this writer's suggestion to the EMP that the second female mummy from KV60 was relocated in the attic of the Cairo Egyptian Museum, where it has last been seen by an American researcher in the late 1970s. It was resting in a coffin made for the early-18th Dynasty royal nurse In-Sitre (left), in whose Valley of the Kings tomb it had been found by Howard Carter in 1902. It was shipped to Cairo ca. 1906 (probably by excavator Edward Ayrton), placed in storage at the Museum & subsequently forgotten. It became a focus of the SCA search for the mummy of Queen/King Hatshepsut early in the first decade of the 21st Century. Salima Ikram photo

the Valley of the Kings Tomb 60, which was identified with In-Sitre, the attested nurse of Hatshepsut (see Appendum Four this volume, for a full discussion of that venture, with its disputed conclusion). When he had satisfied himself with that distraction, Hawass almost immediately formulated a spin-off of the EMP, which he titled the Family of King Tutankamun Project (FKTP), detailed in following Addendum Seven.

The FKTP's scans and DNA analyses took two years' time (2007-2009), with the results finally published in 2010, in the *Journal of the American Medical Association* (*JAMA*), to mixed reactions. In 2015 the Hawass co-authored official full report of the results of the CT and DNA studies of select ones of the Royal Mummies — *Scanning the Pharaohs: CT Imaging of the New Kingdom Royal Mummies* — was formally published, with resultant scientific criticisms of the Project's metologies and conclusions regarding its findings.

Of course, the Egyptian revolution of early 2011 and its subsequent political upheavals affecting the overall Antiquities situation in the country brought what is likely an end to the Egyptian Mummy Project, its ambitious mission far from accomplished. That same year Hawass was dismissed from his post as Minister for Antiquities in the newly created Ministry of State for Antiquities and Heritage, and at this writing no one has stepped forth to carry on the EMP.

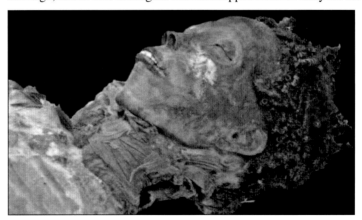

The well-preserved mummy of mid-18th Dynasty royal fanbearer Maiherpri (above & right, resting it his coffin) was not investigated by the EMP, but in 2010 it was included along with 41 other Cairo Museum mummies in "The Horus Study" of arteriosclerosis in ancient Egyptians. Photos of the half-Nubian male (25-30 at death) were posted with an Internet report of the study. The mummy had last been seen in the early 20th Century.

The famous late-18th Dynasty mummy of royal father-inlaw Yuya, found by the EMP resting in his displayed coffin in the Cairo Egyptian Museum. The mummy itself had been fully on view earlier in the 20th Century.

EMP photo

ADDENDUM SEVEN

FKTP: The Family of King Tutankhamun Project*

On February 17, 2010, a press conference — coordinated with the publication on that same date of the *Journal of the American Medical Association* — was held at the Cairo Egyptian Museum, at which were announced the findings of a two-year-long study (September 2007 - October 2009) under the auspices of Egypt's Supreme Council for Antiquities, titled the Family of King Tutankhamun Project (FKTP) — funded partially by an American cable-television channel, Discovery, which aired in North America a two-part, four-hour documentary on the Project the following February 21 and 22 ("King Tut Unwrapped: Royal Blood" and "King Tut Unwrapped: Life & Death"). The Project's formal findings were published in the American medical journal as "Ancestry and Pathology in King Tutankhamun's Family."[1]

The SCA press release for the event was titled "The Discovery of the Family Secrets of King Tutankhamun" and focused on four principal conclusions of the FKTP investigations: (1) the identification of the bones from KV55 as *"almost certainly"* belonging to Akhenaten, and the latter being the father of Tutankhamen; (2) Tutankhamen's mother was the anonymous female mummy from KV35 (Tomb of Amenhotep II) known as the "Younger Lady," KV35YL, who was also the full sister of Akhenaten (KV55) and the daughter of the other anonymous female mummy from KV35 — long known as the "Elder Lady" (KV35EL) — although KV35YL's identity still remains a question mark; (3) KV35EL *"can now conclusively be identified as Tutankhamun's grandmother, Queen Tiye"*; and (4) that DNA from a parasite causing malaria was found in the mummy of Tutankhamen, and *"it is likely that the young king died from complications resulting from a severe form of this disease."*

To quote further from the SCA press release: *"The primary analysis was carried out in a newly built DNA laboratory at the Egyptian*

Above, Digitally adapted Internet photo of the head of Tutankhamen's mummy about to be CT-scanned for the FKTP. Opposite, Detail of the first (outermost) gilded-wood coffin of Tutankhamen, in situ KV62.

George B. Johnson photo

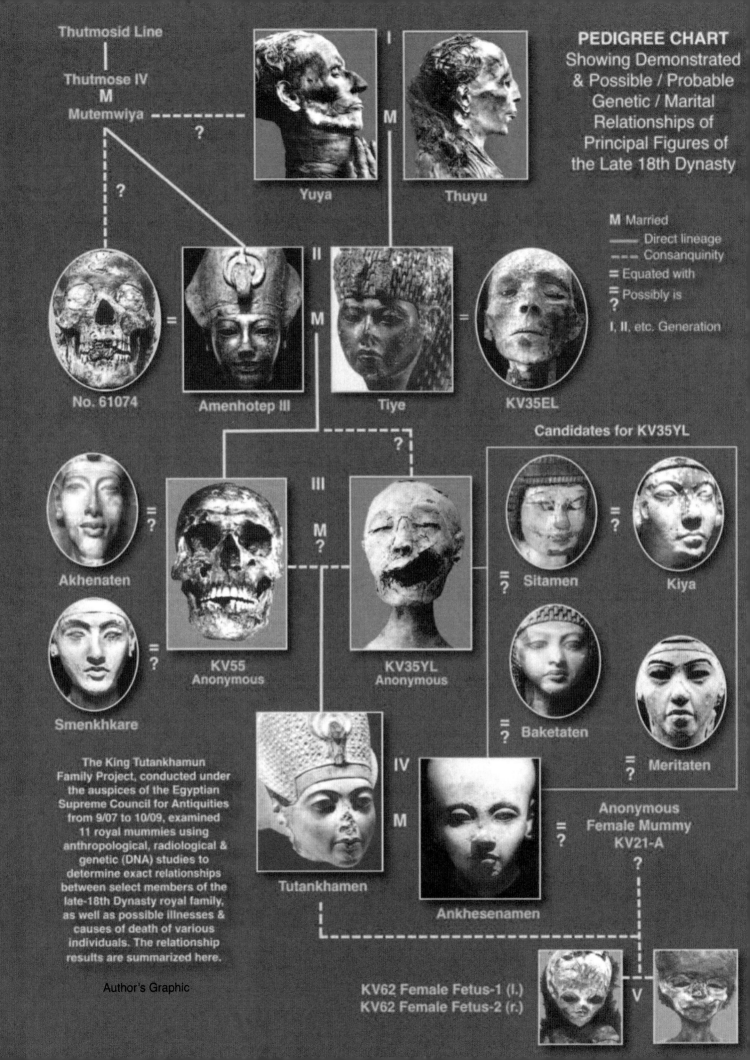

Thutmosid Line

Thutmose IV
M
Mutemwiya

?

?

Yuya **M** Thuyu

I

PEDIGREE CHART
Showing Demonstrated
& Possible / Probable
Genetic / Marital
Relationships of
Principal Figures of
the Late 18th Dynasty

M Married
—— Direct lineage
--- Consanquinity
= Equated with
≞ Possibly is
?
I, II, etc. Generation

No. 61074 = Amenhotep III **M** Tiye = KV35EL

II

Candidates for KV35YL

Akhenaten
=
?

=
?
Smenkhkare

III

M
?

KV55
Anonymous

?

KV35YL
Anonymous

=
? Sitamen =
? Kiya

=
? Baketaten

=
? Meritaten

The King Tutankhamun
Family Project, conducted under
the auspices of the Egyptian
Supreme Council for Antiquities
from 9/07 to 10/09, examined
11 royal mummies using
anthropological, radiological &
genetic (DNA) studies to
determine exact relationships
between select members of the
late-18th Dynasty royal family,
as well as possible illnesses &
causes of death of various
individuals. The relationship
results are summarized here.

Author's Graphic

Tutankhamen

IV

M

Ankhesenamen

=
?

Anonymous
Female Mummy
KV21-A

?

KV62 Female Fetus-1 (l.)
KV62 Female Fetus-2 (r.)

V

Museum, Cairo, dedicated to ancient DNA; this was donated to the Project by Discovery [American cable-television channel]. *Two types of DNA analyses were performed on samples taken from the bones of these mummies: analysis of specific nuclear DNA sequences from the Y-chromosome, which is passed directly from father to son, to study the paternal line; and genetic fingerprinting from the autosomal DNA of the nuclear genome that does not directly decide a person's sex. To authenticate the DNA results, the analyses were repeated and independently replicated in a newly equiped ancient DNA laboratory staffed by a separate group of* [Egyptian] *personnel. The CT* [computer tomography] *scans were carried out with a movable multi-slice CT unit C130KV, 124-130 ms, 014-3mm slice thickness, Siemens Somatom Emotion 6 donated to the Project by Siemens and the National Geographic Society."*

Continuing the SCA press release: *"Both the Y-chromosome analysis and the genetic fingerprinting were performed successfully, and have allowed the creation of a five-generation kindred for the young king* [Tutankhamen]. *The analysis proves conclusively that Tutankhamun's father was the mummy* [bones] *found in KV 55. The Project's CT scan of this mummy* [skeleton] *provides an age at death of between 45 and 55 for this mummy, showing that this mummy (previously thought to have died between ages 20 and 25) is almost certainly Akhenaten himself, as the Egyptological evidence from the tomb has long suggested. In support of this lineage, the DNA also traces a direct line from Tutankhmun through the KV 55 mummy to Akhenaten's father Amenhotep III. DNA shows that the mother of the KV 55 mummy is the 'Elder Lady' from KV35. This mummy is the daughter of Yuya and Tjuya* [Thuyu], *and thus definitely identified as Amenhotep III's great queen Tiye."*

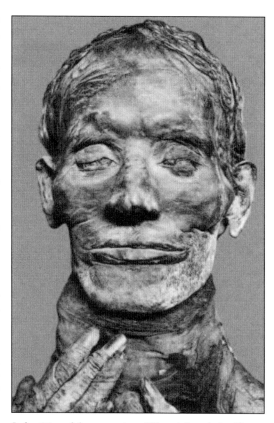

Indentities of the mummies of Yuya (above) & wife Thuyu (below) are indisputable, having been found in their all-but-intact Valley of the Kings tomb (KV46) in 1905. The 2007-2009 SCA FKTP study confirmed that they are the genetic parents of the "Elder Lady" mummy from KV35, who is now to be seen as definitely Tiye, Great Wife of Amenhotep III & mother of Akhenaten.

Both adapted from archival photos

Further from the press release: *"Another important result from the DNA analysis is that the 'Younger Lady' from KV 35 has been positively identified as Tutankhamun's mother. The Project is not yet able to identify her by name, although the DNA studies also show that she was the daughter of Amenhotep III and Tiye and thus Akhenaten's full sister. Thus Tutankhamun's only grandparents, on both his paternal and maternal sides, were Amenhotep III and Tiye.*

"Two stillborn fetuses were found mummified and hidden away in a chamber of Tutankhamun's tomb. Preliminary DNA analysis supports the Egyptological belief that these were children of the young king's [sic]. *This analysis has also suggested a mummy known as KV-21A, a royal female whose identity was previously unknown, as the most likely mother of these children and thus as Tutankhamun's wife, Ankhsenamun* [sic]."*

And concluding from the SCA press release: *"The Project studied the CT scans of the family carefully to look for inherited disorders, such as Marfan Syndrome and gynecomstial/craniosynostoses syndromes, that have been previously postulated based on representations in Egyptian art. No evidence was found for any of these diseases, thus the artistic conventions followed by the Amarna period royal family were most likely chosen for religious and political reasons.*

"Another important result of the DNA studies was the discovery of material from Pasmodium falciparum, *the protozoon that causes maleria, in the body of Tutankhamun. The CT scan also revealed that the king had a lame foot, caused by avascular bone necrosis. The Project believes that Tutankhamun's death was most likely a result of malaria coupled with his generally weak consistution. The CT scan of the pharaoh earlier confirmed the presence of an unhealed break in the king's left thigh bone; the team speculates that the king's weakened state may have led to a fall, or that a fall weakened his already fragile physical condition."*[2]

The SCA press release included the names of the Family of King Tutankhamun Project personnel, which numbered fifteen SCA Egyptologists and Egyptian medical professionals, plus two foreign (German) consultants.

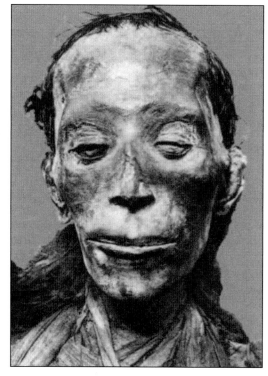

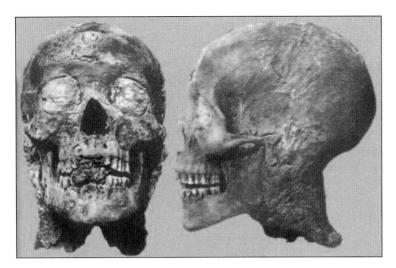

AMENHOTEP III The identity of the badly damaged mummy found in a sideroom of KV35 & labeled in antiquity as belonging to Nebmaatre Amenhotep III has been disputed chiefly due to its embalming technique — which included stuffing the limbs with resinous material, a practice not otherwise attested until the 21st Dynasty. The FKTP accepted the ancient identification, but did not DNA-test the remains against the mummies thought to be Thutmose IV & Amenhotep II, his father and grandfather. It has been pointed out that No. 61074 (the Cairo Museum identification assigned the Amenhotep III mummy) bears no craniofacial similarity to his male Thutmosid ancestors. The mummy's head is detached & all soft tissue — save for some of the mostly bald scalp — has disappeared from the latter (seen at top in frontal & side views *Royal Mummies*, 1912), reducing it essentially to a skull, the eye orbits & mouth stuffed with pads of gummy cloth. Amenhotep III's likely appearance in life is seen in a plaster head found in a sculptor's workshop at El Amarna (above & top right *Ägyptisches Museum, Berlin*). The king would have suffered dental abcesses, his upper incisors having been lost prior to death. Although the mummy's feet are badly damaged, the FKTP concluded that Amenhotep III had a slightly clubbed foot — a deformity to also be seen in his grandson, Tutankhamen. Short at 1.561 meters, the remains indicated that the seventh ruler of the 18th Dynasty was between 40 and 50 at the time of his death, which fully accords with the historical record.

In conjunction with the SCA press conference, reporters were allowed to view, photograph and film three of the featured remains, displayed — modestly covered with white sheets to their clavicals — a few inches off the Cairo Museum floor in large wood-and-glass showcases: Left to right, still-anonymous KV35YL; KV35EL, now Queen Tiye; and the KV55 skeleton, declared *"almost certainly"* Akhenaten.

By the time the FKTP news from Cairo was hitting the international wire-services, a pdf copy of the official JAMA article was being circulated on the Internet. This included only the main body of the article (pages 638-647, with references); an appendix and full-body CT reconstructions of the mummies, as well as interactive kinship analyses and pedigrees, were available online (<http://www.jama.com>), but only to *Journal* subscribers or for a user fee).

The *JAMA* article revealed that the FKTP had been funded by — in addition to the Discovery Channel — the Brando Quilici Production Group and two German sources. There was an accompanying disclaimer: *"The funding organizations had no role in the design and conduct of the study; the collection, analysis, and interpretations of the data; or the preparation, review, or approval of the manuscript."* As stated in the *JAMA* article, the objectives of the FKTP study were: *"To introduce a new approach to molecular and medical Egyptology, to determine familial relationships among 11 royal mummies of the New Kingdom, and to search for pathological features attributable to possible murder, consanquinity, inherited disorders, and infectious diseases."*[3] A "Morphological and Genetic Control Group" of four other Eighteenth Dynasty mummies (including Thutmose II and the so-called Hatshepsut) were examined, as well.

"To authenticate DNA results, analytical steps were repeated and independently replicated in a second ancient DNA laboratory staffed by a separate group of [Egyptian] *personnel."*[4] The Outcome Measures of the study were: *"microscopic-based haplotypes in mummies; generational segregation of alleles within possible pedigree variants; correlation of identified diseases with individual age; archaeological evidence; and the written historical record."*[5]

Laypersons (i.e., without scientific or medical backgrounds, which includes this writer) reading and re-reading the *JAMA* article found themselves confronted by scientific/medical terminologies which might as well have been in Sanskrit, so were generally at a loss to evaluate the accuracies of or flaws in the presented technical data. However, close reading did raise red flags for many, regarding basic methodologies and assumptions of the study. Off the top there was clearly a large discrepancy between the SCA press release and the *JAMA* article regarding the FKTP's new aging of the skeletal remains found in KV55 in 1907, the identity of which long has been disputed by Egytologists (Smenkhkare or Akhenaten?). The SCA announced the age at death of the individual as *"between 45 and 55,"* whereas the official *JAMA* report placed the revised age at 35-45.[6] Both state that this reassessment for the bone age was determined by computer tomography (CT-scanning). Bone rings?

Going online this writer was unable to find any reference to CT-scanning being used to determine the age of bones. However, in the Discovery Channel documentary, one of the German geneticists and the Egyptian radiologist independently are seen physically examining (eyeballing) the KV55 bones, in the same manner as had been done by anatomists G. Elliot Smith[7] and R.G. Harrison[8] and, more recently, Egyptologist/physical anthropologist Joyce M. Filer.[9] All of them and others — based on visible criteria, such as lack of fusion of bone epiphyses and cranial sutures, minimal dental wear and an unerupted molar — had placed the age of the bones in question at between 18 and 25 at death, with a possible high of 30. Harrison's study was particularly detailed (and persuasive).

In the Discovery program, the German (A. Zink) is seen holding the KV55 skull and commenting that the lack of cranial-suture fusion indicates a *"younger individual."* Whereas the radiologist (A. Selim), handling a KV55 femur, announces that it comes from a *"an older individual, say 45-55, even 60."*[!] Perhaps it is their clear difference of personal and professional opinion which accounts for the age discrepancies referred to above.

The age of the KV55 individual at death is critical to determining his true (as opposed to wished-for) identity. Clearly Akhenaten can be KV55 only

Below, Three views of an under-life-size, uninscribed quartzite head from a composite statue in the collection of the Metropolitan Museum of Art, New York, generally thought to depict King's Great Wife Tiye. Author's photos

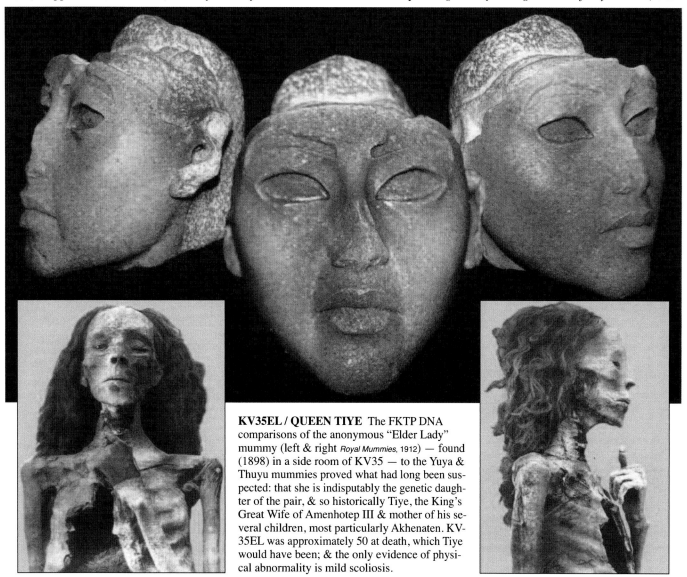

KV35EL / QUEEN TIYE The FKTP DNA comparisons of the anonymous "Elder Lady" mummy (left & right *Royal Mummies*, 1912) — found (1898) in a side room of KV35 — to the Yuya & Thuyu mummies proved what had long been suspected: that she is indisputably the genetic daughter of the pair, & so historically Tiye, the King's Great Wife of Amenhotep III & mother of his several children, most particularly Akhenaten. KV-35EL was approximately 50 at death, which Tiye would have been; & the only evidence of physical abnormality is mild scoliosis.

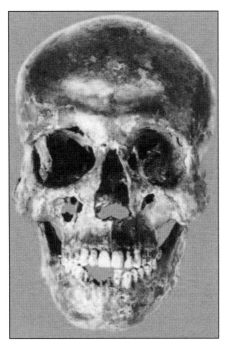

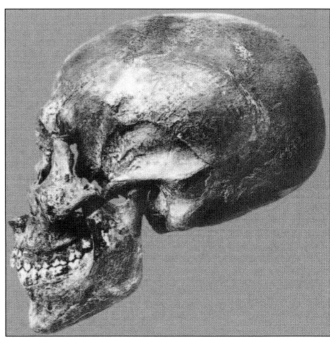

THE KV55 SKELETAL REMAINS have been a matter of controversy since their discovery in 1907, when they were initially — if briefly — declared to be those of a female, because of the wide pelvis. Subsequent analysis by antomist G. Elliot Smith (*The Royal Mummies*, 1912) determined that the bones were those of a young adult male not likely more than 30 years of age; & he concluded — because of the circumstances of their interment — that they belonged to Akhenaten, despite their seeming age at death. The age-range of 20-30 years (lowered by others' later examinations & assessments to 18-25) was based on immaturity of certain bones (non-union of epiphyses), unfused cranial sutures & lack of dental wear (as well as an unerupted wisdom tooth). Because the historicial Akhenaten (seen above left in two different plaster studies from El Amarna, reflecting his more-probable facial appearance, rather than the caricaturized features of the art style earlier in his reign Ägyptisches Museum, Berlin) would have been most likely at least 35 years at death, a younger candidate for the bones' owner was to be found in Djoserkheperure Smenkhkare, Akhenaten's putative brother & coregent, thus another offspring of Amenhotep III & Tiye). The FKTP DNA studies concluded that the KV-55 remains were those of a son of Amenhotep III & Tiye, as had been posited all along. The Project's conclusions were that the bones were considerably older than previously thought — 45, 55, even 60 years at death — apparently based on the same sort of visual assessments of earlier antatomists/physical anthropologists. Thus, the original conclusion of 20-30 years at death arbitrarily were thrown out, in favor of the new higher ones; & the FKTP declared in the article published in the *Journal of the American Medical Association* that the person found in KV55 was, in fact, *"most likely"* Akhenaten, after all. What is more it was determined that the KV55 individual was genetically the father (by KV35YL, a full sister!) of Tutankhamen, as many had hoped to be the case. A Smenkhkare identification wasn't considered because, allegedly, not enough is known about him.

if he was at least 35 at death, assuming he did not begin his religious revolution as a young teenager or even a prepubescent (but at 55 or 60, he would have been born before his mother!). Smenkhkare is the obvious candidate (as presumed son of Amenhotep III and Tiye), if KV55 died between 18-30, and still could have been as old as 35 at death, since he very well might have been only a year or two younger than his brother, Prince Amenhotep (IV/Akhenaten).

Another red flag of the *JAMA* report is the Project's blank acceptance of the Amenhotep III-identified mummy (No. 61074) as actually that king, without having DNA-compared those remains with the mummies of Thutmose IV (his father, Royal Mummy No. 61073) and Amenhotep II (his grandfather, No. 61069). This would have been highly desirable, inasmuch as the identity of the Amenhotep III mummy has been seriously questioned because of its mummification technique — artificial padding of the limbs — is otherwise not seen until the Twenty-first Dynasty; and its craniofacial characteristic are unlike those of the Thutmosids who were Amenhotep III's male ancestors.[10]

There has never been any question, however, as to the correct identification of the husband/wife mummies Yuya and Thuyu, found in their rifled-but-essentially-intact tomb (KV46) in 1905. Thus they form the first generation of FKTP's Tutankhamen pedigree. Although Yuya manifests no physical malformations, his wife was shown by the Project's study to have severe scoliosis (curvature of the spine), a problem found to varying degrees in several of her descendents, including Tutankhamen. Surprisingly, both of the couple had evidence of *maleria tropica* in their systems, although this infection may have been a dormant condition rather than the actual cause of their deaths — which occured when they were 50-60 years old.

The first important revelation of the FKTP research was the positive DNA/genetic identification of the daughter of Yuya and Thuyu, Amenhotep III's Great Wife Tiye, as KV35EL, the "Elder Lady" found (1898) in a side room (J-c) of the Tomb of Amenhotoep II. This identification has been speculated for some time, although it also has been proposed that she might be Hatshepsut or even Nefertiti.[11] A corresponence between a hair sample from KV34EL and the "heirloom" lock presumed to be from Queen Tiye found in Tutankhamens tomb (KV62) had been noted; but this identification was subsequently challenged[12] — mistakenly, as it has turned out. The FKTP posited that Tiye was around 50 at

A STRONG CASE FOR SMENKHKARE as the individual who was interred in KV55 can certainly be made. In the Discovery Channel documentary about the FKTP, it was stated quite erroneously, *"We have no evidence, no clue about him, except his name."* Certainly there are plentiful examples of Smenkhkare's name, particularly in association with funerary goods originally prepared for his use & subsequently appropriated & re-inscribed for the interment of Tutankhamen (second or middle coffin, canopic chest & stoppers, canopic coffinettes, mummy bands, to name but the most obvious). The Discovery statement ignores actual depictions of Smenkhkare — admittedly only one of which is (or was) inscribed with his name. This is, of course, the now almost-faded-away pre-carving ink sketch in the El Amarna Tomb of Meryre II (seen at right in reverse), which depicts a small figure of the tomb owner before much larger-in-scale standing figures of a male ruler, wearing a *Khepresh*, in the company of a royal woman — the pair identified by an inscription (cut away in the 1890s but recorded before that) as King Smenkhkare & King's Great Wife Meritaten.

Additionally there is a quartzite head of a composite statue in the Brooklyn Museum collection which is thought to quite possibly represent Smenkhkare (below Author's photo). Most particularly there is a life-size plaster "mask" or study (below right Ägyptisches Museum, Berlin) — among several others found in a sculptor's workshop at El Amarna — which clearly represents a male ruler, judging from the brow band & a few bosses of the *Khepresh* crown. But the individual is certainly neither Akhenaten nor Amenhotep III & especially not the boy Tutankhaten. So, by process of elimination, this leaves only one other attested male-king of the period who is possibly the subject of the study — & that would be Smenkhkare. Interestingly, the bow-lips of this king also suggest a Tiye connection.

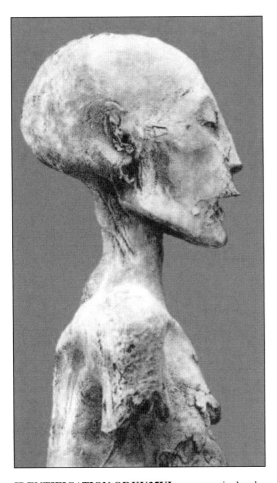

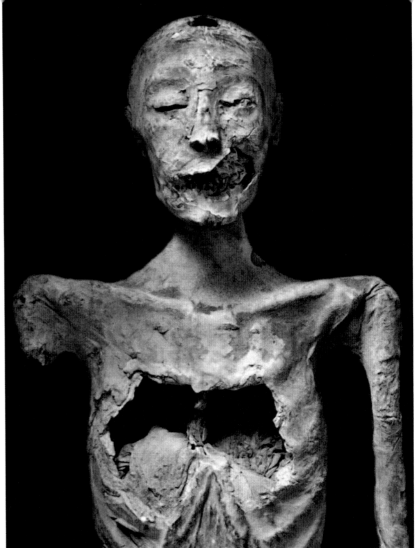

IDENTIFICATION OF KV35YL as a genetic daughter of Amenhotep III & Great Wife Tiye did not come as a particular surprise, although that she was a full sister of the male individual in KV55 was unexpected — as was the DNA determination that she was the genetic mother of Tutankhamen. When first found by Victor Loret in a side room (J-a) of the Tomb of Amenhotep II (KV35) in 1898, he misidentified the bald mummy as that of a male. This was corrected by G. Elliot Smith to a young woman *less than 25 years of age.* Recently the Younger Lady became the focus of an effort to identify the mortal remains of Queen Nefertiti; this conclusion was rejected by the SCA, which issued a report that KV35YL was male after all! A sex reasssignment by the Family of King Tutankhamun Project back to female & the conclusion that she had died at 25-35 with scoliosis, was KV55's sister & Tutankhamen's mother — albeit anonymous — has resulted in an evaluation of the various candidates who might fit the new criteria for her identity. *Royal Mummies*, 1912 & digitally adapted Internet photo

her death, which accords with the historical record. She manifests a mild form of scoliosis, inherited from her mother.

Not surprisingly the FTKP studies show that KV35EL/Tiye is the genetic mother of the KV55 individual, inasmuch as historically it is well documented that she and Amenhotep III are the biological parents of Akhenaten; and it has always been presumed that the somewhat shadowy Smenkhkare was also their younger son.[13]

Arguably the most provocative of the FTKP's findings/conclusions is that KV35TL ("Younger Lady") is not only the daughter of Amenhotep III and Tiye (again speculated previously) but the full sister of the KV55 individual — and also the genetic mother of Tutankhamen! The FTKP wisely did not propose an identity for KV35YL — for, realistically, there is no scientific way of determining that. But only a handful of candidates meet the necessary criteria, leaving aside an unknown person who never made it into the Amarna-period record. These are, most obviously, any one of the attested daughters of Amenhotep III and Tiye, of which there were five: Sitamen (presumably the eldest), Aset (or Iset), Henuttaneb, Nebetiah and Baketaten (presumably the youngest). Leaving out of any real consideration the middle three (because their documentation is minimal, at best), the eldest daughter, Sitamen, is a prime candidate.

She is best known for her contribution of two armchairs to the funerary goods of her maternal grandparents, Yuya and Thuyu, on each of which she is both named and depicted.[14] Princess Sitamen is also recorded as having become her father's second King's Great Wife, at the time of Amenhotep III's first renewal *Heb-Sed* in his Year 30, when Sitamen herself may have been as old as 16 (assuming she would not have been born before her father was 14). This marriage is seen by most scholars as having been for religious reasons associated

THE CASE FOR SITAMEN AS KV35YL

Eldest and best-attested daughter of Amenhotep III & Great Wife Tiye, Sitamen may be the prime candidate for sister-wife of the KV-55 individual (whether Smenkhkare or Akhenaten), as well as mother of Tutankhamen — although it has been proposed that the latter would then have been sired by Amenhotep III, inasmuch as Sitamen was her father's second King's Great Wife, having been married to him at the time of the aging ruler's first *Heb-Sed* in his Year 30 — an arrangement likely more ceremonial than consumated. So, certainly, Sitamen marrying her younger brother (whether Akhenaten or Smenkhkare) would had to have taken place following the demise of Amenhotep III (just prior to Amenhotep IV/Akhenaten's ascent to the Horus Throne, probably following an Amenhotep III/IV coregency of some years). A move to her brother's new capital at Akhetaten ("Horizon of the Aten") would have necessitated a name change for the widowed Sitamen the *-amen* element of her name (*"Daughter of Amen"*) by then being proscribed. Unless she became the shadowy Kiya (see next page), a newly named sister-wife of Akhenaten is not present in the historical record. Sitamen is represented on two armchairs probably contributed by her to the (KV46) funerary goods of her maternal grandparents, Yuya & Thuyu. One of these depicts her twice in 3-dimensional gilded finials (one at left) & in a double-facing gilded raised-relief on the chair's interior back (above), in which she wears a unique crown. Author's photos

THE CASE FOR BAKETATEN AS KV35YL

Amenhotep III & Tiye parented four daughters after Sitamen (the middle three, Iset, Henuttaneb & Nebetiah, barely attested), with the youngest, Baketaten, known only from depictions in the Tomb of Huya at El Amarna, showing her accompanying her mother on a visit (or move) to Akhetaten; but perhaps she is also to be seen in a small painted-limestone statue-bust of an Amarna princess in the collection of the Louvre (left above), where the heart-shaped face, pouty bow-lips & overall dour expression echo 3-dimensional representations of Tiye. It may be objected that Baketaten appeared on the Amarna stage too late — & then as a young girl — to have been the mother of Tutankhaten (by either Smenkhkare or Akhenaten). Counter to that argument is the distinct possibility that Baketaten was actually a teenager — or even a young adult — at the time of her mother's arrival at Akhetaten, & that she was shown in Huya's tomb on a scale relative to the older daughters of Akhenaten & Nefertiti (as in a banquet scene — above in reverse — Baketaten alongside Tiye [r.] & two princesses next to Nefertiti) for purely visual/balance reasons, regardless of the reality of her age at the time. Artistic license in representing the princesses' ages is evident in the famous "Durbar" scene of Year 12 in the Tomb of Meryre II, where all six royal daughters are shown on the same scale, despite their age spread. If Baketaten did bear Tutankhaten by one of her brothers, perhaps she died in childbirth & is to be seen in one of the deathbed tableaux of the El Amarna Royal Tomb. Smenkhkare would have then married his niece, Meritaten.

WHAT ABOUT NEFERTITI? Recently at least one Amarna scholar — arguing *ex silencio* — has seriously proposed that Nefertiti (in addition to producing a brood of six daughters) was, in fact, also the mother of Tutankhaten by Akhenaten, making the boy-king a full-brother of his wife, Ankhesenpaaten/amen. There is no physical proof to support such wishful thinking. Nefertiti, simply enough, does not meet two necessary criteria in order to be taken seriously as KV35-YL. In addition to the seeming age of the Younger Lady mummy (25-35), the small limestone statuette from El Amarna, now in Berlin (detail right) likely depicting a haggard woman of 40 or more, there is the problem of Nefertiti never having —or at least being recorded as having — the titles "King's Daughter" & "King's Sister," which would have been her bragging rights if Amenhotep III & Tiye were her parents & Amenhotep IV/Akhenaten her full brother. Thus, even had the effort of a few years ago to identify KV35YL as Nefertiti had been accepted by the Supreme Council for Antiquities, this would have to be thrown out, now that the FKTP research has shown the DNA-genetic connection between KV-35EL (Tiye) and KV35-YL. Berlin Ägyptisches Museum

AND THEN THERE IS KIYA Since her marginal existence was first recognized, the apparently non-royal "other woman" secondary wife of Akhenaten has been an odds-on-favorite candidate for the mother of Tutankhaten — with the Heretic as father, of course. Perhaps she is to be seen in two plaster "studies" from a sculptor's workshop at El Amarna (one at right, Ägyptisches Museum, Berlin). She is thought to have likely died in childbirth (as depicted in one of the deathbed-&-infant scenes in the El Amarna Royal Tomb), with several of her relief images at Ahketaten sites being subsequently usurped to represent the eldest Akhenaten/Nefertiti princess, Meritaten (an example above Ny Carlsberg Gyptotek). It would be attractive to think that Sitamen transmorgrified into Kiya at Akhetaten, taking a nickname echoing those of the Akhmim family with close royal ties (Yey, Yuya, Thuyu, Tiye, Aye). The problem is that Kiya — like her rival Nefertiti — is never called a "King's Daughter" or "King's Sister," so would not be a daughter of Amenhotep III &, therefore, not KV35YL.

with the *Heb-Sed* ceremonies, in which the King's Great Wife would have presumably enacted ritual roles of various goddesses. If so, this would not have necessarily meant that the father/daughter marriage was actually consummated. Some who would like to believe otherwise had therefore posited that Tutankhaten might have been the result of such an incestuous union (which would have necessitated a long coregency between Amenhoteps III and IV).

With the passing of his father, it is tempting to see Akhenaten, on the other hand, taking his "widowed" older (but not necessarily all that much older) sister as a second Royal Wife, with perhaps the sole purpose of fathering on her a son — which he had not succeeded in doing with his King's Great Wife, Nefertiti. This would have required that Dowager Great Wife Sitamen moving (from the Royal Residence at Waset) to Akhetaten and taking a new Aten-acceptable name — inasmuch as "Daughter of Amen" would have been proscribed, certainly. Therefore, it is the stuff of a novel to see Sitamen becoming the mysterious Kiya, who definitely is recorded as Akhenaten's secondary wife (and Nefertiti's presumed "rival"). "Kiya" seems to echo names of the royal-associated Akhmim (Ipu) family of the period (Yey Yuya, Thuyu, Tiye, Aye) and already might have been a nickname by which Princess Sitamen had been known. A problem with this scenario is that Kiya is never labeled a "King's Daughter" or "King's Sister," which Sitamen would have been; and she likely would have retained at least those titles in her new circumstance. Of course, allowing that KV55 is Smenkhkare rather than Akhenaten, Sitamen may have found herself married (unrecorded) to her younger (although not necessarily all that much younger) brother, by whom she mothered a son (Tutankhaten), dying in childbirth, thereby necessitating Smenkhkare marrying his niece, Meritaten, when he became his brother's coregent in or about the latter's Year 16-17.

The other Amenhotep III/Tiye daughter who would be an attractive candidate for KV35YL is the presumed youngest of the lot, Baketaten. Having an "Aten" name, she possibly would have been born sometime (perhaps soon) after Amenhotep IV became Akhenaten (his Year 5?) and Amen, et al., were outlawed (as it were). In which case she would have been only about 4 or 5 at at Tutankhaten's birth in Year 9 or 10, so obviously not his mother. She is pictured as a young child in several scenes in the El Amarna tomb of Tiye's steward, Huya, which record the Dowager Great Wife's visit (or more probable relocation to) Akhetaten in about Year 12.[15]

There is, of course, the possibility that the final (love?) child of Amenhotep III and Tiye was actually a teenager (or even young adult) at the time of

FINALLY, DARK-HORSE KV35YL CANDIDATE: PRINCESS-QUEEN MERITATEN, A.K.A. ANKH(ET)KHEPERURE NEFERNEFERUATEN

Allowing for the distinct possibility — given all the inbreeding of the late-18th Dynasty royal family — that the DNA of KV35YL reflects a generational leap & the Young Lady mummy from KV35 is the *granddaughter* of Amenhotep III & Great Wife Tiye, rather than their daughter, & so the niece of the KV55 individual rather than his full sister as the FKTP data suggests. Thus, she might be none other than the Akhenaten/Nefertiti eldest daughter Princess Meritaten, who is also the documented King's Great Wife of Djoserkheperure Smenkhkare, her uncle, depicted as such in the Tomb of Meryre II (see p. 205).

It is possible — although improbable — that Akhenaten might have subsequently fathered Tutankhaten on his firstborn. Judging from from Meritaten's depiction as a child approximately 4-5 years old (impossible to be sure) in reconstructed relief scenes of the Aten temples Amenhotep IV built just east of the Amen precinct at Ipet Isut (Karnak) at the outset of his reign, she would have been 14 or 15 at the time Tutankhaten was born in Akhenaten's Year 9 or 10, certainly childbearing age. Inasmuch as Meritaten was married to her putative uncle, Smenkhkare, during (& likely before) his brief coregency with his brother, Akhenaten, it is equally possible — & realistically more probable — that she would have borne Tutankhaten to her husband. This would give Smenkhkare primacy as the son of Amenhotep II & Tiye whose bones were found in KV55. Smenkhkare could have been only a year or two younger than brother Prince Amenhotep (Akhenaten), so possible as old as 35 at death (the minimum age assigned to the KV55 bones by the new FKTP studies). Which does not mean he could not also have been as young as 18-25 when he died, after co-ruling briefly with Akhenaten (probably during final Year 17), if the several previous anatomists'/physical anthropologist's assessments of the bones' age-at-death are, in fact, correct after all. Photos Berlin Ägyptisches Museum

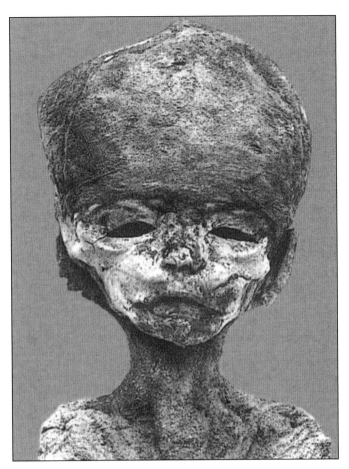

AND THEN THERE ARE THE TWO FEMALE FETUSES FROM KV62 which generally had been presumed — since their discovery in the tomb's Treasurey — to be the offspring of Tutankhamen & his Great Wife, Ankhesenamen. The smaller one (above left, adapted detail of a Harry Burton photo) was stillborn probably in the fifth month of gestation & mummified with its internal organs present. The larger (above right, Harry Burton) reached seven months, so possibly died after being born prematurely: there was no umbilical cord present & the internal organs had been removed through an abdominal incision.

While it has been suggested that the infants possibly were placed in KV62 only as magical agents for Tutankhamen's rebirth in the Afterlife, the FKTP study shows that both are, in fact, genetic offspring of the boy-king &, surprisingly, possibly a female partial-mummy found in KV21 & now known as KV21-A (there being a second, more-complete-but-badly-damaged female mummy from the same tomb, KV21-B).

If these weak DNA-genetic identifications are correct, the missing mummy of Great Wife Ankhesenamen may have been identified. But, if so, it is disturbing that KV21-A has a severely deformed right foot (much like in a Chinese binding), which would have made it impossible for her to have walked in her lifetime. It is hard to imagine Ankhesenpaaten/amen as a total cripple.

her visit or move to her big brother's Aten capital, and that she changed her name on the occasion for "religous correctness." (Might she have been Henuttenab or Nebetiah?) Her depiction as a young girl in the Huya tomb may very well have been a matter of artistic license (or visual balance), so that she was on the same scale as her nieces in the same or parallel scenes. Certainly the older daughters of Akhenaten and Nefertiti themselves would have been more than mere youngsters in Year 12. So it is within the realm of possibility that a renamed Baketaten might have mothered Tutankhaten by either of her elder brothers, perhaps dying in childbirth (as depicted in one of the El Amarna Royal Tomb deathbed scenes). In any case, nothing is known of Baketaten in the closing years of Akhenaten's reign.

Two other KV35YL candidates have to be considered, if briefly: King's Great Wife Nefertiti and King's Wife Kiya. Despite recent efforts to argue (*ex silencio*) the former as Tutankhaten's mother, the fact that the KV35 Younger Lady would seem to be a genetic descendent of Amenhotep III and Tiye pretty much rules out Nefertiti as that individiual. It has been posited that Akhenaten's Great Wife was a daughter of the commoner-later-king Aye, so she would have had third-generation blood ties to Yuya and Thuyu —however only if Aye was, in fact, that couple's unrecorded son (which has been assumed, without proof). But she would not have had a direct genetic link to Tiye, in any case. More importantly, Nefertiti never claimed to be a King's Daughter or King's Sister, if she had those relationships with Amenhotep III and her husband.

Kiya — unless she had once been Sitamen —must summarily be ruled out as a KV35YL claimant, on the same grounds of not being called a King's Daughter or King's Sister.

This leaves the final — and in this writer's view best, if dark-horse — candidate for the identification of KV35YL: Princess-Queen Meritaten, who later briefly ruled as the shadowy female king Ankh(et)kheperure Nefernefera-aten. But it will be protested, Meritaten was neither the daughter of Amenhotep III/Tiye nor the full sister of her father, Akhenaten (nor her uncle, Smenkhkare, for that matter). What with all of the inbreeding of the late-Eighteenth Dynasty royals, it would seem fully within the realm of scientific possibility that the DNA/allele link betweeen KV35EL/Tiye and KV35YL jumps a generation, so that the latter is the granddaughter of the former, rather than her daughter.[16]

Meritaten would have been as old as 14-15 in her father's Year 9-10, so easily enough might have mothered Tutankhaten. This assumption is based on her appearance as a youngish child (and the then-only Amenhotep IV/Nefer-titi daughter) in scenes on Aten monuments raised east of the Amen complex at Ipet Isut (Karnak) at the outset of the future heretic's reign. Which means she would have been born a few years before Amenhotep IV became king (or pos-sibly/likely his father's coregent).

Frustrated by not having produced a son with Great Wife Nefertiti (by Year 9 he would have had at least three, even four daughters from her), it is fully possible that Akhenaten may have turned to his eldest offspring for a solution to his lack of an heir (Horus-in-the-Nest). It makes more practical sense that he, instead, put his ego aside and married Meritaten to his younger brother, Smenkhkare, with hope of continuing the Thutmosid royal line through him.

AND WHAT OF THE KV35 BOY? It has to be (& has been) wondered why the well-preserved mummy of a prepubescent boy (aged around 11) found lying denuded between the female mum-mies KV35EL & -YL in KV35 side room J-a (be-low left, photo adapted from *Royal Mummies*, 1912) was not included in the FKTP studies. From the style of mummification & nature of postmortem damage (large hole in the head, hacked-open chest cavity), & the boy's precise placement by those who res-cued the Royal Mummies in the 21st Dynasty, it would seem a good bet that he is, in fact, Prince Thutmose, eldest son of Amenhotep III & Great Wife Tiye, who served as high-priest of Ptah prior to his premature demise (as depicted below in a relief from Sakkara now in Berlin, A. Dodson photo). DNA comparisons would prove (or not) that the KV35 Boy was the son of Tiye, brother of KV55 Bones & so uncle of Tutankhamen; or else, as also speculated, a prince of KV35's owner, Amenhotep II, one Prince Webensenu.

That he was at visually examined *in situ* by then-director of the FKTP, Zahi Hawass, is evi-denced by a photo published in *National Geograph-ic* magazine in 2010 (below, © National Geographic).

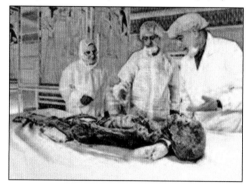

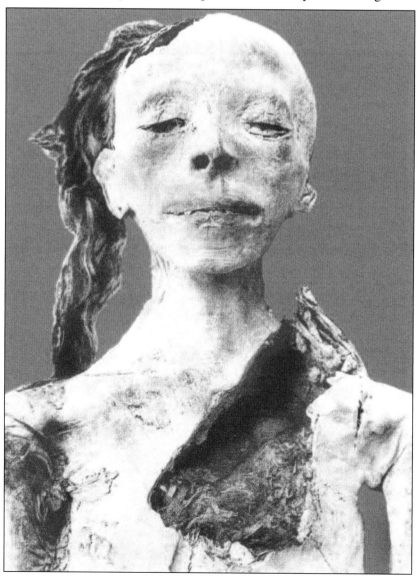

TUTANKHAMEN'S WOUNDS The FKTP's CT-scanning of Tutankhamen's mummy (below, before the gold brow band was removed and the eye sockets punched in, Adapted Harry Burton photo) revealed a severe fracture of the femur near the left knee, which could have been caused by a fall —possibly from a moving chariot. Interestingly the Project's formal report (*Scanning the Pharaohs*) reported that the left padella (kneecap) had been completely detached and was found in the left hand of the mummy. Whether this happened prior to mummification or occurred during its "unwrapping" in 1926 was not commented on, however.

But the Project characterized the large, coin-sized lesion on the mummy's left cheek (indicated at right, Adapted Burton photo) as possibly indicating an *"aleppo boil, plague spot, an inflamed mosquito bite, or a mummification artifact."* Could this instead have been a healing wound that had resulted from the same fall, indicating that Tutankhamen may have lingered for a time before succumbing to blood poisoning caused by the leg fracture?

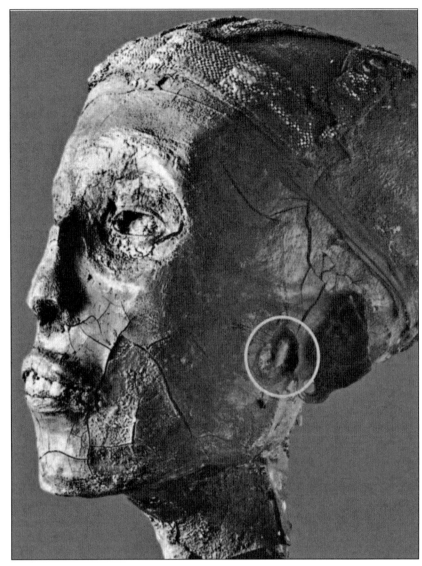

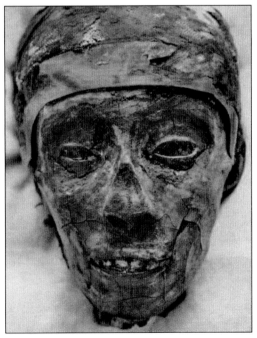

That this union took place, in any case, is a matter of record (at least in the Tomb of Meryre II scene of King Smenkhkare and Great Wife Meritaten together). If KV55 and KV35YL are the parents of Tutankhaten/amen, as the FKTP study concludes, then the DNA genetic relationship between them would have to be uncle-niece rather than brother-sister.

A mother-of-Tutankhaten role for Meritaten was proposed by this writer in 1998,[17] based on the purely circumstantial evidence of the seemingly special placement of Princess Meritaten's ivory writing/painting palette in Tutankamen's tomb: it was found resting perfectly centered between the forelegs of the life-sized jackal figure atop the Anubis Shrine situated just inside the doorway to the KV62 Treasury. While this certainly could have been placed there (so perfectly centered?) by the necropolis officials who reordered the tomb following one of the two break-ins, it seems more probably that this object was originally so prominently positioned (instead of being deposited in one of the chests where Tutankhamen's personal scribal gear was discovered) because those who buried the young king meant to acknowledge a special relationship between him and Akhenaten's eldest daughter. It would have been fully appropriate for the boy-king to have retained the palette belonging to his mother as a memento (Meritaten was very likely long deceased by the time Tutankhamen was at the end of his own somewhat-brief life).

It is assumed that coregent Djoserkheperure Smenkhkare either prede-

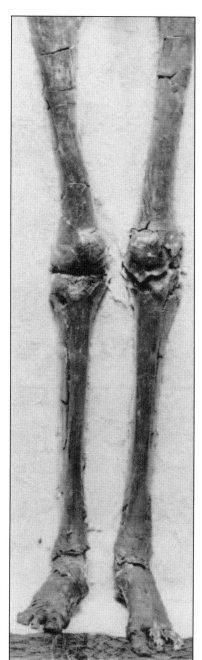

TUTANKHAMEN'S LEFT-FOOT DEFORMITY — revealed by CT-scanning & x-ray — was determined by the FKTP to be juvenile aseptic Frieberg-Kohler syndrome, causing the left foot to be significantly longer than the right (which is visually apparent in Harry Burton's photo, above, of Tutankhamen's reassembled mummy on a sand tray taken just prior to its re-interment), which would have almost certainly caused the young king a walking disability, probably neccesitating the use of a supportive staff, as is shown in a scene of the king & his queen, Ankhesenamen, on the lid of an ivory-inlaid casket from KV62 (above right, Cairo Egyptian Museum). The *JAMA* article characterized this condid-tion as a "clubfoot," bringing to mind the image of the deformed foot of the mummy of King Siptah (No. 61080), which is far-more severe than in Tutankhamen's case. The same article indicated the clubfoot condition is also present in the mummy of Amenhotep III (No. 61074) & the two anonymous badly damaged female mummies found in KV21 (-A & -B), one of whom has been tentatively identified as Ankhesenamen. An uninscribed painted-limestone relief in Berlin (right, A. Dodson photo) depicts a royal couple, the king supporting himself with a crutch under his right armpit & favoring his left foot. Long thought to depict Smenkhkare & Meritaten, perhaps it instead portrays an Amarna-ized Amenhotep III & Queen Tiye!

ceased Akhenaten by a few months or outlived him by no more than a year — both rulers probably dying as a result of a plague which seems to have been ravaging Egypt at this time (introduced in Year 12, that saw the so-called "Durbar" tributes by foreign client-kings). In Year 17 of Akhenaten, Horus-in-the-Nest to King Smenkhkare (and by extension to Akhenaten himself) Prince Tutankhaten would have been only 7 or 8 years of age, so too young to reign without a regent (who traditionally would have been his mother). Due to the likely political turmoil at the time, it is not unreasonable to suggest that Dowager Great Wife Meritaten found it expedient to co-opt two of her late husband's names and rule, fully king in her own right, as Ankh(et)khperure Neferneferuaten. (Smenkhkare seems to have also used the Akhkheperure and Neferneferuaten prenomen and nomen.)

She then either herself died after a brief two or three years occupying the throne (another plague victim?), or else had 10-year-old Tutankhaten crowned as Nebkheperure, married him to her younger sister, Ankhesenpaaten,[18] and continued as her son's coregent until the capital at Akhetaten was finally abandoned and the court transferred north to Mennufer (Memphis), on which occasion 12-year-old Nebkheperure changed his Atennomen to Tutankhamen, signaling a full return to the old orthodoxy. If renamed Meritaten lived on, she would have likely gone into voluntary retirement (as possibly Hatshepsut had done several generations earlier, thus setting a precedent for female kings stepping down in the modern-day Dutch manner), even surviving the duration of her son's 10-year reign (KV34YL may have been as old as 35 at death, according to the FKTP findings).

One further comment regarding Meritaten's possible maternal relationship to Tutankhamen is in order. This is the disputed E.A.W. Budge reference in his *Amenism, Atenism and Egyptian Monotheism* to a scarab found by A. Mariette at Abydos which purportedly names a "Merit-Ra" as the mother of a "(Neb)kheperure," which was cited again by C. Desroches-Noblecourt in her popular 1963 study, *Tutankhamen, Life and Death of a Pharaoh*. There has been objection to this theory, on the grounds that the ruler's name in question had been mis-copied by Mariette and that the actual king is (A)kheperure (Amenhotep II), whose mother's name was Meritre(-Hatshepsut). But perhaps this should be reconsidered now. Meritre would have been the perfectly logical name alteration for Meritaten post her father's demise.[19]

The fifth generation of the "Amarna" royal family in the FKTP study needs some discussion: the two female fetal mummies found together in KV62 and presented in the Discovery documentary as if being uniquely discovered by the Project (*"No one has examined these* [fetal] *mummies for decades"*), which (perhaps cluelessly) ignored the fact that they, indeed, had been featured on two different television documentaries in recent years (1998 and 2004), as well as discussed (and pictured) in companion books to those programs.[20] In both instances the tiny mummies — in storage at the Kasar El Ainy Faculty of Medicine of Cairo University — were shown to be pathetically deteriorated; or as said in the "King Tut Unwrapped" documentary, *"Crumbling to pieces."*

The two fetal mummies (the smaller one only five months in gestation; the larger, at seven months, so possibly born alive prematurely) were found — fully mummified and carefully wrapped, housed in miniature anthropoid double coffins and laid together in a large chest — in the Treasury of KV62. While it was logically presumed that they were offspring of Tutankhamen and Ankhesenamen — with known instances of royal children being interred with their father whom they predeceased in other 18th Dynasty royal tombs — it was also proposed that the two infants' presence was for ritual purposes associated with Tutankhamen's rebirth, rather than because they were his actual offspring (and in fact were not necessarily related to him in any way).

Such theorizing has been laid to rest once and for all, with the Project's demonstration that the fetuses are genetically Tutankhamen's daughters. The surprise of the fetuses' DNA analysis was that they may possibly also be genetically related to a greatly damaged (even headless) female mummy found (in 1817 by G. Belzoni and refound again in 1989 by D. Ryan) in a well-cut-but-uninscribed 18th Dynasty Tomb 21 in the Valley of the Kings, which has been given the designation KV21-A (there being a second badly desecrated female mummy from the same tomb, KV21-B).

The *JAMA* article cautiously states, in the caption to Figure 2: *"...the mother* [of the KV62 fetusues] *is not yet genetically identified. The data obtained from KV21A suggest her as the mother. However, the few data are not significant to find her as Ankhesenamun."*[21] This, of course, did not prevented the media from jumping to just such a conclusion. Unsettling is the *JAMA* article's indications that both KV21-A and -B have clubfeet (as well as scoliosis), the one remaining foot of KV21-A so severely deformed (much like a Chinese bound one) that she likely could not have been able to walk in her lifetime. The Discovery narrator drolly observed: *"A picture is emerging of a royal family with genetic problems"*[!].

A good portion of the *JAMA* article is devoted to the condition of the mummy of Tutankhamen himself. When the excavator-dismantled, "unguent-charred" KV62 remains were subjected by the SCA to CT-scan scrutiny in early 2005, the stated ojective was to determine the cause of the boy-king's death. Because of a milky area seen in the two earlier x-rays of Tutankhamen's cranium (Harrison, 1968; Harris, 1978), it had been speculated that he had died from a blow to the base of same, thus probably murdered.[22] The CT-scan revealed that this aberration was a consequence of the mummification process and not a premortem trauma contributing to death; thus, the murder theory was disproven to the SCA's satisfaction.

The scan did reveal a severe fracture of the left femur just above the knee, the kneecap (patella) having become detached. Part of the team conducting the CT-scan believed that this fracture (and associated detached kneecap?) was premortem and possibly caused by a fall, likely from a moving chariot. Others of the investigating team believed that the fracture was postmortem and had resulted from the forsible removal of the mummy from the coffin by H. Carter, et al. The majority view of an accident and subsequent fractured femur — leading to blood poisoning and death — prevailed in the SCA released findings.

Additionally it was reported that Tutankhmen had *"a small cleft in his hard palette"* and a *"slight bend in the spine"* (scoliosis). It also was noted that the sternum and *a large percentage of the front ribs* [of the mummy] *are missing,"* a condition which the investigators blamed on Carter and his team, who they concluded had removed the ribs *"in order to collect the artifacts present."* The clear probability that this was done following Tutankhamen's 1926 reinterment in KV62 (when photographic evidence proves the ribs were present, covered by a beaded bib/collar) and before the 1968 disinterment for the purpose of x-raying the mummy (when both bib and ribs were gone) was blantantly ignored by the investigators, apparently with the sole motive of demonizing Carter.[23]

When the existing CT-scans of the Tutankhamen mummy were re-evaluated by the FTKP researchers, two additional serious problems with the boy-king's state of health were discovered (apparently having been missed by the 2005 SCA study of the mummy). The *JAMA* article rreveals that, at the time of his death, Tutankhamen was crippled by a clubfoot manifested in *"congenital aseptic bone necrosis"* of the second and third metatarsals (toes) of his left foot — which is significantly longer than the other one (the arch of which was flattened, caused by shifting weight to the right foot when the young king stood and walked). The article said that the presence in KV62 of 130 sticks and staves supported the hypothesis of Tutankhamen's *"walking impairment."*

A second health condition of the boy-king, which had been missed in 2005, was the presence in the mummy of the parasite causing *malaria tropica* — which had also been observed in Tutankhamen's great-grandparents, Yuya and Thuyu. While the royal inlaws may have had an immunity to such an infection, the FKTP researchers concluded that, when his leg was broken in a fall, the king's weakened physical state (resulting from his detriorating foot situation) *"might have resulted in a life-threatening condition when a malaria infection occurred."*

The Family of King Tutankhamun Project also included in its study a "Morphological and Genetic Control Group of 18th-Dynasty Mummies." These four were: the now-anonymous No. 61065 (formerly identified as Thutmose I); Thutmose II (No. 61066); the so-called "Hatshepsut" (KV60-A); and the presumably non-royal "In-Sitre" (KV60-B). Not much has been said about the study of these individuals — generations removed from the "family" of Tutankhamen," and two not even royal — in the popular press; but the data collected will certainly add, in a published scientific format, to the morphological (form and structure) and genetic data of the SCA's earlier "search for the mummy of Hatshepsut" (in 2007). By 2016 this had not been forthcoming, perhaps a victim of the 2011 revolution in Egypt and the subsequent reorganization of the Supreme Council for Antiquities into the Ministry of State for Antiquities and Heritage.

Clearly the FKTP *Journal of the American Medical Association* article represents a "rush to judgment" of sorts, at least as far as one of its major conclusions is concerned — that being the less-than-certain identification of the KV55 skeletal remains as belonging *"almost certainly"* to Akhenaten. But the basic willingness of the SCA to undertake a DNA study of Egypt's unique ancient royals in a multidisciplinary approach should be applauded. This valuable data will undoubedly be open to re-evaluation in coming years, and it is only to be wished that such

scientific research will continue in the future and that further identifications and familial links will be made.

Notes

1. *Journal of the American Medical Association*, Vol. 303, No. 7, 638-647+.
2. Released by the Arab Republic of Egypt Ministry of Culture Supreme Council for Antiquities, February 17, 2010.
3. *JAMA*, 303:7, 638.
4. Ibid.   5. Ibid.   6. Ibid. 640, Table 1
7. G. Elliot Smith, *The Royal Mummies* (Cairo, 1912), 51-56.
8. R.G. Harrison, "An Anatomical Examination of the Pharaonic Remans Purported to be Akhenaten," *Journal of Egyptian Archaeology* 52 (London, 1966), 95-119.
9. Joyce M. Filer, "Anatomy of a Mummy," *Archaeology* (March/April 2002), 26-29.
10. James E. Harris, Edward F. Wente, eds., *An X-Ray Atlas of the Royal Mummies* (Chicago and London, 1980), 352-353.
11. Susan E. James, "Who is the Mummy Elder Lady?", *Kmt* 12:2 (summer 2001), 42-50; and by the same author, "In a 'Secret Chamber' in the Valley of the Kings: Dueling 'Nefertitis'!", *Kmt* 14:3 (fall 2003), 22-29.
12. Renate Germer, "Die Angebliche Mumie de Teje: Problem interdisziplinaren Arbeiten," *Studien zur Altägyptischen Kultur* 11 (1984), 85-90.
13. Except for the creative suggestion by Marc Gabolde that he was the Hittite prince Zannanza!
14. T.M. Davis, et al., *The Tomb of Iouiya and Touiyou* (London, 197); also D. Forbes, *Tombs.Treasures.Mummies.* (Sebastopol & Santa Fe, 1998), 155-157.
15. N.D. Davis, *The Rock Tombs of El Amarna, Part III - The Tombs of Huya and Ahmes* (London, 1905).
16. This intergenerational jump of DNA alleles between KV35EL and KV35YL is discussed in detail and at length by Kate Phizackerley, in her paper "DNA Shows the KV55 Mummy Probably Not Akhenaten," posted March 2, 2010, on her website (<http://egyptology. blogspot. com>). This writer's similar, if-non-scientific conclusions were reached independently prior to Ms. Phizackerley's Internet publication.
17. Forbes, 511, for discussion and photo.
18. A great deal is made on the Discovery "King Tut Unwrapped: Royal Blood" documentary of an inscribed block in storage at Ashmunein — broken in halves rejoined for the camera — on which Tutankhaten is titled "King's Son of His Body" and Ankhesenpaaten is similarly called "King's Daughter of His Body." The conclusion presented is that this is proof-positive that Tutankhaten was the son of Akhenaten, inasmuch as Ankhesenpaaten was definitely the latter's daughter. This leap of logic did not take into consideration that the king referred to in both instances is unnamed and so may be two different individuals, i.e., Smenkhkare and Akhenaten, respectively. The inscription (there is no depiction of the subjects) may possibly reflect the occasion of the marriage of juvenile Tutankhaten and his few-to-several-years-older aunt.
19. For a discussion of this scarab, see the "Readers' Forum" in *Kmt* 9:2 (summer 1998).
20. See B. Brier, *The Murder of Tutankhamen: A True Story* (New York, 1998), 115-119+ and figs. 13c, 14b and 15; also M.R. King and G.M. Cooper, *Who Killed King Tut?* (Amherst, NY, 2004), 99, 100+.
21. *JAMA* 303:7, 645.
22. See note 19, above.
23. For a detailed discussion of what likely happened to the sternum and ribs, see D. Forbes, S. Ikram and J. Kamrin, "Tutankhamen's Missing Ribs," *Kmt* 18:1 (spring 2007), 50-56.

* This Addendum was originally published in a different format as "Tutankhamen's Family Ties Full of Knots," *Kmt* 21:2 (summer 2010), 19-35.

Dennis C. Forbes, the author, has been an ardant Egyptophile since childhood. In 1990 Forbes created the quarterly *Kmt, A Modern Journal of Ancient Egypt*, & he continues today as its editorial director, having contributed numerous articles, photographs & graphics to the Journal during its 27 years of publication. In addition to *Tombs.Treasures.Mummies.*, he is the author of *Imperial Lives, Biographical Sketches of Famous New Kingdom Egyptians* (2005); & seven volumes of his black & white photography of the Egyptian monuments are published as *Intimate Egypt* (2009-2016). A native of Des Moines, Iowa, & for a quarter century resident in San Francisco, Forbes has lived for the past 17 years in rural North Carolina near Asheville.

Photo: George B. Johnson

Made in the USA
San Bernardino, CA
14 February 2020